st.george

Good with people. Good with money.

St.George Bank occupies a unique position in the Australian banking industry, with a reputation for great customer service, innovative products and strong community ties. We value this reputation and strive to live up to it each and every day. We aim to develop genuine personal relationships with our customers, assisting them throughout their life with their banking and investment needs.

Perhaps nothing binds a community more strongly than its children. Our hope for their future wellbeing and desire to provide them with best possible chance in life are feelings that we all understand and share.

It is for this reason that St.George Bank's primary community focus is directed towards the St.George Foundation. The Foundation was established in 1990 to provide financial support to charitable organisations throughout Australia, to help them assist young people with special needs. To date, the Foundation has provided more than $8 million to help thousands of Aussie kids to be the best they can be.

For similar reasons, St.George Bank is proud to support Young Queensland, a showcase of the State Library of Queensland's unique collection of historical memorabilia – with a particular focus on the life of young people in Queensland. We hope it brings back pleasant memories of your youth.

Rhyll Gardner
General Manager, Queensland
St.George Bank Limited

slq **state library of queensland**
www.slq.qld.gov.au

FOCUS PUBLISHING
PTY LTD

A Focus Publishing Book Project
Focus Publishing Pty Ltd
ABN 55 003 600 360
Level 3, 100 William Street, Woolloomooloo, NSW, 2011
Telephone: 61 2 9336 7000
Fax: 61 2 9357 2501

Email: focus@focus.com.au
Website: www.focus.com.au

Editorial Project Manager Diane Jardine
Senior Designer Jason Cupitt
Production Manager Karen Young
Client Services Manager Kita George

Publisher and CEO Jaqui Lane
Managing Director Gordon Hinds
Associate Publisher Andra Müller
General Manager Publishing Peter Hock

Copyright © 2006 State Library of Queensland
This book is copyright. Apart from any fair dealing for the purposes of private study, research, criticism or review, as permitted under the Copyright Act, no part may be reproduced by any process without written permission. Enquiries should be addressed to the State Library of Queensland.

While all reasonable attempts at factual accuracy have been made, Focus Publishing accepts no responsibility for any errors contained in this book.

Saunders, Kay, 1947- .
    Between the covers: revealing the State Library of
    Queensland's collections.

    Bibliography.
    ISBN 1 921156 05 8.

    1. State Library of Queensland. 2. State libraries -
    Queensland - Special collections. 3. State libraries -
    Collection development - Queensland. I. Title.

    025.21875943

Between the covers

Revealing the State Library of Queensland's collections

Author Kay Saunders
Research Librarian Dianne Byrne

4 | Between the covers

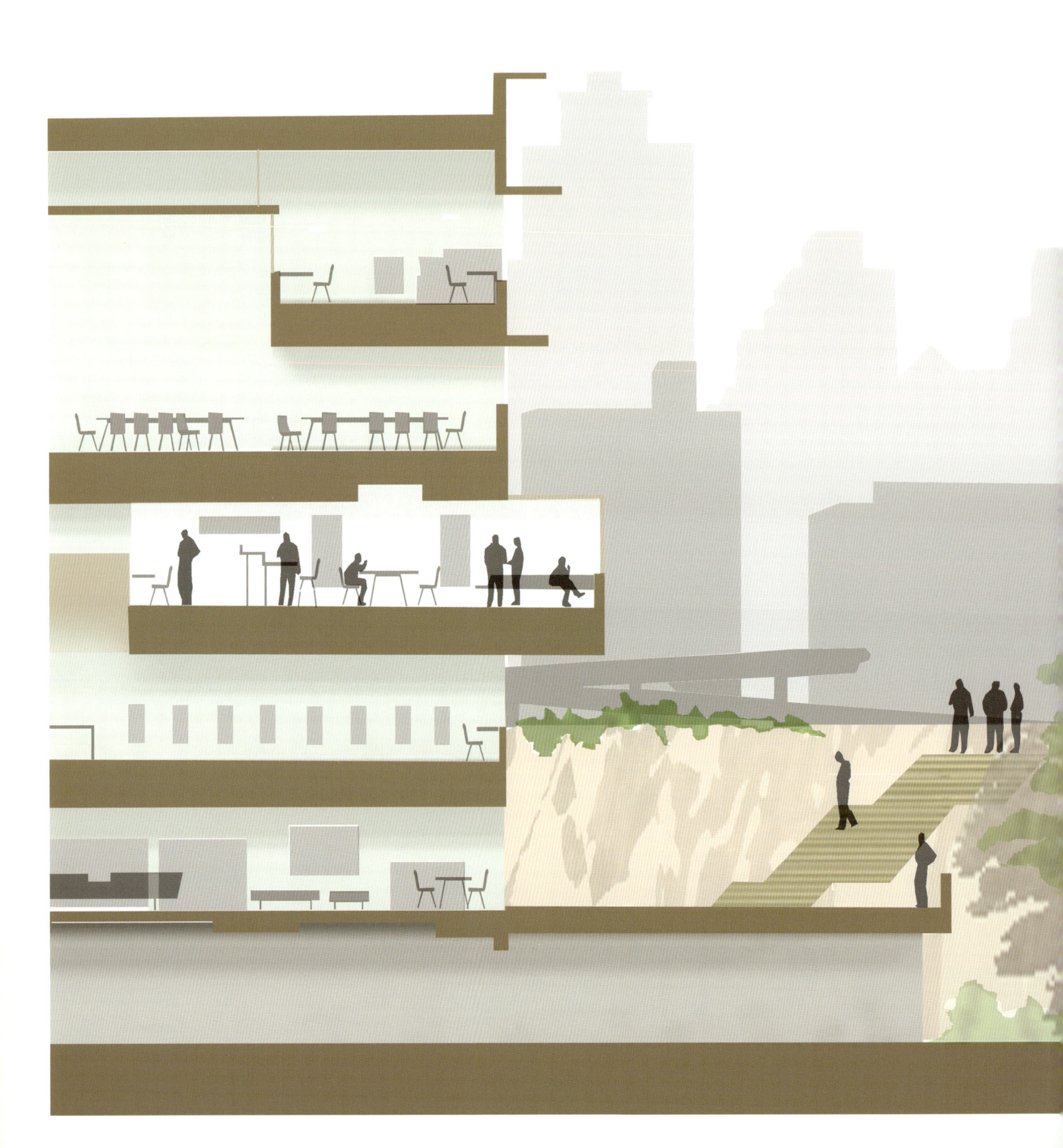

Foreword

Heralding a milestone in Queensland's history – the reopening at South Bank of the State Library of Queensland – this beautiful book celebrates the diversity of the State Library's collections and highlights our role as Australia's most important repository of Queensland's documentary heritage.

In one of the Australia's premier cultural and education precincts, South Bank now boasts a contemporary leisure and knowledge destination responsive to the changing world of information and ideas.

Destined to play an integral role in the lives of Queenslanders for generations to come, the State Library has undergone a transformation to a dynamic physical and virtual library, providing access to a vast array of information for leisure and learning. All members of the community are encouraged to participate in the development of knowledge and the sharing of ideas through the State Library.

The redeveloped and expanded State Library building at South Bank features well-appointed galleries and a Treasures Wall where many of the items featured in *Between the covers: revealing the State Library of Queensland's collections* can now be exhibited and appreciated in all their splendour. Our touring exhibition program will extend the enjoyment of these treasures to communities throughout Queensland and globally, online, through state-of-the-art digital technology.

The items exquisitely presented here convey just a taste of the treasures contained in our extensive collections.

On behalf of the Library Board of Queensland, I take this opportunity to acknowledge the ongoing support of the State Government and the commitment of many generous benefactors, both individuals and corporations, in acquiring items of significance to the heritage of the state of Queensland. In this connection, the Queensland Library Foundation has provided sustained and imaginative support, both through acquisitions and by greatly enhancing the renovated building.

On behalf of the State Library, I also thank most warmly the generous sponsors of this significant publication.

I invite you to visit the new State Library of Queensland and take a fascinating journey experiencing the full richness of the collections so well represented in *Between the covers.*

Emeritus Professor Roy Webb AO
Chairperson, Library Board of Queensland

Opposite An artist's impression of a cross section of the new State Library of Queensland building at Brisbane's South Bank. The building was officially opened by the Hon Peter Beattie MP, Premier of Queensland on 24 November 2006.

6 | Between the covers

INTRODUCTION

In 1902, when the Public Library of Queensland opened in William Street in Brisbane, its holdings consisted of around 20,000 volumes and the annual book budget was less than £800. With an interior that was described as "unpretentious", and an Australian collection that occupied only a few shelves, it lacked the grandeur of the established public libraries in Sydney and Melbourne. For much of its early life, the Public Library of Queensland was a remote and forbidding place. *The Brisbane Courier* described it as such:

> *The doors open on the stroke of 10, and they march with solemn shuffling gait up the dingy shabbiness of the entrance steps in the wide Hall of romance – second-hand romance, vicarious romance, packed neatly on grimy, friendly shelves … The stream of these regulars – as much a part of the Library as its faded walls – has emptied itself by this time in the nooks and corners of the library. You can almost hear its sigh of contentment, as it reaches out for its collective book, giving a final creak, a cough, and a rustle before settling down to a morning's unbroken silence …*
>
> Brisbane Courier, 17 September 1932

Today's State Library of Queensland is a very different place. It offers a huge variety of services and resources, and its contents range from newspapers, maps and music, to multimedia and audiovisual materials. There are items of interest to be found in all parts of the State Library, but the rarest and most intriguing are located within the Heritage Collections.

Heritage Collections comprises three main collections. The John Oxley Library, originally established in 1923, has been a part of the State Library since 1946. It contains works of Queensland and Australian literature, Australian exploration and discovery, and Queensland biography, as well as material on Aboriginal and Torres Strait Islander culture, anthropology, myths and legends. It is rich in photographs, paintings and drawings, items of ephemera, and collections of personal and family letters, memoirs and diaries, as well as the records of Queensland businesses, clubs and organisations.

The Australian Library of Art collects material relating to Australian art and artists, especially Queensland art, and incorporates the James Hardie Library of Australian Fine Arts, the Lindsay Collection of Pat Corrigan and the History and Art of the Book (incorporating Rare Books). The holdings include limited edition Australian art books, private press publications and over 7,000 exhibition catalogues, as well as bookplates, designer bindings and printing blocks acquired for the insight they offer into the art of book production. The State Library also houses one of the country's largest holdings of Australian and international artists' books.

The Map Collection features historical and current published maps, atlases and other cartographic materials, particularly relating to Australia, Queensland, and other states. Early pastoral maps of Queensland and estate maps of early Brisbane are among the strengths of the State Library's local history resources.

Between the covers: revealing the State Library of Queensland's collections features outstanding examples from all of these collections. However, this publication is not intended to be simply a celebration of the State Library's treasures. The items have been specially selected for the

Opposite This miniature pocket globe, entitled *A correct globe with the new discoveries*, was made in London in 1774. It is the first globe to show Captain James Cook's voyage around the world from 1768 to 1771. A dotted line marks Cook's journey from England to the Pacific Ocean and then south to New Zealand, up the east coast of Australia, through the Torres Strait and back to England. The globe measures 7 cm in diameter and is enclosed in a sharkskin case.
[RB 910 1774]

Ihrem hochverehrten Mitcolonisten
Herrn J.C.Heussler
Consul des deutschen Reiches und der Niederlande,
Mitglied des Queensländer Oberhauses,
widmen dieses Album bei Gelegenheit
seiner als Kommissär der queensländer
Regierung zu unternehmenden Reise
in's deutsche Heimatland mit dem ergebenen
Ausdrucke der
Hochachtung
Die Deutschen Queenslands.
August 1897 A.D.

insights they offer into our history and for their ability to illustrate and tell a story.

Beginning with "Queensland style", the chapters look at the people, places and influences that have contributed to the distinctive Queensland way of life. Topics include the impact that the landscape has exerted on the Queensland outlook ("Our landscape", "Beach and bush"), the role of sport in our society ("The greatest game under the sun"), the interaction between the sexes ("Life and love"), and the changing role of young people from the colonial period to recent times ("Young Queensland"). Queensland visionaries and innovators are considered in "Dreamers and yarners", and the comings and goings of tourists and travellers is the subject of "The great escape". The State Library's unique collection of rare and fine books is showcased in "The art of the book".

Between the covers is illustrated with over 200 items, ranging from sheet music, scrapbooks and silk theatre bills, to sporting programs, tickets, illuminated addresses, manuscripts, posters and photograph albums. Many of these works have been acquired through the generosity of corporate and private donors. The Queensland Library Foundation also has played a crucial role in obtaining material of national significance. One outstanding example is the Rawson Archive relating to the family who were among the first European settlers in the Mackay area.

The continuing growth and use of the collections is a vital part of today's State Library. At a time when the internet has revolutionised the delivery of information and is transforming collection building and service delivery, the State Library is responding with the development of online services to engage the community.

These services include Picture Queensland, which contains thousands of digital images of historic photographs from our collections, as well as images from other Queensland cultural institutions and libraries.

Through participation in national initiatives such as Picture Australia and PANDORA (Preserving & Accessing Networked Documentary Resources of Australia) the State Library is contributing to the preservation of electronic websites and web pages that reflect Queensland culture and society.

Between the covers offers a taste of the world of information waiting within the State Library of Queensland. It will excite your interest. I encourage you to visit us online, or to come in person to our wonderful new State Library.

Lea Giles-Peters
State Librarian

Opposite Album presented to Johann Christian Heussler, Commissioner of the Queensland Government, by the German inhabitants of Queensland on the eve of his return voyage to Germany, August 1897. Heussler was Queensland's first Emigration Agent in Europe, Consul for Bavaria and the Netherlands and a member of the Queensland Parliament. [ACC 5478]

10 Between the covers

Sponsors' Roll of Honour

Lead

Knight Frank

St.George Bank

Major

Alcan

Channel Seven Brisbane

Wilson HTM Investment Group

Key

Clayton Utz

John Wiley & Sons Australia, Ltd

Xstrata Queensland Limited

Opposite Album presented to Johann Christian Heussler, Commissioner of the Queensland Government, by the German inhabitants of Queensland on the eve of his return voyage to Germany, August 1897. Heussler was Queensland's first Emigration Agent in Europe, Consul for Bavaria and the Netherlands and a member of the Queensland Parliament. [ACC 5478]

CONTENTS

4 Foreword

6 Introduction

10 Sponsors' roll of honour

16 State Library of Queensland acknowledgements

Chapter one

17 Queensland style

With its vast distances, terrain, economic base and colonial ethnic mix, Queensland developed a distinctive and fascinating style.

Chapter two

33 Our landscape

Queensland's relationship with its land, flora and fauna ranged from enchantment and curiosity to domination and exploitation.

Contents 13

Chapter three

49 Beach and bush

The beach and the bush remain at the heart of how Queensland sees and expresses itself to the outside world.

Chapter four

65 Queenslanders

Large distances and a decentralised and widespread population nurtured individuals with ambition to pursue their dreams.

Chapter five

81 Young Queensland

Queensland's wealth was always measured in the physical and moral strength of its children despite changing social ideas.

Between the covers

Chapter six

97

Life and love

Shared enterprise was the basis of any enduring pact between Queensland men and women.

Chapter seven

113

The greatest game under the sun

Warm climate, abundant playing fields and healthy population encouraged the enthusiastic development of sport in Queensland.

Chapter eight

129

The great escape

Newcomers travelling for pleasure, curiosity or necessity have been an important part of Queensland's history.

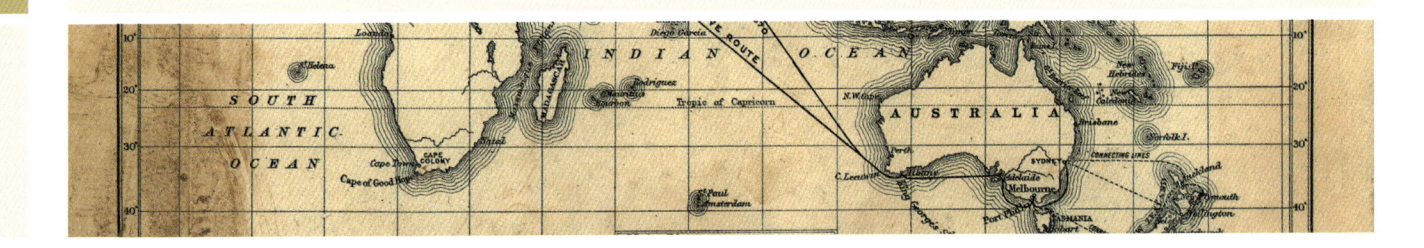

Contents 15

Chapter nine

Dreamers and yarners

145

Dreamers and yarners gave voice to the hopes of everyday people and connected a vibrant and emerging Queensland identity.

Chapter ten

The art of the book

161

The history of the book is one of artistic and technical innovation, driven by the desire to document the world in a lasting record.

177   Sponsors' gallery of excellence

182   Further reading

184   Author acknowledgements

State Library of Queensland acknowledgements

Project Director: Vicki McDonald
Project Manager: Deborah Stumm
Research Librarian/Coordinator: Dianne Byrne
Research Librarians/Officers: Elizabeth Fa'Aoso, Sharon Nolan, Margaret Warren
Designer: David Ashe
Photographers: Reina Irmer, Leif Ekstrom

The State Library thanks the following individuals and organisations for their generous support and for permitting items to be reproduced.

Alecto Historical Editions, Mr Dimple Bani (estate of Ephraim Bani), Mr Keith Bartholomew, Mr Benjamin Brown, the Bundanon Trust (estate of Arthur Boyd), Mr Michael Callaghan and Redback Graphix, Mr Pierre Cavalan, Mr Tony Champ, Mrs Dorothy Collins, Mr Kevin Collins (estate of Clyde Collins), Mr Hugh Cornish, Ms Bernadette Crockford, Mr Ray Crooke, Ms Kate Dickson, Mrs Alison Drake (estate of Romeo W Lahey), Ms Sun Evrard, Mr Andrew Glad, Ms Catherine Glad, Ms Helen Glad (the estate of Norman Lindsay), the editor and staff of the *Gold Coast Bulletin*, Mr David Gwynne, Mrs Anneliese Harris (estate of William Julius Harris), Mr Henry Howell, Miss Shirley Lahey (estate of Vida Lahey), Mrs Meta Lindsay (estate of Jack Lindsay), Mrs Margaret Lock, Mrs Bettina MacAulay, Mr Ron McBurnie, Mr Michael McMartin, Ms Helen Malone, Mrs Carole Mooney (estate of Clyde Collins), Mrs Ann Neale (estate of Romeo W Lahey), News Limited, Mr Garth Nix, Ms Katharine Nix, Mr Mark O'Connor, Ms Adele Outteridge, the Hon Justice Anthe Philippides SC, Mr Friedhelm Pohlmann, Ms Janet Prowse, the editor and staff of Queensland Newspapers, Shoog Enterprises, Mr Michael Stafford, Mrs Paula Stafford, Ms Kylie Stillman, Ms Robin Tait, Mr Simon Target (estate of William Bustard), Mrs Denise Thorpe (estate of Dorothy Coleman), Mr John Tonkin, Mr Russ Tyson, Mr Leonard Waia (estate of Mr Kala Waia), Ms Judy Watson, Mrs Leonie Watson (estate of Olive Ashworth), Mrs Anthea Wieneke (estate of James Wieneke), Mr Frank Wiesner, the Wildlife Preservation Society of Queensland (Sunshine Coast).

Sponsored by
Knight Frank

Chapter one
Queensland style

Author Kay Saunders Research Librarian Dianne Byrne

Between the covers

> "With its vast distances, and terrain ranging from desert to tropical rainforest to mountain coolness, Queensland never possessed a singular style ... Civilisation and chaos produced a distinctive and fascinating originality."

Opening image Original fabric designs and commercial artwork inspired by tropical north Queensland, created by Olive Ashworth. [TR1947]

On her first trip outback in the early 1890s, Lady Lamington reported on her visit to Barcaldine Downs where there had been big strikes the year before. "When I arrived [the shearers] … drew a chalk line across the floor of the shed and said I must "pay my footing" (alias a drink all round) which we gladly did, and they showed us everything …" She noted that one man (Jackie Howe) sheared 327 sheep in one day. Her curiosity and enthusiasm have given us a rare insight into an evolving Queensland style.

With its vast distances, and terrain ranging from desert to tropical rainforest to mountain coolness, Queensland never possessed a singular style. Its enduring economic structure, with pastoralism, sugar production and mining as the central base, alongside its diverse colonial ethnic composition with Indigenous people, Pacific Islanders, Japanese, Chinese, Italians, Afghans, Britons, Germans and Danes, meant that Queensland would always be "different". The intense class conflicts that might erupt into armed industrial warfare, the destruction of the natural environment and the exploitation of its resources gave a particularly aggressive character to the society. Civilisation and chaos produced a distinctive and fascinating originality.

Queensland architecture contributed notable genres to the emerging Australian vernacular. In 1849, William Pickering's store and house in Queen Street contained "… verandahs back and front, eight feet wide, protected by a substantial and ornamental palisade. The roof is shingled with ironbark shingles". The wealthy squatters' grand homes like Jimbour, Nindooinbah, Bromelton and Gracemere convey graciousness and ease with the beauty

Right The contrast of old and new: Brisbane's landmark colonial General Post Office building, completed in 1879, is overlooked by the Bank of Queensland's state-of-the-art BOQ Centre, opened by Premier Peter Beattie on 18 November 2004. [Image courtesy Knight Frank, the appointed managing agent for this building.]

Far right Two views of the GPO and Queen Street c. 1897 [top] [Image No. 108052] and c. 1918 [bottom] [Image No. 38582]. The site now occupied by the Bank of Queensland was the location of the Commonwealth Bank.

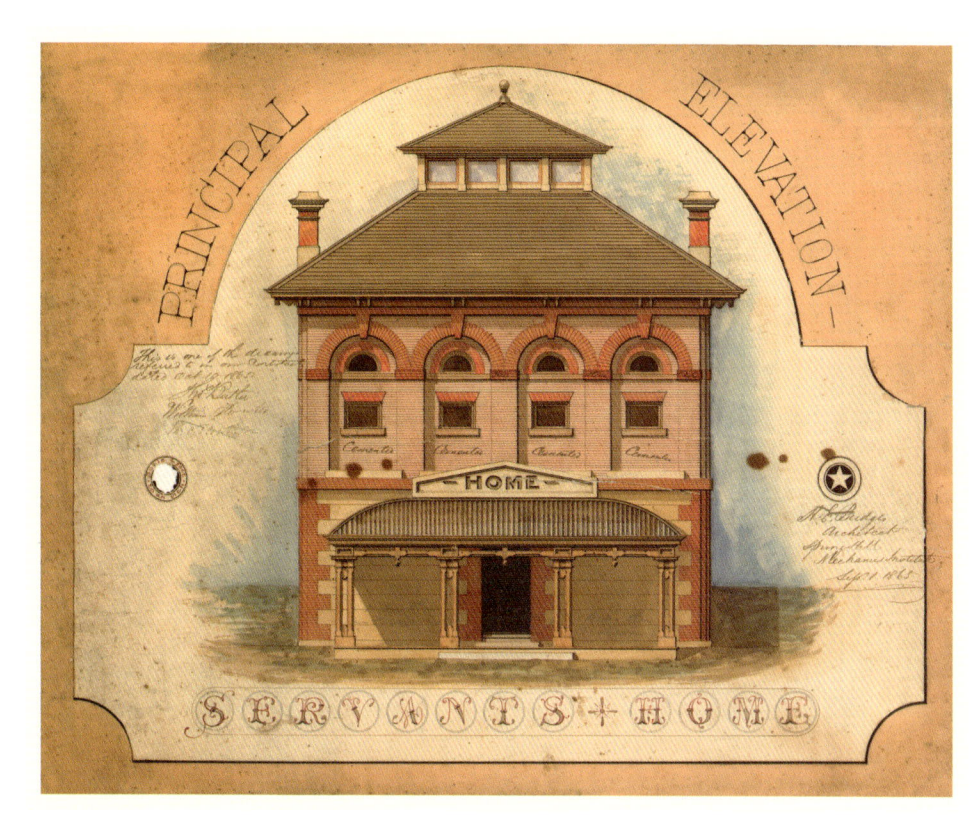

of the local environment that cannot be rivalled. With some borrowing from grand plantation homes of the West Indies and verandahs of India, these magnificent homes were transformed in an authentic reaction to new conditions. The Rawsons' The Hollow maintained a verandah on all sides of the wooden construction. An elegant desk, replete with candles, sat on the front side, along with a barometer to record the blistering heat of Mackay.

The distinctive domestic Queenslander house, "… perched upon stilts like teetering swamp birds … that made southerners think of us like bayside-dwelling Papuans", as novelist Thea Astley wrote, remains a local icon. The feel of these wooden houses with their dark nooks and breezes coming through the French doors from spacious verandahs is captured in David Malouf's evocative *12 Edmondstone Street* (1985).

The Rawson Archive contains a unique photographic record of the early dwellings in Mackay. The watercolours of CGS Hirst depict properties such as the Junction Hotel (1886) on Boggo Road and Jerriestown, the Laidley Creek Farmstead of John Campbell (1873) with its verandah and the Danish flag flying from the shingled roof. The Danish influence in Queensland extended to Danish photographer Poul Poulsen, whose collection of 144 original glass plates document the period from the 1880s to the 1920s, capturing the distinctive housing and alignment within streetscapes.

The State Library possesses a magnificent collection of architectural drawings and plans from the Italian architect Andrea Stombuco, who designed buildings such as St Andrew's Anglican Church in South Brisbane, Her Majesty's Imperial Opera House and parts of All Hallows Convent School in Brisbane. His style, although largely derivative, also responded to Queensland genres with his grand house, Sans Souci (later Palma Rosa). In 1894, a unique coloured supplement from the *Telegraph* featured one of the major works of another landmark Queensland architect, FDG Stanley. Prominent among these images is the Queensland National Bank Building in Queen Street, which still ranks among the state's finest colonial buildings. The Heussler album (1897) also featured important architectural

Above left Proposed design by architect Henry Edwin Bridges for the Servants Home at Ann Street in Brisbane, September 1865. Bridges won the design competition with this work. The completed building was extended by Richard Gailey 1877–78 and became the School of Arts. The building was restored in 1983 and it remains a Brisbane landmark. [ACC 3109]

Above right Architectural plans by Italian-born Andrea Stombuco, who moved to Queensland in 1875 and executed a variety of important commissions including houses, theatres, schools, churches and convents buildings. Well-known works by Stombuco that survive today include St Patrick's Catholic Church in Fortitude Valley and Palma Rosa, in the Brisbane suburb of Hamilton. [ACC M 321; ACC 3225]

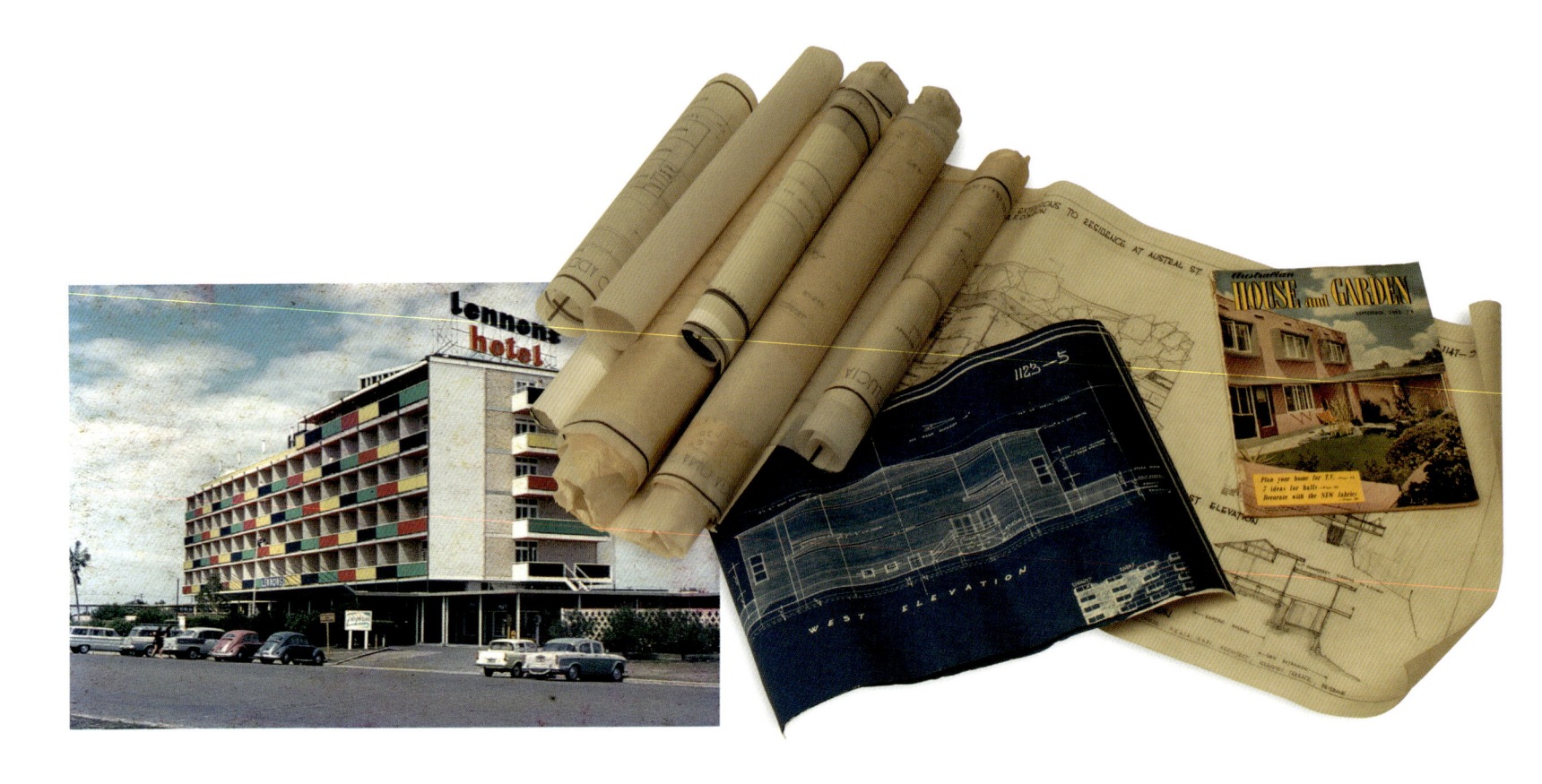

Above left The new Lennon's Hotel at Broadbeach, September 1962. Set among sand dunes on five-and-a-half acres of Crown land, it quickly became a landmark with its bright, multicoloured balconies. [Image No. 00198]

Above right Architectural plans by Karl Langer for RF Condon's residence in St Lucia, c. 1962. [R 83-30]

landmarks, such as Parliament House, the Supreme Court building, and the convict-built Observatory. The Archer Album contains images of the 1860s interior of the Bank of New South Wales in Brisbane.

The Karl Langer collection links Queensland design into world trends. A Viennese refugee from the Nazis, Langer arrived in Brisbane with his wife, art critic Gertrude Langer, in 1938. His appreciation of Queensland's climate, combined with his sleek modernism, produced buildings like the Lennon's Hotel at Broadbeach and poet Val Vallis's house in St Lucia. His advocacy of the state's architectural heritage made Langer a force within the National Trust. The impact of modernism continued with the construction of the 1960 high-rise apartments Torbreck in Highgate Hill, and Australia's first drive-in shopping centre at Chermside in 1957. Gabriel & Elizabeth Poole Design Company's recent architecture has responded to the "heat and dust and benefits of the sub-tropics", as Astley remarked of the Queensland climate.

Impressive modern buildings were not only constructed in the more populated south-eastern corner. The Delta Hotel in Ayr and Corones Hotel in Charleville are among the finest examples of Art Deco interior design in Australia. Built on the site of the original Hotel Norman in 1929 at the immense cost of £50,000 with local labour, the Corones' exterior used the idiom of wide, cool verandahs alongside venetian blinds to create a building of extraordinary beauty. The original brochure proclaimed the delights of "hot bore water …", so that the local environment and cutting-edge international design were combined. Visitors to Australia, such as aviator Amy Johnson and Gracie Fields, stayed at this notable hotel. In its first years, despite the Depression, guests in the latest Paris fashions danced to music from imported orchestras and dined in a magnificent dining hall that seated 320 people. Its owner, Harry Corones, originally from Kythera in Greece, was one of the earliest shareholders in Qantas and a consummate host. His impact on the life and style of western Queensland was matched by other Greeks who opened cafes, oyster bars and hostelries throughout the state.

Queensland also produced professional cabinet-makers of the highest quality. Born in Toowoomba in 1887, Edmund Rosenstengel worked in New Zealand, in Vancouver, Canada and in the United States before setting up a business in

Queensland style

Above *Torbreck, a new concept in modern living*, a pamphlet produced by developers Reid Murray, to promote the new structure, the first reinforced concrete building in the southern hemisphere. [P 728.31 rei]

Above right *"Torbreck" under construction*, by Cyril Gibbs, watercolour, 1959. Torbreck was the first high-rise unit complex built in Queensland and remains architecturally and historically significant. Constructed between 1958 and 1960 by builder Noel Kratzmann, the complex consisted of 150 units in a seven-storey "garden block" and a 20-storey tower. [ACC 4610]

Right An artist's impression of one of the apartments in Torbreck, c. 1960. [Image No. BC 920]

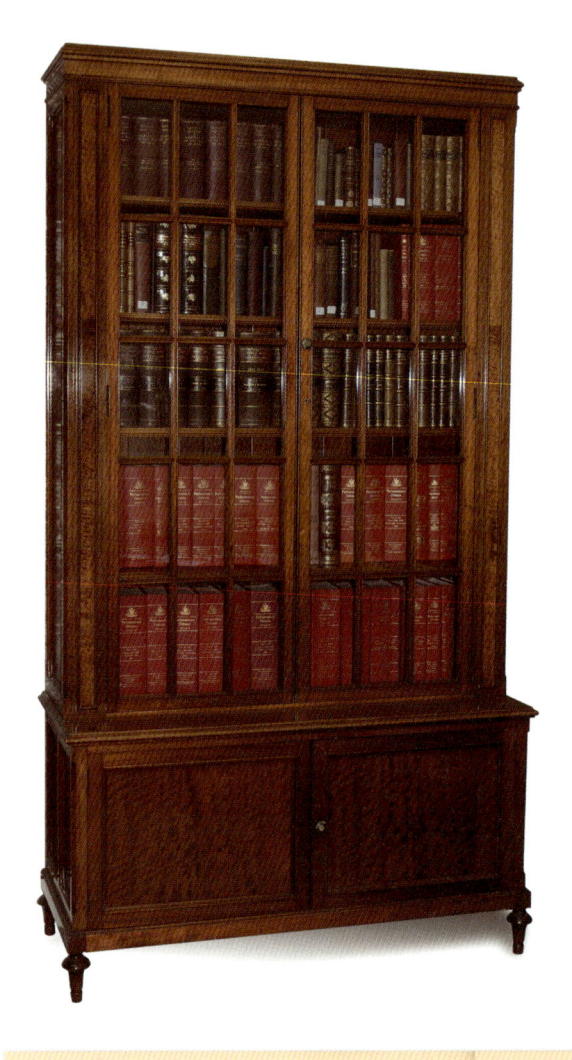

22　Between the covers

Above Souvenir tulipwood wall plaques with handpainted scenes of north Queensland, 1940s. [ACC 6265]

Left Bookcase of Queensland maple and silky oak manufactured by Edmund Rosenstengel and presented to the State Library of Queensland by his daughter, artist Paula Rosenstengel. [ACC 3125]

Below Pamphlet produced for the opening of Corones Hotel at Charleville, completed in 1929 at a cost of £50,000. The hotel, with its jazz hall, elaborate plaster ceilings and ensuite bathrooms became an oasis for graziers, wool-buyers and commercial travellers. [RBJ 647 HOT]

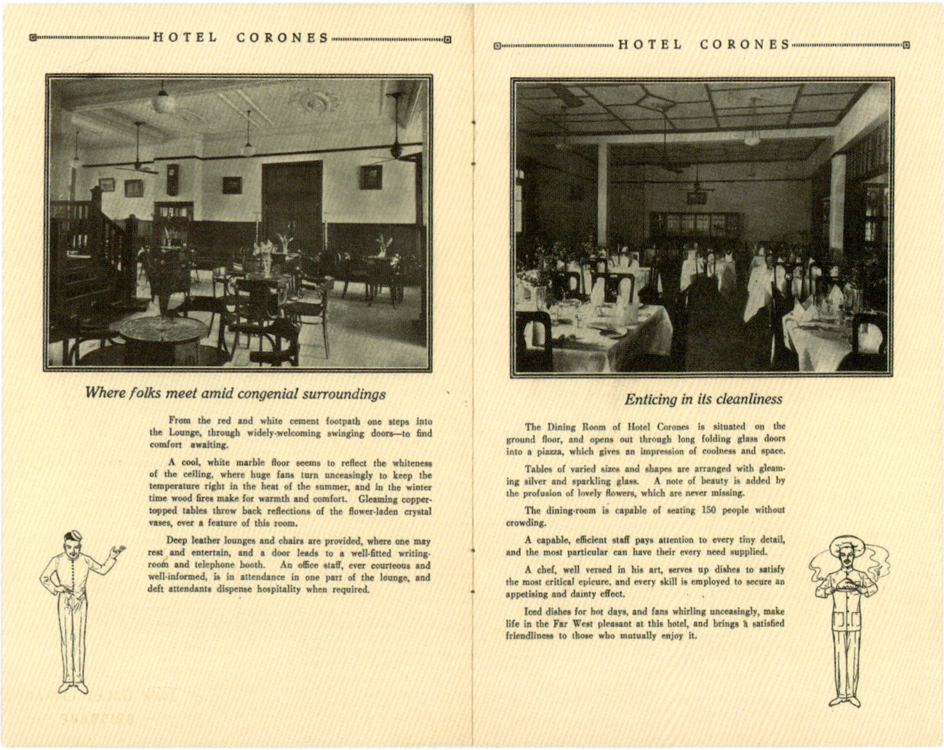

Brisbane in 1922. His work is celebrated for his fine use of Queensland timbers, along with elaborate carving and marquetry inlay. The furniture he made for Parliament House for the use of the Duke of Gloucester (1934) and the jewellery box for the Duchess of York (later Queen Elizabeth, the Queen Mother) are among his finest works. The State Library also owns many photographs of the work of manufacturer FH Byrne, as well as Tritton's and John Hicks' catalogues. These publications depict domestic interiors designed for a conservative but discerning clientele.

People with more modest incomes also cultivated beauty in their household environments. Paul Grano's 1938 poem "The tree planter" captured women's longing to transform their domestic environments into welcoming spaces:

She so often planted trees,
tidy orange and cool-leaved custard apple,
shrubby mulberry, and dark-shadowed mango,
but ever her sorrow she saw no fruit;

From Mrs Rawson's advice on parrot-decorated firescreens to the tulipwood wall plaques of the 1940s, interiors were made familiar and comfortable. Lady Lamington was appalled by the decoration of Government House when she arrived. As she noted: "I went around the house, which had been freshly done up for our arrival and I found a brown plush on the top of my bedroom, and peacock-blue plush porteries and curtains in the drawing room … I got hold of the man in charge from the Board of Works … I said it did not seem to do for everyday use … He said brown Holland covers would answer the purpose nicely!! … By degrees the house got so pretty with varnished floors and basket tables and chairs in the hall, while aboriginal weapons were around the walls …" Her reaction to the immediacy of a new climate was intelligent, radical and unexpected.

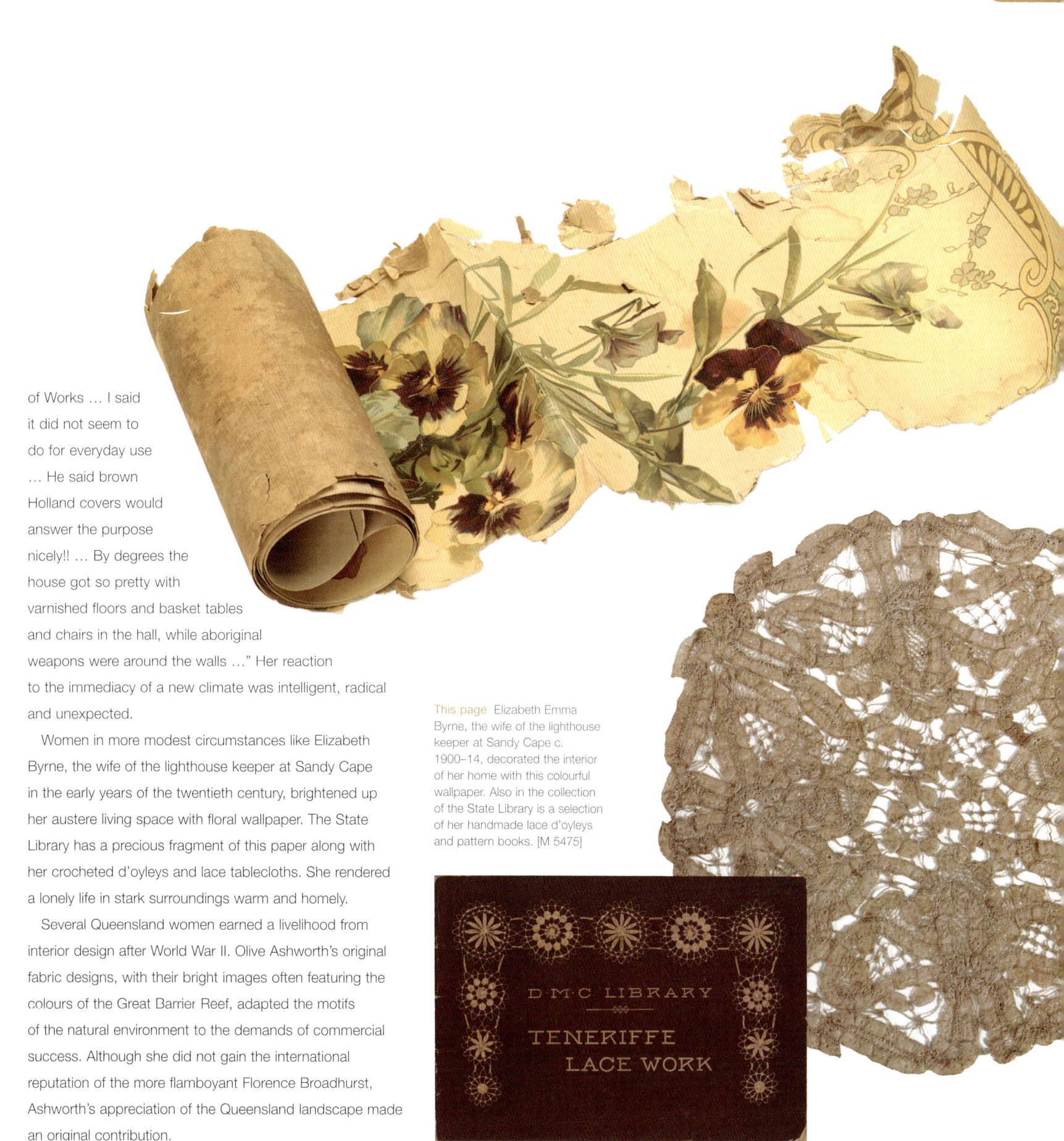

Women in more modest circumstances like Elizabeth Byrne, the wife of the lighthouse keeper at Sandy Cape in the early years of the twentieth century, brightened up her austere living space with floral wallpaper. The State Library has a precious fragment of this paper along with her crocheted d'oyleys and lace tablecloths. She rendered a lonely life in stark surroundings warm and homely.

Several Queensland women earned a livelihood from interior design after World War II. Olive Ashworth's original fabric designs, with their bright images often featuring the colours of the Great Barrier Reef, adapted the motifs of the natural environment to the demands of commercial success. Although she did not gain the international reputation of the more flamboyant Florence Broadhurst, Ashworth's appreciation of the Queensland landscape made an original contribution.

This page Elizabeth Emma Byrne, the wife of the lighthouse keeper at Sandy Cape c. 1900–14, decorated the interior of her home with this colourful wallpaper. Also in the collection of the State Library is a selection of her handmade lace d'oyleys and pattern books. [M 5475]

Below Plans for the historic semi-circular shearing shed at Isis Downs station in Queensland's central-west, the first electrified shearing shed in Australia and the largest structure of its kind in the southern hemisphere. The shed took two years to build and the first shearing took place in July 1914. [OM DS 47] [R 762]

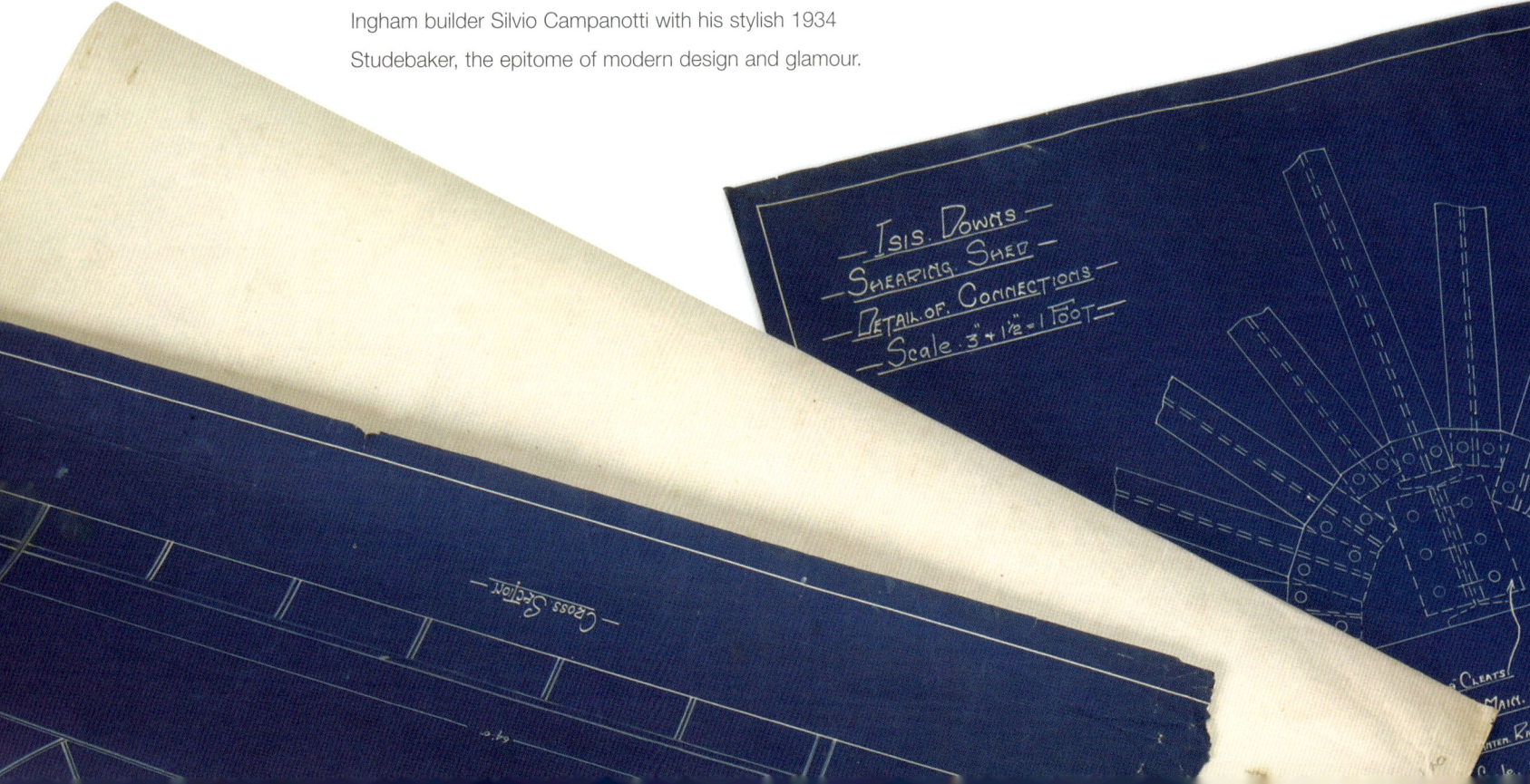

The years following World War I witnessed an emphasis upon health and vitality. The Helidon Spa, established in 1879, became popular in the interwar years. Despite its claims that its products were "more beneficial than those at many of the glamorous European resorts", the modesty of the surroundings gave consumers no misunderstanding they were entering Baden-Baden or Biarritz.

The plans for the semi-circular shearing shed at Isis Downs – the first electrified shed in Australia with its steel girders manufactured in England and painstakingly transported by Australia's first road train in 1912 – reveal an enduring commitment to innovation and new technology. Ten years earlier, James Trackson, the proprietor of an electrical firm, demonstrated the first steam Locomobile to Governor Sir Henry Norman. This is reputedly the first car introduced into Queensland. This enterprise was beset by difficulties as the municipal authorities insisted upon travel only when accompanied by a man walking ahead holding a red flag. A century on, we can speculate on the environmental wisdom of the steam car, the production of which ceased in 1903. Queensland's love affair with the petrol-driven automobile is evident in the photograph of Ingham builder Silvio Campanotti with his stylish 1934 Studebaker, the epitome of modern design and glamour.

Some local icons have an enduring and popular appeal. A recent Castlemaine XXXX beer advertisement featuring two Australian bushmen heading for a tiny pub, declaring "Australians wouldn't give a XXXX for anything else", was inducted into the prestigious international Advertising Slogan Hall of Fame. The original XXX Sparkling Ale from 1878 was produced through the joint efforts of two young Irish brothers, Nicholas and Edward Fitzgerald, with the Brisbane firm of Quinlan and Donnelly. Mrs Quinlan took over from her husband as a brewer. These partnerships formed the basis of the original Castlemaine Brewery. In 1916 the brand product added an extra X to become the label that still exists, marked out in huge fluorescent lighting on the roof of the Milton Brewery. In 1928 it joined with former competitor Perkins to become Castlemaine Perkins.

In 1979 the company became part of the Toohey's business and later part of the Bond conglomerate. Alan Bond's injudicious decision to place his logo on the brewery wall caused outrage to locals. "Mr Fourex", dressed in his distinctive boater, was a celebrity in his own right, appearing at important events such as the opening carnival at Doomben Racecourse in 1933.

The years following World War I witnessed an emphasis upon health and vitality.

Above Queensland's first motor car, a steam-powered model owned by businessman James Trackson. [ACC 6147; Album APA-3]

Right Taking the waters at the award-winning Helidon Spa, c. 1924. [Image No. 43379]

Above Local builder Silvio Campanotti posing with his Studebaker roadster at Ingham, 1940. [Image No. 61281]

The consumption of food and beverages has held a long fascination in Queensland. Dr Lang's immigrants arriving on the *Fortitude* in 1849 were greeted with a poem:

… Lov'd land of plenty, – land of wealth and ease,
'Land of vintage' – queen of the southern seas …
Here, far from poverty and fractious broil,
Plenty and peace repay the labourers toil: –
… Welcome, then, strangers, to our Eden shore, –
And for its joys indulgent heaven adore.

This theme of abundance endured, but in reality food often left much to be desired. Henry Stuart Russell in *Genesis of Queensland* (1888) noted the meat was "tough teeth-task" at the Brisbane Victoria Hotel in the mid-1840s.

Hailed by the Danish immigrant Thorvald Weitemeyer as "Kind people! – Good Queensland! – Happy Country – No starvation here or smell of poverty … Who said Australia was a desert?", his description of the diet again leaves us to wonder on the health of those "kind people". "… In the morning we generally had fried steak, white bread, and butter." He recalled in the 1870s, "No beer or schnapps are put on the table in this country, but instead of that one drinks tea by the quart at every meal." Out in bush pubs, rough alcohol was consumed in vast quantities. The Reverend George Carrington, an itinerant Anglican priest around Weitemeyer's time, noted in his memoirs, *Adventures of a university man*, that men would drink so much they might literally drop dead in the dusty Queensland townships.

Within a few decades the raw and dangerous potency of bush-bingeing made way for more civilised modes of consumption. Rather than an insistence on steak at every meal as a sign of the abundance and prosperity of colonial life, cuisine was adapted to local produce. In the northern regions of Queensland, the Chinese residents provided welcome nutritious vegetables. Later they farmed bananas in the Cairns region. The State Library's photograph

Queensland style 27

Above "Mr Fourex" makes an appearance at the opening carnival at Doomben Racecourse, May 1933. [Image No. 102672] **Left** Label for Castlemaine XXXX Sparkling Prize Ale. [RBF 741.692 lab; Image No. 190334]

Above Plan of the Pineapple Estate at Kangaroo Point, offered for sale 28 March 1885. [ME 846; Image No. est 00080]

collection contains images of Chinese workers transporting the heavy banana bunches onto wooden river vessels.

Lady Lamington, as the vice-regal vessel made its way down the Queensland coast, enjoyed both hospitality and the new cuisine. The ladies of Townsville organised a garden party in her honour "where they presented me with a lovely basket of blue water lilies … and gave me such a good fruit compote or salad, and where I first made the acquaintance of sand flies". The pineapple, a symbol of hospitality and welcome since the eighteenth century, became a motif of prosperity in colonial Queensland. It appeared in advertising and invitations, and even became the inspiration for developers marketing real estate.

Pineapple as a principal ingredient in tropical fruit salad also became a distinctive Queensland dish. At the Royal Ball held on 10 March 1954 to honour the visit of Queen Elizabeth and Prince Phillip, it was served with ice-cream. The banquet featured Queensland specialties such as barramundi. Much of the rest of the meal, comprising dishes like Lobster Cocktail Parisienne and Hot Ham Crescents, might have stepped out of Mrs Beeton's books nearly a century before.

The State Library also owns a rare book by Tasmanian resident Edward Abbott, *The English and Australian cookery book: cookery for the many, as well as for the "upper ten thousand"* (1864) which first combined Antipodean and English cuisine.

Queensland cuisine has a long tradition, with the Victoria Hotel in Brisbane serving fresh turtle soup in the mid-1840s. The recent interest in "bush tucker" with crocodile, possum, wattle seed and kangaroo on menus, adds a contemporary dimension to Mrs Rawson's recipes for bandicoot and flying fox in the late colonial years.

The hot climate also required an adaptation of conventional European attire. The theme of the conflict between an informality of dress, appropriate to the climate, and more formal attire still continues. John Sweatman, a clerk on the surveying vessel *Bramble,* noticed in Brisbane in 1846 "the thermometer during our stay was frequently above

> Rather than an insistence on steak at every meal as a sign of the abundance and prosperity of colonial life, cuisine was adapted to local produce.

Right Menu for the Royal Ball at the Brisbane City Hall, March 1954. [Ephemera Collection]

100 degrees Fahrenheit in the shade and the inhabitants going about in their shirt sleeves". Gentlemen did not dress so informally in this period. For those who wished to maintain the standards of Europe, in 1854 William Cairncross imported £5,000 worth of "well-selected, fashionable, and extensively varied Drapery Goods".

Some emigrants began shedding European conventions while in transit. The author of a ship's diary on the *Southern Cross* recorded that: "The intense heat has induced rather airy costumes among the gentlemen; the favourite being – no coats-shirts mimic Collars; sleeves rolled up to the elbow … We noticed many novelties in the Ladies Attire – Crinolines are collapsing … hats look generally as if they had been sat upon or slept in …" A few wealthy Queenslanders always maintained formal dress codes. The elegant Major Bertram Bell played polo in the 1920s in full kit including military-style puttees.

Somewhat irreverently the eccentric Bundaberg parliamentarian, "Bomber" Barnes often wore a full topee

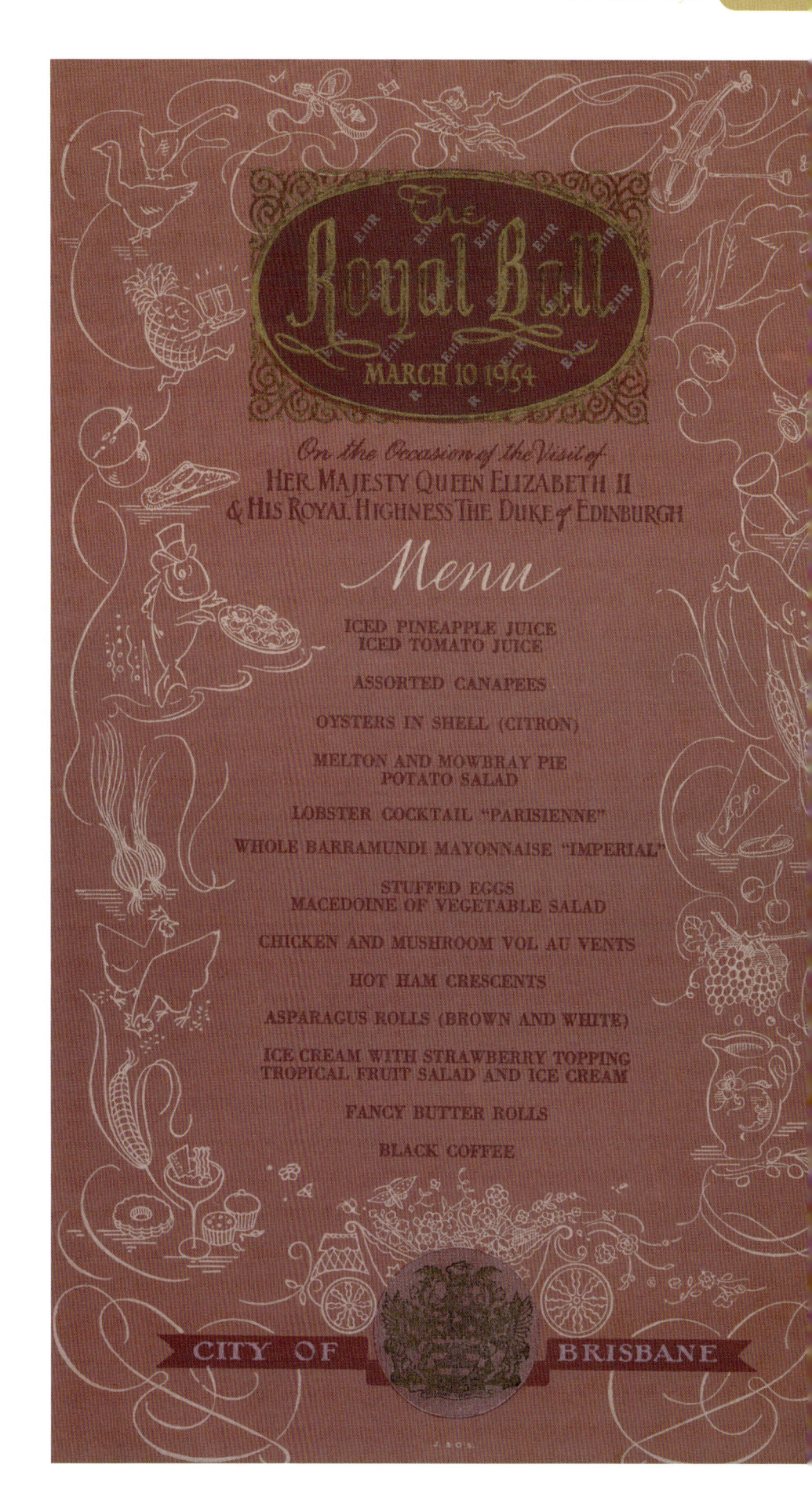

The hot climate also required an adaptation of conventional European attire. The theme of the conflict between an informality of dress, appropriate to the climate, and more formal attire still continues,

regardless of the occasion. Governor Sir Henry Abel-Smith kept up the formal tradition of perfectly tailored suits despite the weather conditions.

For women, the decision of what to wear could present a series of dilemmas. With the boyish figure made fashionable by Coco Chanel after World War I, underwear began to adapt from the previous heavy whale-boning. At first flappers, with their disregard for conventional modes of dress and behaviour, were condemned. This did not last long as the State Library's splendid collection of *Vogue*'s precursor, *La Gazette du bon ton* (1912–25), a beautifully illustrated exclusive magazine, shows.

New modes of women's underwear had a direct Queensland connection with Hickory, the manufacturers of lightweight brassieres and girdles. Its owner, Bernard Dowd, aligned his company (which revived the Miss Australia Quest) as sponsor for the Queensland Spastic Children's League in 1954. The records of this organisation are recent State Library acquisitions. Part of the prize for state and national title-holders included travelling wardrobes from other generous sponsors such as department store Allan and Stark (later Myer). State title-holders were instructed by experts in the department stores in make-up techniques, grooming and dress sense as a preparation for the national competition. A posed photograph of Ann Miscamble, Miss Queensland 1965, demonstrated this process.

The dilemma of how to dress comfortably but fashionably in the Queensland climate continued to be a challenge in the 1930s when Helen Hughes, daughter of former Prime Minister William Morris Hughes and Dame Mary Hughes,

Above Major Bertram Charles Bell, son of a distinguished Queensland pastoral family, with members of his polo team, Cressbrook A, runners-up in the Dudley Cup at Goondiwindi, 1924. [M 780-35]

Below Queensland's most dapper dresser, Governor Sir Henry Abel Smith, takes over the role of ABC cameraman, c. 1959. [Image No. BC 045]

Queensland style 31

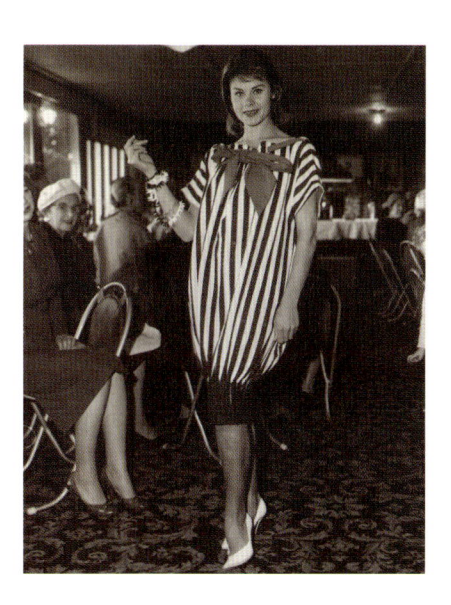

Above Some of Paula Stafford's early style-setting beach and party fashions. [Image Nos. BC 057, 055, 056]

Right Material from the collection of the Cerebral Palsy League of Queensland documenting the history of the Miss Queensland competition and the Miss Australia Quest. Included is a photograph of Miss Queensland 1965, Ann Miscamble, receiving make-up advice from a visiting expert. [ACC 5590]

Between the covers

Above left Program for the French fashion parade presented in Brisbane in 1956. [Ephemera Collection]

Above right Scrapbooks containing photographs of Paula Stafford's beach and leisure wear fashions, and the paper pattern for trousers she created for visiting American entertainer Sammy Davis Junior. [ACC 6491]

was working as a mannequin. The State Library possesses a series of photographs with the glamorous Miss Hughes modelling expensive fur coats, items hardly appropriate for the Queensland climate. The French fashion parade presented by *Trois Hirondelles Groupe* in 1956 at McWhirters department store contained a tradition of haute couture in the European style.

Paula Stafford's beach and leisure wear solved the problem of what fashionable Queensland women could wear in their everyday lives in the 1950s. Like the American designer Lilly Pulitzer, who dressed wealthy women on vacation at Palm Beach, and Emilio Pucci in Florence with his light clothes that travelled well, Stafford carved out an important niche in design. When the diminutive Sammy Davis Junior was unable to find trousers while touring Australia, he turned to Stafford. Along with RM Williams, with his distinctive menswear begun in the Depression, Stafford is a Queensland designer who produced a unique mode of dress, appropriate to both climate and consumers. The Sunday Sun Collection contains many images of international fashion and its local adaptation. The photographs of the first miniskirts in Brisbane in July 1967 demonstrated how Carnaby Street made its way south.

The State Library holds a wealth of fascinating material about Queensland Style. The scrapbooks of the Johnstone Gallery contain rare catalogues, newspaper clippings and greeting cards sent by gallery artists, while the Leonard and Kathleen Shillam Collection documents the careers of two of Queensland's most important sculptors. The State Library also has extensive holdings of the influential journals *Barjai* and the *Meanjin papers* both produced in Queensland in the 1940s, and the publications of Queensland-born writers such as Rodney Hall, Humphrey McQueen and Thomas Shapcott. The works of emerging writers like Venero Armano, Andrew McGahan, and Rebecca Sparrow are recent additions to the collection, along with the creations of inventive visual artists such as Davida Allen, Mona Ryder and artist/jeweller Barbara Heath.

Chapter two
Our landscape

Author Kay Saunders Research Librarian Dianne Byrne

> *These mountains are very remarkable. Out of the low ranges they rise like needles, like castles, like those fantastic isolated rocks in the ocean ...*

On a three-day excursion to the Glasshouse Mountains in 1843, Dr Ludwig Leichhardt captured the majesty of the environment: "These mountains are very remarkable. Out of the low ranges they rise like needles, like castles, like those fantastic isolated rocks in the ocean ..." This wonder of the natural environment was also caught in the splendid drawings in Joseph Banks' *Florilegium of Captain Cook's first voyage to Australia* (1771–84), Anthony Alder's *Queensland birds*, and John Gould's *The mammals of Australia*.

Queensland history did not always follow these paths of enchantment and curiosity with the land and its flora and fauna. For many colonists intent upon material success, the environment and its peoples had to be conquered and dominated. Grazier Donald Gunn reported "the old pioneering days seemed to consist of fights against nature the whole time". Frank Baily, a tutor at Jimboomba station sent back letters to his relatives in England recounting his frequent killing

Above John Gould's *The mammals of Australia* was published originally in 13 parts from 1845 to 1863. The plate shown here depicts the bridled nail-tailed wallaby, an animal which has been driven to the point of extinction in Queensland. Its natural habitat was brigalow country, most of which has been cleared. [RBF 599.0994 gov]

Right and opening image Oil painting depicting 17 of Queensland's best-known birds executed in 1892 by Anthony Alder, a taxidermist, who provided specimens for the Queensland Museum. [ACC 4100]

The Moreton Bay Penal Settlement, New South Wales, by Henry Boucher Bowerman, pen and ink with wash, 1835. This is the earliest signed and dated painting of the future township of Brisbane. [ACC 3944]

of those parrots so lovingly depicted by both Alder and Gould. He sent his sisters feathers for their hats in 1868, having seen the new fashions in the *Illustrated London News*. These tensions between wonder and destruction thread through the narrative of how Europeans engaged with the environment.

Initially what became Queensland in 1859 had unpromising beginnings in the Moreton Bay Penal Settlement established in 1824. In 1835, Henry Bowerman could not have imagined its future development that relied upon wool, beef, cereals, sugar, timber and minerals. Often, this wealth was extracted after deep conflicts with the land itself, its original owners, introduced pests and conflicts with workers.

Initially explorers charted the vast country, unknown to Europeans. The most successful were those who came to understand the land and how to exploit its resources. When Surveyor General Sir Thomas Mitchell explored the interior of southern and central Queensland in 1846 he was heavily dependent on the expertise of his Aboriginal guides, particularly Yuranigh. His treatise, *Journal of an expedition into the interior of tropical Australia* (1848) remains a valuable account of exploration.

Whilst Willem Janszoon in the *Duyfken* in 1606 and Jan Carstenszoon in 1623 sought new markets for the Dutch East India Company, it was British navigators like James Cook in 1770 and Matthew Flinders in 1802 who brought back accurate knowledge of the coast. The State Library of Queensland holds rare books and memorabilia depicting early European exploration in the Pacific. Alexander Shaw's *Catalogue of specimens of cloth* (1787), containing actual pieces of tapa cloth, gives an immediacy to Cook's voyages. *A correct globe with the new discoveries* (1774), showing Cook's first voyage around the world from 1768 to 1771, is a miniature pocket-size globe carried by fashionable gentlemen. Lieutenant George Edward's journal recorded his journey through the Timor Straits in 1831. Henry Bowerman's sketch of Edwards, along with his telescope and regimental badge, are valuable items in the State Library's collection. Charles James Card's journals from HMS *Rattlesnake* (1846–50) recorded scientific voyages to Australia and New Guinea.

Joseph Bradley's *Adventures of a native of Australia, when astray from his ship, the barque "Lynx" (a whaler)* provides

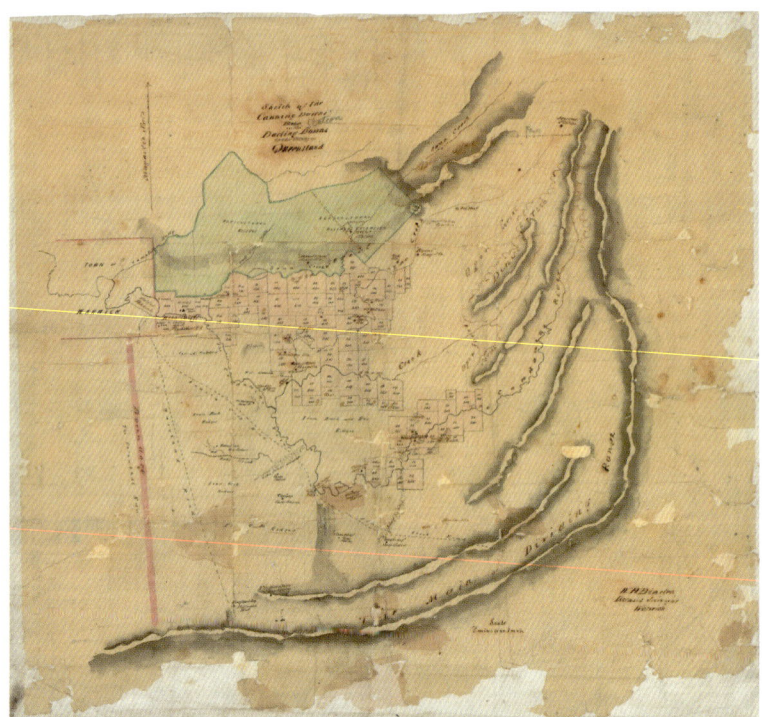

Above *Sketch of the Canning Downs station on the Darling Downs in the colony of Queensland*, by William Henry Binsted, c. 1865. This is a unique, original record of one of Queensland's most historic stations and includes notes on vegetation and topography. The creator of the map was a private surveyor who practised in Toowoomba, Warwick and Dalby. [ACC 6263]

Above *Sketches in Australia and the adjacent islands*, produced by Harden Sidney Melville, expedition artist on the surveying voyage of HMS *Fly* and HMS *Bramble*, 1842–46. This volume contains an outstanding collection of lithographed Australian views, including some of the earliest depictions of the Queensland landscape. [RBQ 994.02 mel]

a rare insight into early commercial shipping in the 1830s. As a burgeoning market to China and India developed at this time, more accurate maps of the dangerous reefs of the Great Barrier Reef were needed. The offshore waters of north Queensland were surveyed between 1842–46 by HMS *Fly* and HMS *Bramble* under Captain FP Blackwood. The draftsman for that survey was Harden Melville, who published *Sketches in Australia and the adjacent islands* (1849). The waters remained dangerous. Lieutenant John Gowlland's logbook documented the search for *Maria* survivors off Cardwell in 1872.

The extent and possibilities of the land also called for expert knowledge. Writing in June 1843, Leichhardt reported that: "All this country from the Condamine to the range is called the DARLING DOWNS [*sic*]. There is no equal to them in the colony for sheep rearing …" Patrick and George Leslie were the first pastoralists who responded to earlier reports of these lush pastures. They established Canning Downs station in 1840, a sprawling property that embraced the future townships of Warwick and Killarney. Local surveyor William Binsted sketched the homestead around 1865.

One extraordinary Scottish-Norwegian family contributed much to the development of the new industries. David and Thomas Archer also brought their flocks through the Darling Downs in 1841, travelling north to take up land on the headwaters of the Brisbane and Stanley Rivers. Durundur proved to have exceptionally fertile soil, allowing the cultivation of wheat, corn, pumpkins and sweet potatoes. Charles Archer's watercolour of Durundur, painted in 1843, is among the State Library's treasures. His letters (1834–55) rank among the earliest surviving correspondence from the free settlers in the Moreton Bay district.

The wool industry expanded rapidly throughout Queensland. However, there was a major swing to beef cattle from the 1870s. The Archer family was at the forefront of this shift, later taking up Eidsvold station in the Burnett district and Gracemere station near Rockhampton. The early family saga is recorded in Thomas Archer's *Recollections of a rambling life* (1897). The Archers still own the magnificent property of Gracemere.

The cattle industry underwent further improvements in the following century, particularly after the introduction of the hardy Santa Gertrudis breed from Texas in 1952. Tom Lea's *In the crucible of the sun* (1974), highlights the role of the American-based King Ranch in these later developments.

Pastoralism did not go unopposed. Indigenous peoples did assert their ownership. Mary McConnel cited a conversation with Long Kitty who "would look proudly over the country and

Above *Durundur*, by Charles Archer, watercolour, 1843. Durundur station in the Brisbane Valley was established by the Archer brothers in 1841. This painting shows the property around the time when the brigalow scrub had been cleared and the first slab huts erected. [ACC 4624]

Between the covers

Above *Portrait of King Sandy*, by Oscar Fristrom, oil, 1899. "King Sandy" of the Toorbal Point or Ningi Ningi tribe was one of the last surviving Brisbane district Aborigines. He is thought to have died at Wynnum in 1900. [Colour Image No. 110962]

Opposite page *Noosa sawmill*. Two watercolour views of the mill at South Brisbane by itinerant artist Charles Gordon Sebastian Hirst, 1876. This mill was owned by Messrs McGhie, Luya and Company who also operated the Cootharaba sawmill on the Noosa River. Three times a fortnight the company's paddle steamer *Culgoa* brought down shipments of kauri and hoop pine, cedar and beech from Tewantin. [ACC 5797]

> By 1899 Queensland sawmills produced over 90 million super feet of timber, including nearly 2 million super feet of cedar, which was largely exported.

say, stretching out her arms, 'All this *yarmen* [land] belonging to me'". Justifying European occupation, McConnel continued: "It did seem hard to have it all taken from them, but it had to be. They cultivated nothing; they were of no use on it". Across the expanding frontier, sporadic violence flared as the Indigenous peoples defended their territories. The government responded by creating the Native Mounted Police in 1849, consisting of detribalised Aboriginal troopers led by white officers whose duty it was to "disperse" (a euphemism for destroy) local clans. In 1852, a detachment of men from the Edward and Murray Rivers, under the control of Frederick Walker, was stationed in Brisbane.

Earlier in October 1846, after the fatal spearing of Mary Shannon and Andrew Gregor, Thomas Dowse recorded in his diary that he "went this evening with a number of other Townsfolk out after the Blacks who murdered Mr Gregor ... returned at 8 am from the bush, no success ..." Sub-Collector of Customs, WA Duncan complained that his servant "a peaceable old man ... was fired on by a constable in the public street ... the camp was burned ..." The oil painting by Swedish artist Oscar Fristrom (1856–1918), *Portrait of King Sandy* (1899), depicts one of the last surviving members of the Toorbal or Ningi Ningi people, whose territory lay immediately north of Tom Petrie's old property. *Tom Petrie's reminiscences of early Queensland* (1904) contains much valuable material on early conflicts over land, from a settler unusually sympathetic to Indigenous peoples.

Our landscape

Above and above right Garden book from East Talgai station, 1869–1913. The ledger records the names of the trees and shrubs, fruit and flowers planted in the gardens of the property situated on the Darling Downs. It also tells much about the desire of Queensland's early settlers to recreate familiar horticultural surroundings. [R1152]

Mary McConnel identified the settlers' desire to cultivate the land and exploit its resources. She reported that one of "Dr Lang's immigrants was a first-class cabinet maker, Towill by name … [who made furniture from] cedar and stained pine, and it was very much admired by our visitors". Richard Daintree's magnificent photographs detail the majesty of the forests.

These timbers were regarded primarily as commodities. Timber was exported from the penal settlement as early as 1826. Two watercolours by CGS Hirst depicting one of Brisbane's early sawmills show the development of the industry fifty years on. There are many photographs of saw millers and bullock drivers with carts laden with cedar in the Johann Heussler album from 1897. The Queensland National Bank headquarters, built in 1882, was a tribute to the industry with its magnificent cedar interiors.

CH Barton's important assessment in 1885 entitled, *The Queensland timber industry and its prospects*, advocated development on a large scale. By 1899 Queensland sawmills produced over 90 million super feet of timber, including nearly 2 million super feet of cedar, which was largely exported. EHF Swain, in his report *The timber and forest products of Queensland* (1928), noted that Queensland had become an importer of softwoods.

William Senior in *Near and far: an angler's sketches of home, sport and colonial life* (1888) outlined the sentiment that "the first duty [of a colonist] is to take an axe and ring as many trees as he can". Earlier in 1879, Government Botanist

Left Cutting book documenting the history of the battle against prickly pear. In 1927 the poison SOS (Save Our Soil) was introduced, but ultimately, it was the appetite of the cactoblastis moth which brought about the destruction of the pear pest. [TR 1831]

Below An album of photographs produced by the Queensland Department of Agriculture and Stock showing prickly pear destruction at Tara, Chinchilla and Goondiwindi, 1926–33. [ACC 6189; Album API-101]

Walter Hill was dismayed by logging practices. Flora Shaw (Baroness Lugard) in *Letters from Queensland* (1893) was shocked by ringbarking. She noted, "[s]ometimes an entire hill-side will be white with such a ghostly forest".

The protection of forests and timber reserves has been a significant environmental issue since Romeo Lahey's initiatives in the 1910s. More recently, sites of intense struggles in environmental campaigns included the Cape Tribulation protests of 1984. Photographs in the Ron and Ngaire Gale Collection document the splendour of the environment and those who sought to protect its beauty.

Many established pastoralists wanted to beautify their immediate environment. The creation of English gardens was a means to render the alien environment familiar. Prospering on their Darling Downs pastoral run, George and Colin Clark of East Talgai Station duly planted a garden around their homestead to remind them of 'home'. Their horticultural experiments were recorded in the East Talgai garden book. Lady Lamington, in her first encounter with local citizens on Thursday Island on her journey there as a vice-regal presence, reported one sad woman who presented her with a rose "To remind me of home".

Exotic plantings frequently went horribly wrong. The cactus known as prickly pear was brought to Australia in 1788 with the First Fleet in the hope of establishing a cochineal industry. (The cochineal insect is a parasite which lives on cacti.) The experiment failed; but the "dye" was cast from the 1880s when prickly pear found conditions in northern New South

Between the covers

Wales and Queensland perfect for regeneration. By the time it was brought under control by the Argentine moth *Cactoblastis cactorum*, introduced in 1925, prickly pear had devastated more than 24 million hectares of land as far north as Mackay. This biological catastrophe is documented in both Arthur Temple Clerk's *The prickly pear problem in Queensland* (1913) and *The prickly pear cutting book* (1926–27). James Wieneke's charming painting shows an amusing side to this devastation. While the battle still raged in 1935, foolishness continued with the introduction of the cane toad. Accidental introductions more recently, such as fire ants, may have even graver consequences.

Animals like rabbits and foxes, introduced as shooters game, caused immense damage when released into the environment. William Senior's account detailed the passion for game hunting in colonial Queensland. The introduction of the exotic occasionally went to bizarre lengths. A posed image in the Trackson family album features wealthy patriarch James Trackson supposedly "shooting" a big cat on Charles Higgins' Toombul Tiger Farm in 1884. A heavy chain ensured there was no danger to the sportsman.

Climate, limited markets, poor transport, and the pastoral monopoly initially stifled agriculture in Queensland. In 1837, JW Mayo used female convicts to plant cotton and sugar cane. Dr Lang's early proposals to establish a cotton industry set forth in his *Cooksland* (1847) came to nothing. A marked change occurred in the early 1860s when the American Civil War erupted, leading to a search for

Below left The prickly pear infestation became the inspiration for this *Queenslander* cover by artist James Wieneke in 1936. The original artwork is also in the collection of the State Library. [RBF 079.943 QUE]

Below right James Trackson "shooting" tigers at Charles Higgins' Toombul Tiger Farm, 1884 [ACC 6147; Album APE-21]

Our landscape

> By the early 1870s Mackay was producing one-third of Queensland's output, an expansion underwritten by the use of Melanesian indentured labour.

alternative supplies of raw cotton to supply the English textile mills. The Queensland Government offered potential growers a substantial subsidy. Plantations sprung up between the Tweed River and Rockhampton. Captain Robert Towns was convinced that cheap non-white labour was essential. In August 1863 he introduced the first shipload of Melanesian indentured labourers to work his cotton plantation on the Logan River. Despite extraordinary opposition from missionaries in the New Hebrides and Queensland Liberal parliamentarians, the introduction of Pacific Islanders continued until 1904. A few other wealthy landowners, including the Honourable Louis Hope, uncle of the Commonwealth's first governor-general, followed Towns' lead at Cleveland. Hope and Captain Claudius Whish also experimented with another tropical crop — sugar cane — while wet conditions and insect pests continually plagued cotton.

When the American south revived, Queensland growers directed their attention to sugar production. John Spiller planted his first crop in 1865 in Mackay. By the early 1870s Mackay was producing one-third of Queensland's output, an expansion underwritten by the use of Melanesian indentured labour.

Plantations contained a rigid social hierarchy with wealthy, often aristocratic, landowners at the apex. Along with Pacific Islanders, Chinese, Japanese, Ceylonese and Piedmontese were added to the workforces. An understanding of this unique way of life in the Mackay district can be gleaned from images in both the Brandon album and the Rawson Archive. The Brandon collection has a unique photograph of an early election meeting in Mackay where the newly enfranchised white workers are dubbed "The Great Unwashed". The State Library possesses rare *cartes-de-visite* of the Melanesian labour force, produced by travelling photographer William Boag in the 1870s.

Sweeping political and economic changes altered the old way of life based upon immense wealth and privilege. The scourge of sugar cane rust ended early prosperity in 1875,

Above Photograph album owned by Henry Brandon, manager of the Mackay branch of the Australian Joint Stock Bank from 1874 to 1884, who, together with sugar planter John Spiller, was a partner in Ashburton and Pioneer plantations. In 1881, when the sugar boom reached its zenith, Spiller and Brandon sold both properties for £95,000. In 1884, Brandon left Mackay and returned to England where he eventually became a London director of BHP. [ACC 6298]

Above Original labels for wine produced by Robert William Le Grand, 1880–90. Robert Le Grand emigrated to Australia in 1871 and settled in Ipswich. In 1873 he took up 840 acres on Purga Creek where he grew grapes and began making wine and spirits. [RBQ 741.692 leg]

with severe depression leading to the fragmentation of large plantations from the late 1880s. Legislation ensured that small farmers, co-operative mills as well as the major operation, Colonial Sugar Refining Company (CSR), became the backbone of the restructured industry. The concept of a rural yeomanry held a long attraction in Queensland, extending through post World War I soldier settlement to the failure of the Peak Downs Scheme in the early 1950s, when distance to markets and adverse environmental conditions repeated this familiar story of adversity.

There were success stories in unexpected places. Among the State Library's treasures is the silver medal awarded to Henry Franklin of the Upper Albert River for a sample of maize he exhibited at the 1878 Paris Exposition. Other crops signaled new industries. Missionary Gerler of Nundah imported 500-year-old vine cuttings in the early 1850s. The Ipswich district also figures prominently in relation to the pioneer vigneron, Robert Le Grand. Having made a small fortune on the Victorian goldfields in the 1850s, Le Grand returned to Europe where he studied winemaking in France and Germany before returning to Australia in 1871. Two years later, Le Grand took up 340 hectares of land on Purga Creek at Milbong, where he planted vines. The State Library contains a collection of original labels from his winery, dating from 1880–90.

Just as gold provided Le Grand with the means to engage in winemaking, Gracemere station was built around the original gold rush at Canoona in 1852. James Nash's discovery of gold at Gympie in 1867 was the later salvation of Queensland, gripped in severe financial crisis. More gold rushes followed including Ravenswood (1868), Etheridge River (1870), Palmer River (1873) and Charters Towers (1882). Gold triggered massive emigration from the United States, Europe and China and the creation of numerous towns in the wilderness. While the prosperity for many was brief, solid foundations were laid for others, exemplified by William Jamieson Allom's 1895 oil painting of capital-intensive Charters Towers.

Gold triggered massive emigration from the United States, Europe and China and the creation of numerous towns in the wilderness.

Right Silver medal from the 1878 Paris Exposition awarded to Henry Franklin of the Upper Albert River for a sample of maize included in the Queensland exhibit and produced from a crop "matured with little or no rain". The importance of the accomplishment is not diminished by the misspelling of Franklin's name. [M1173]

Below *View of Charters Towers*, by William Jamieson Allom, oil on board, 1895. The painting shows the mining centre at the height of its prosperity when it was known as "The World". At the left is the Mills Day Dawn United Mine, known as the "Show Mine of the Colony". WJ Allom was a local artist and auctioneer. [ACC 4606]

46 Between the covers

Above and below Photograph album presented to Sir Herbert Chermside, Governor of Queensland, by the Mount Morgan Town Council in May 1903. It contains a series of original images of the Mount Morgan mine which yielded vast quantities of gold and copper for more than 100 years. [ACC 6188][Album APU-14]

> Mining was not limited to gold, for many other non-ferrous metals made their own valuable contributions.

Croydon now bears little resemblance to the boom town of the 1890s when population peaked at seven thousand. Although mining continued until 1906, poor management, lack of transport and environmental difficulties were significant factors in its demise. When Gold Warden and Police Magistrate Frederick Parkinson was transferred from Croydon to Georgetown in 1897, friends and well-wishers presented him with an illuminated address.

Discovered by a stockman in 1880, Mount Morgan remained untapped for six years until the formation of the Mount Morgan Gold Mining Company. Although immense wealth was extracted, technical difficulties caused erratic production until the company finally went into liquidation in 1927. The golden days of this central Queensland town are nevertheless recalled in an album of photographs presented to Sir Herbert Chermside, Governor of Queensland from 1902 to 1905. As a parting gift from the women of Queensland, Lady Lamington was presented with "the most beautiful solid gold set of brushes, bottles, comb etc that I have ever seen, and best of all it was made in Brisbane … at Messrs. Hardy, the jewelers".

Mining was not limited to gold, for many other non-ferrous metals made their own valuable contributions. Tin was discovered at Stanthorpe in 1872, where an enterprising Scot named John Moffat expanded his small storekeeping business. When extensive deposits of tin were found at Herberton seven years later, Moffat relocated north to establish a mining empire which embraced silver mines at Montalbion, copper at Chillagoe and Cloncurry, Wolfram mine at Mount Carbine, coal at Mount Mulligan and oil shale south of Gladstone. Moffat died in 1918, just five years before an itinerant prospector named John Campbell Miles stumbled on the rich silver-lead, zinc and copper deposits of Mount Isa. Miles' find was to have a major

Above Illuminated Address by John Sands of Sydney, presented to Frederick Philip Parkinson, Gold Warden and Police Magistrate at Croydon, April 1897. In his long career, Parkinson also served on the Etheridge and the Palmer goldfields. [ACC 6556]

Above left *Symbolic representation of transport and industries in Queensland*, by Noel Pascoe Lambert, watercolour, 1939. This brilliant work of political propaganda depicting Labor Premier William Forgan Smith, illustrates the achievements of his government (1932–42) and celebrates the bounty of the Queensland landscape. [ACC 4678]

Above right An important early move in the battle for recognition of Aboriginal land rights was the stand taken by the Mapoon people who, in the early 1970s, began returning to the land from which they had been removed by mining interests in 1963. [Poster Collection]

impact on Queensland's economy right to the present. The State Library contains several important photographic collections on early Mount Isa, including the Plass Album (1932) and the record of Home Secretary Hanlon's tour in 1933.

Mining was also essential for the development of secondary industries, the growth of which is reflected in Noel Lambert's watercolour, *Symbolic representation of transport and industries in Queensland* (1939). Moreover, mineral exploitation continued its economic prominence, with the state's first open-cut coal mine at Blair Athol near Clermont operating from 1946. It was the beginning of a boom in coal extraction, with large-scale deposits worked at Moura and Blackwater.

Bauxite brought together the twin themes of displacement and development. Essential for the production of aluminum, enormous reserves of bauxite were discovered on the west coast of Cape York Peninsula in 1955. Two years later the new Coalition government was elected on a slogan "A new deal for the Far North". Although much of it was located on Aboriginal reserves, the government granted leases to multinational mining corporations. Extraction went ahead. When passive resistance occurred at Mapoon in November 1963, traditional custodians were forcibly evicted. Their exile imposed by government regulation did not mean defeat, as the poster *The Mapoon people demand their land back* shows.

For its time, Comalco was a forward-thinking company with positive employment practices. The State Library owns the magnificent Weipa-Comalco Collection with seven volumes of photographs outlining developments from 1959–67.

The State Library holds in its myriad collections many superb manuscripts, photographs, paintings and drawings which detail both the beauty of the Australian land and its flora and fauna, as well as its destruction. Tales of heroism, struggle, conflict and achievement mark a complex ongoing story of the habitation of this landscape.

Chapter three
Beach and bush

3

Author Kay Saunders   Research Librarian Dianne Byrne

"The bush is the heart of the country, the real Australian Australia."

The English visitor Francis Adams writing his famous book *The Australians* believed "[t]he bush is the heart of the country, the real Australian Australia." By 1893 popular attitudes towards the bush were undergoing transformations. Queenslander AG Stephens' *Bulletin* magazine, the bible of the new, proud Australian nationalism, created a mythical landscape of the bush. The outback was a place of regeneration, far from the contamination of the coastal-dwelling effete city dwellers. Sitting around campfires reciting bush ballads, manly itinerant workers stood for justice against rapacious squatters. Vance Palmer in *The legend of the nineties* (1954) brought these views to new generations, keeping the bush legend alive.

Yet there were discordant views at the time, with Henry Lawson describing the bush as "a blasted, barren wilderness that doesn't even howl". Official war historian, CEW Bean's earlier work *On the wool track* (1907) took a more conservative view, with his bush workers forming the backbone of the Australian force which later fought on the beaches of Gallipoli. Today these divergent attitudes are still a part of our society with the Stockman's Hall of Fame in Longreach and the Australian War Memorial in Canberra endorsing Bean's precepts, while the Tree of Knowledge at Barcaldine memorialises this radical tradition. The beach, with its fit and healthy lifesavers, took its place in the Australian imagination only after the devastation of World War I.

Opening image Cover image by James Northfield for a pamplet produced by the Australian National Travel Association, c. 1929. [Ephemera Collection]

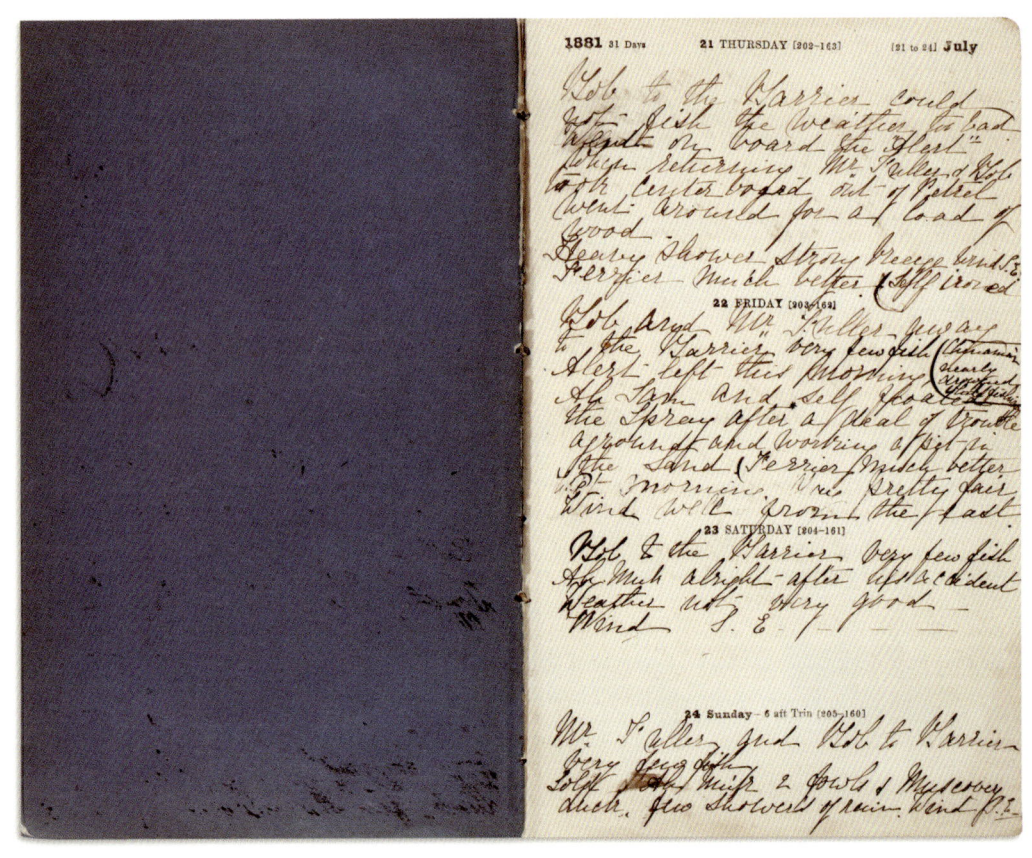

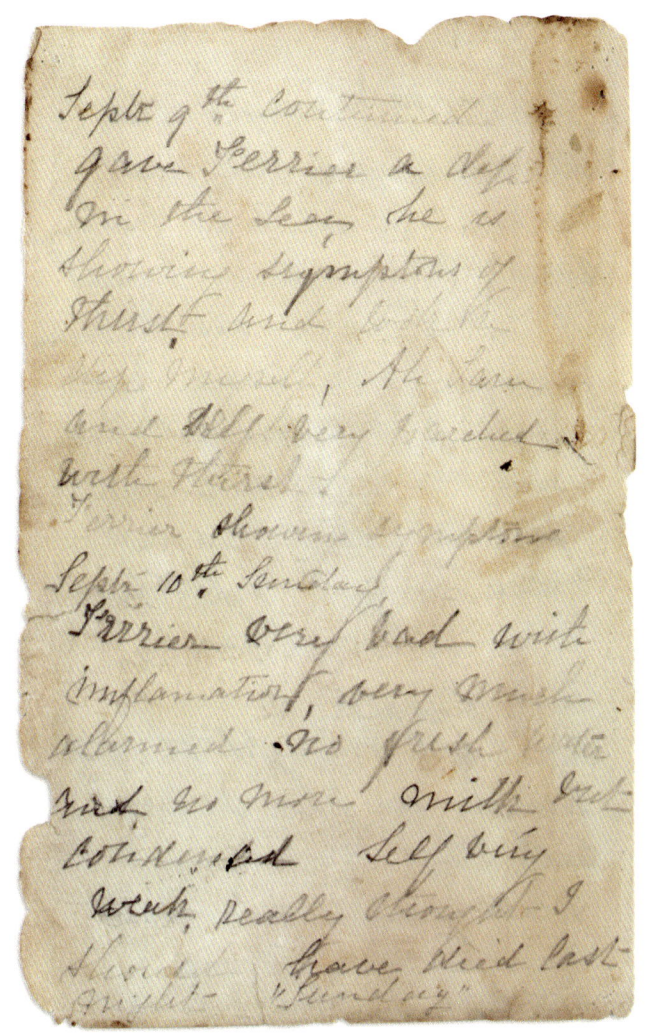

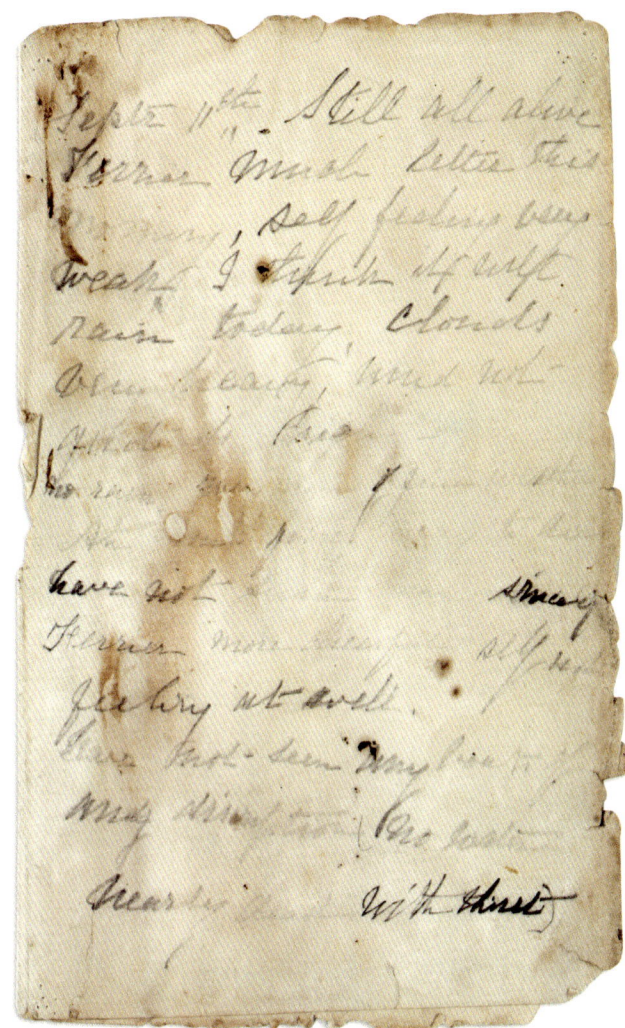

Early explorers were driven by a curiosity to map the contours of the bush's unknown vastness. The heroic figures of their age brought back the first accounts of the environment and its inhabitants which were so foreign to the Europeans' world experience. George Dalrymple, writing to Governor Bowen in August 1864 from Cardwell, envisioned a glorious future: "churches, public buildings, streets, warehouses, &c. spread far along the gleaming shore and back to the base of the mountains, and the taper spires of a merchant fleet give life to the now lonely waters of the harbour".

In reality, for early settlers the themes of the alien character of the new homeland, its vast and forbidding contours, its inherent danger and forbiddingness, dominated accounts. Mary McConnel, arriving from Edinburgh in 1849, wrote: "It seemed really to me as if we had come to the end of the known world, and no other had dawned upon us … We were some hours going up the river to Brisbane. What a dismal waterway it was! Neither sign of house nor hall, nor man, black or white …"

Even for early native-born Queenslanders like Rosa Praed, the bush, though familiar, was forbidding: "Words fail for painting the loneliness of the Australian bush. Mile after mile of primeval forest; interminable vistas of melancholy gum-trees; ravines, along the sides of which the long-bladed grass grows rankly; level, untimbered plains alternating with undulating tracks of pasture, here and there, broken by steep gully, stony ridge, or dried-up creek".

There are fascinating accounts of the adoption of Europeans into Indigenous cultures. Castaway carpenter James Morrill, shipwrecked with Captain and Mrs Pitkethley off Cape Bowling Green in 1846, spent 17 years with the

Above and opposite Diary kept by Mary Watson (1860–81), the wife of Robert Watson, bêche-de-mer fisherman of Lizard Island. Among the entries is her account of the conflict with local Indigenous people which led to her fatal decision to escape over the Barrier Reef in a steel tank with her infant son and Chinese servant. Additional loose leaves record the sad last days of all. [OM 81-120]

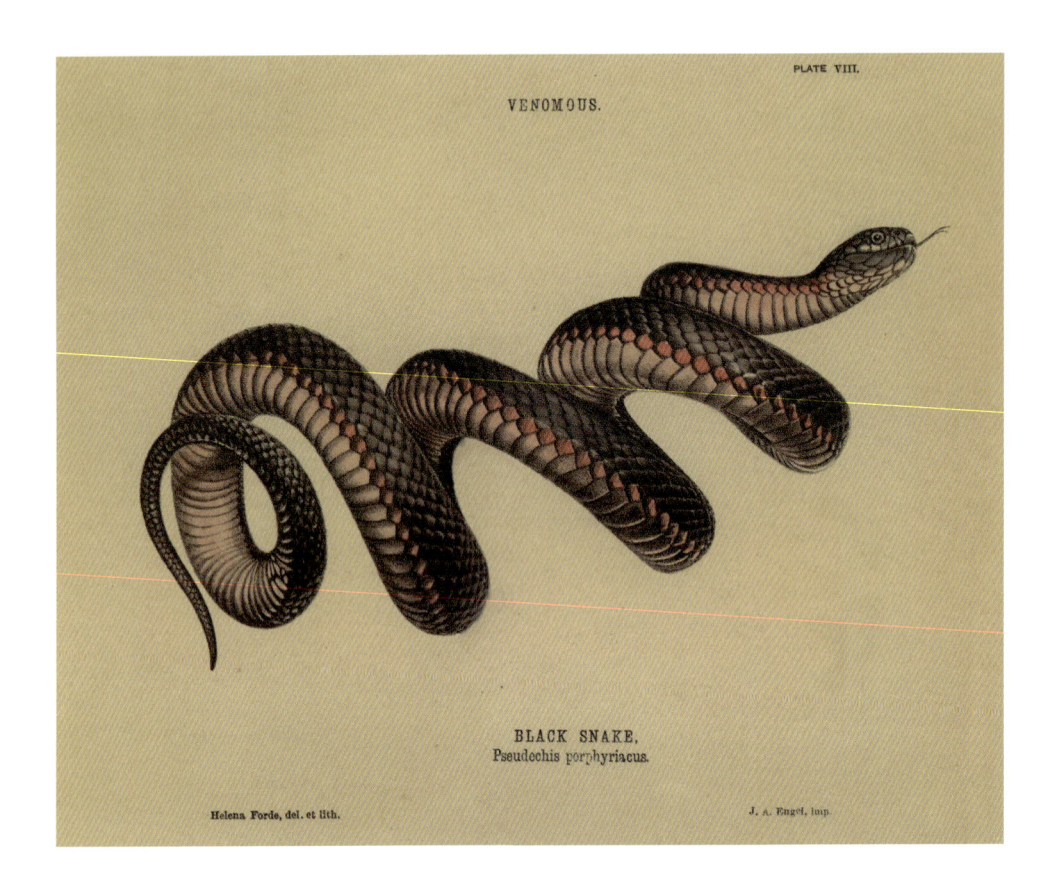

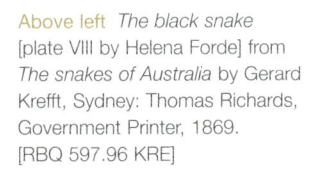

Above left *The black snake* [plate VIII by Helena Forde] from *The snakes of Australia* by Gerard Krefft, Sydney: Thomas Richards, Government Printer, 1869. [RBQ 597.96 KRE]

Above right Crocodile hunter, Dulcie Campbell with two trophies "bagged" at Sunday Gully, North Queensland, c. 1924. [Image No.BC 934]

Burdekin River peoples. Arriving at a frontier sheep station in January 1863 he declared himself to astonished settlers: "Don't shoot, mates, I am a British object!" A year later he joined George Dalrymple's expedition as an interpreter. When he died in October 1865 in Bowen, Indigenous people came from many territories to pay their respects to their sympathetic comrade, as E Gregory's 1866 Brisbane publication attested. David Malouf captured the essence of Morrill's experience in *Remembering Babylon* (1993).

For some settlers, their quest for self advancement led to conflict and tragedy. Cornishwoman Mary Watson, married to a Cooktown bêche-de-mer fisherman in 1880, moved to Lizard Island with her husband and two Chinese servants. In October 1881, Indigenous owners attacked their home, and one servant, Ah Leong, was killed. Mary, with her three-month-old son Ferrier and another injured servant, Ah Sam, fled in a cut-down ship's tank to No. 5 Island where they died. Her poignant diary, not found until January 1882, told the harrowing tale. She became a public hero, honoured with a memorial erected in the main street of Cooktown in 1886.

A contemporary poem, "Dead with Thirst", published in *The Bulletin*, intoned:

Five fearful days beneath the scorching glare,
Her babe she nursed,
God knows what pangs that women had to bear,
Whose last sad entry showed a mother's care.

Europeans often expressed both fear and fascination for the alien bush. Mary McConnel recorded a dramatic encounter with a black snake. She wrote: "I saw a large black snake (at Toogoolawah, now Bulimba) lying in a heap of withered leaves, it was in its winter sleep, but something had disturbed it and it raised it's [sic] head, showing a beautiful scarlet throat. I seemed hypnotised by it, and could not take my eyes away from looking at it. Soon it lay down … I did not feel any fear. Of course in its torpid condition it would not have attacked me". This constant involvement with snakes found a chord in Australian literature with a snake featuring in Lawson's story, "The Drover's Wife". Later another feared reptile, the crocodile, became sport. Dulcie Campbell saw her crocodiles as "kills".

Beach and bush | 53

PLATE 7

This page Plate from OH Rippingale's *Queensland and Great Barrier Reef shells*, published by Jacaranda Press, Brisbane, 1961. Queensland's innovative Jacaranda Press has had a long history of producing works devoted to the unique flora and fauna to be found throughout Australia. With titles relating to marine fishes and wildflowers, bush birds, butterflies and local geology, they have added immeasurably to our understanding of the creatures and characteristics of beach and bush. [Q 594.09943 RIP]

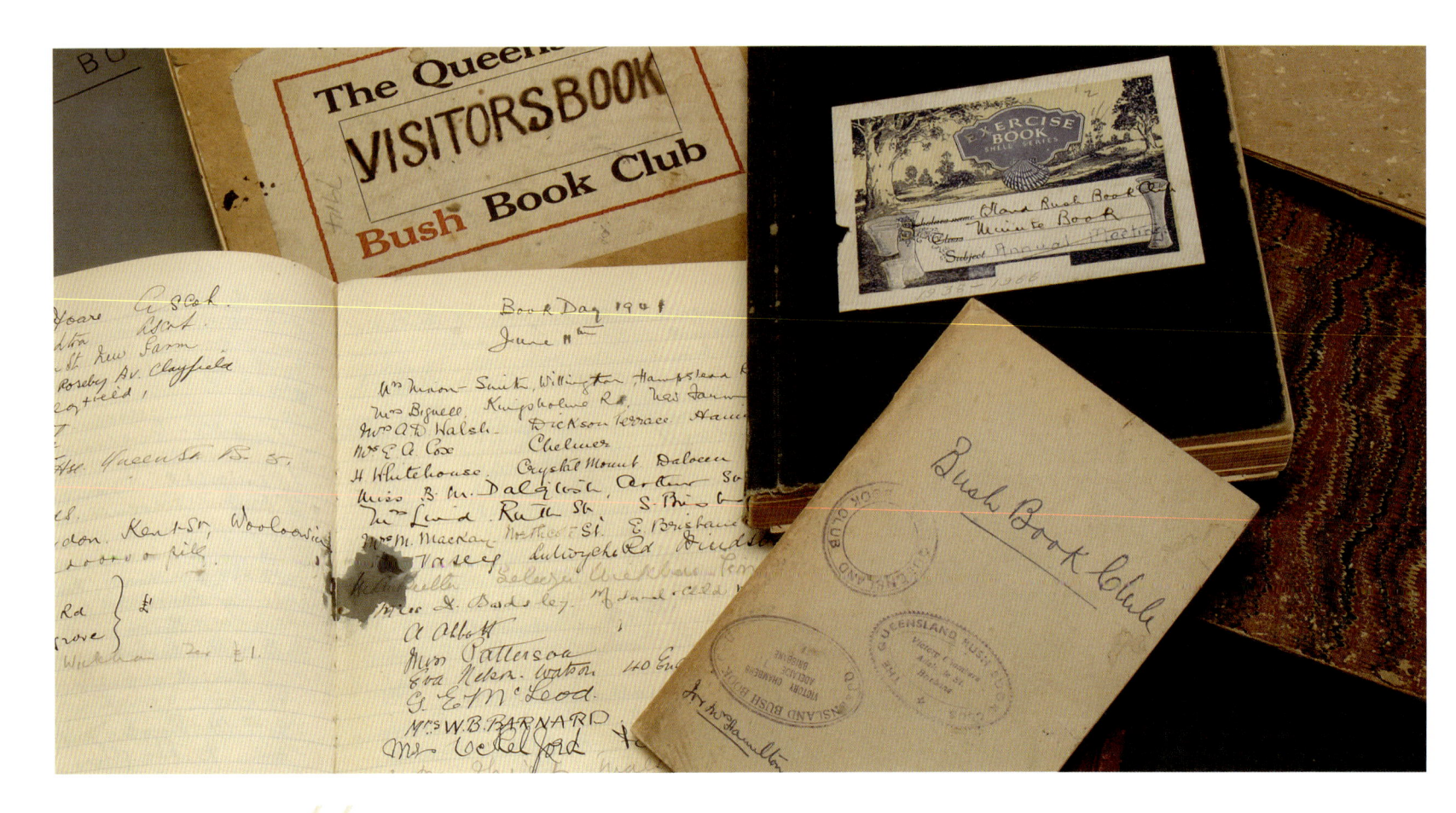

Above Records of the Queensland Bush Book Club, 1921–67. The club was founded to provide general libraries for those who lived beyond reach of a School of Arts in Queensland's bush districts. [OM 78-47]

"... Mrs Fulford of Lyndhurst station on the Einsleigh River papered her rough bush home with copies of the Illustrated London News, poignantly contrasting the cosmopolitan life of England with the remoteness of the Queensland bush."

Sometimes the sheer beauty of the bush and its rhythms appeared almost mystical. Thorvald Weitemeyer recalled his first impression of Queensland from the immigrant ship off Bowen: "Occasionally we saw smoke curling up from among the trees, and at night we could see large fires. This was the dry grass burning among the trees, a very common thing in Queensland; but to us it was a most startling and awe-inspiring event … no one gave thought to its being a bushfire …"

Several influential Queenslanders appreciated and respected the Indigenous understanding of the natural world. EJ Banfield and Thomas Welsby extolled the wonder of unique creatures of Australia in the early twentieth century.

Mostly, however, Indigenous knowledge was ignored. Ancient Aboriginal bark paintings from Melville Island showed the killer box jellyfish (*chironex fleckeri*) and its life cycle, yet it was not until 1955 that Cairns doctor Hugo Flecker scientifically identified the species. The Flecker Botanical Gardens pays tribute to his pioneering work in tropical botany.

For others, the rawness and freedom of the bush stimulated rebellion. The "Wild Scotchman", James McPherson was Queensland's most notable bushranger. An emigrant from Dr Lang's shiploads of worthies in 1849, with his father employed by the McConnels and James apprenticed to Tom Petrie as a stonemason, McPherson became a wild bush lad.

As E Boxall's sympathetic account of his life, published in London in 1899, stated: "… like many other high-spirited young men … the quiet bush life in Australia afforded no escape value to which their desire for excitement might be worked off …" His Queensland biographer, PW McNally claimed in 1899 that the novel, *Robbery under arms* was based upon McPherson's adventures. In the following decades when life was tamer, a sameness settled over bush life. Mabel Forrest's novel, *Hibiscus heart* (1927) captures this: "[h]is lungs were full of dust, his soul of boredom".

For women, the life of a tearaway or a bushranger was far harder to contemplate. Somehow they had to accustom themselves to the deprivations of bush life. In 1871, Mrs Fulford of Lyndhurst station on the Einsleigh River papered her rough bush home with copies of the *Illustrated London News*, poignantly contrasting the cosmopolitan life of England with the remoteness of the Queensland bush. From 1921 to 1967 the Queensland Bush Book Club reached out to country dwellers with books to bridge the isolation.

In the Lawson stories, women like Mrs Howlett in "No Place for a Woman", had a different fate. At the turn of the twentieth century, Lady Lamington visited the lunatic asylum where she reported: "many of the quiet melancholy women were really only the result of the terrible lonely lives they lead in far-out back stations, combined with the sad effect the Colonies' Climate has on all women".

Others took a more pragmatic approach to the difficulties of a bush lifestyle. The redoubtable Wilhelmina Rawson provided practical suggestions to keep out the heat and save the complexion. "In the bush where one need not have regard to appearance and 'what the world says,' the most suitable veil covering is made like a bag of white book muslin." She further recommended for any sunburn "mutton fat rendered down and rubbed on …"

The Queensland bush was also a site for anticipated regeneration in fortune or health. Mary McConnel, on her first journey to Cressbrook along the slow bush tracks, stopped for lunch with Major and Mrs North, "fine old gentlefolk from Ireland" who had "lost their money" and come to renew their fortune. Lunch on damask tablecloths and old silver in a hut were stories not uncommon in the bush.

Below Sheet music for *Sons of the bush: a reminiscent song*, composed by Kelsey Voller, Brisbane, 1900.
[J MUS 782.42 VOL]

Above *On the beach, Sandgate Queensland*, by Louisa Lilias Forbes, watercolour, 1873. One of four works by the artist in the State Library of Queensland's collection, the painting depicts this small seaside resort at a time when it was becoming popular with Brisbane day-trippers and holiday-makers. It is one of the earliest depictions of the beach as a focus of Queenslanders' leisure time. [Image No. 20737]

> Our concept of the island paradise haven is far removed from earlier understandings. The use of beautiful islands as prisons for the outcasts of the new society brought together the themes of beauty and tragedy.

In 1849 Mary met Reverend Thomas Mowbray from Glasgow who had come to Moreton Bay which "… was considered good for chest complaints". This use of the bush for recovery and rejuvenation continued into the next century. The title page of the song, *Sons of the bush* (1900) by Kelsey Voller, ranges across a number of themes connected with bush life – its beauty, its production of livelihoods and its manly strong men. CEW Bean later believed that it was the bush that produced the Anzac warriors.

The State Library of Queensland has the story of Jack Moffatt, a young man from Newcastle-upon-Tyne who migrated to Queensland in 1913. He served in the Army Medical Corps in World War I, helping bring back the severely injured by sea. Contracting tuberculosis, he was admitted to the repatriation hospital at Stanthorpe. The photograph of the handsome Moffatt lying smoking outside the open tent hospital set in bushland is poignant when we learn he died soon after. He is buried in the War Grave Section of Toowong Cemetery.

Our concept of the island paradise haven is far removed from earlier understandings. The use of beautiful islands as prisons for the outcasts of the new society brought together the themes of beauty and tragedy. In the 1840s, Italian priests set up a short-lived mission for the Noonuccal people. The Dunwich Benevolent Asylum, to which the chronically ill, destitute elderly and disabled were despatched, is now the site of expensive real estate on Stradbroke Island. Lady Lamington visited the leper settlement on Peel Island in Moreton Bay with Home Secretary Sir Horace Tozer. She remarked that the afflicted Chinese resided in tents outside of the main building. Late in the 1930s, Home Secretary Ned Hanlon visited the non-European lepers on Fantome Island off Palm Island. St Helena in Moreton Bay housed felons. Lady Lamington also visited the penal station where she reported meeting: "one or two particularly nice men who were finishing their long sentences, having been the leaders of the famous shearers' riots some time before (1891)". These are the workers immortalised by the Tree of Knowledge.

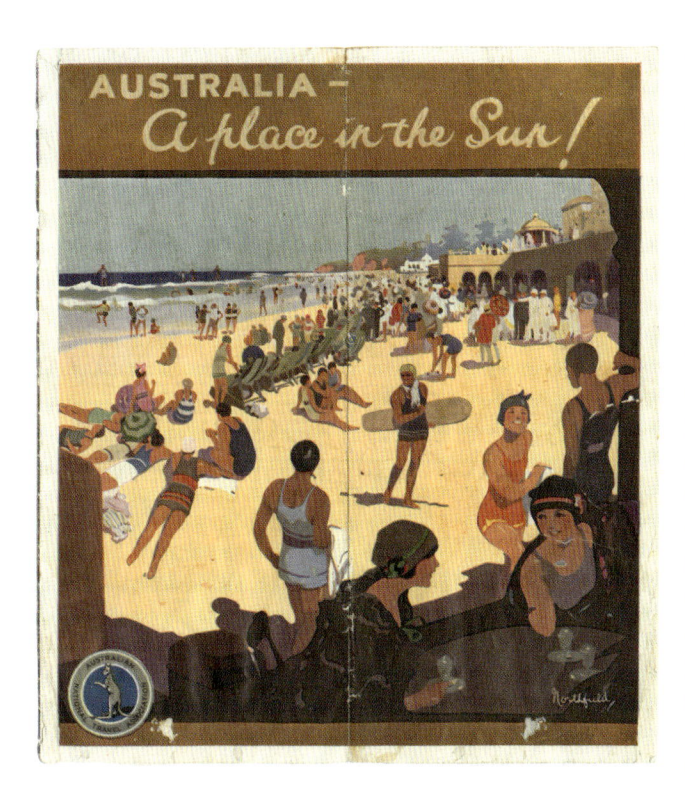

EJ Banfield's books, Confessions of a beachcomber (1908), My tropic isle (1911) and Tropic days (1918) were pivotal in capturing the mystery of the Whitsunday Islands. He wrote: "This isle of dreams, of quietude and happiness, this fretless scene; this plot in the Garden of Eden …" From the 1920s when places like Magnetic Island became modest tourist destinations, this was the dream that fuelled tourism as a new industry and a place for regeneration.

With more urban leisure and new methods of transport in the late 1870s, Sandgate and Redcliffe were developed as destinations for enjoying sea breezes. It was not until the early decades of the twentieth century that the beach became a place of hedonistic pleasure; rather, visitors promenaded in full city dress. The music sheet, Down on the sands at Emu Park, showing the men's bathing area, demonstrates the gradual transformation of the beach as a destination. First, men and women in modest but heavy

Above left Artist James Northfield's glamorous image of the beach as a meeting place for society, from a pamphlet published by the Australian National Travel Association (ANTA), c. 1929. [Ephemera Collection]

Above right In contrast, is Northfield's view of the bush, produced for another ANTA publication. People are absent and it is the preserve of shy, but noble animals. [Ephemera Collection]

Below Early campers in the bush at Burleigh Heads, c. 1907. [Image No. 33940]

Above left Plan of allotments on the Bulcock Estate Caloundra, named after pioneering landowner Robert Bulcock who settled permanently in the area in 1885, building a house called The Homestead. [ME 0034]

Above right *Gem of the Pacific estate, the Nobbys North Burleigh*, c. 1920. [ME 0003]

woollen costumes separately donned in beach cabins on the water's edge, paddled in the water. With the publication of Annette Kellermann's *How to swim* (1918) beachgoers began the process of liberation. People learned to swim and embrace the water and the surf without fear. A photograph in the State Library shows young nuns in the 1950s in full black habits paddling in their stockings. It is a reminder of how everyone once experienced the beach.

By the end of the nineteenth century, holidays could encompass both the beach and the bush. The concept of the hill station was prominent, taken from the British experience in India. Usually going to Toowoomba in summer, Lady Lamington tentatively appreciated sea breezes. She remarked that Premier Sir Hugh Nelson loaned her his beach home at Southport though "I shall never forget the heat and the mosquitoes". Around the same period, campers were more likely to use destinations we now associate as beach holidays to enjoy the bushland, as the photograph of campers at Burleigh Head on the previous page demonstrates. By 1915, as the Anzacs mounted the beaches at Gallipoli, the Queensland beaches were in the process of redevelopment from sites of unspoiled nature to domestic and holiday dwellings. The Bulcock Estate at Caloundra shows this process in 1917.

As the bush was cleared and 'tamed', not everyone celebrated this process as progressive. The engineer and sawmiller Romeo Watkins Lahey, who had served on the front in World War I, later built the Mount Cainable Road celebrated in Charles Chauvel's film, *Heritage*. He was a passionate conservationist who campaigned in 1915 to preserve the McPherson Range area as Queensland's first national park. His original glass slides are among the treasures of the State Library's collection. The National Parks Association was formed in 1930 through his advocacy. With Arthur Groom he built Binna Burra Lodge in 1933. A witty guest menu captures some of the atmosphere at this lodge. Lahey also established the "Save the Trees" campaign in 1946.

By 1915, as the Anzacs mounted the beaches at Gallipoli, the Queensland beaches were in the process of redevelopment from sites of unspoiled nature to domestic and holiday dwellings.

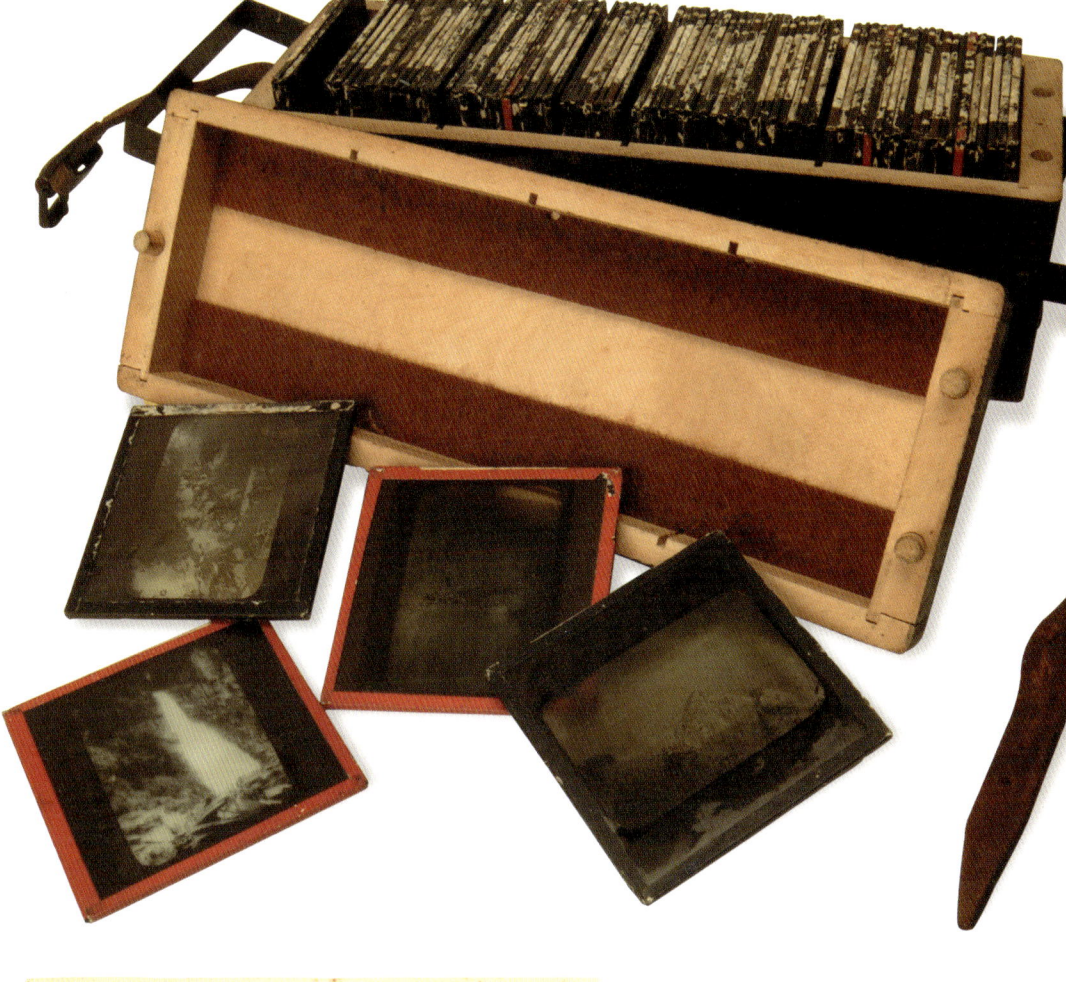

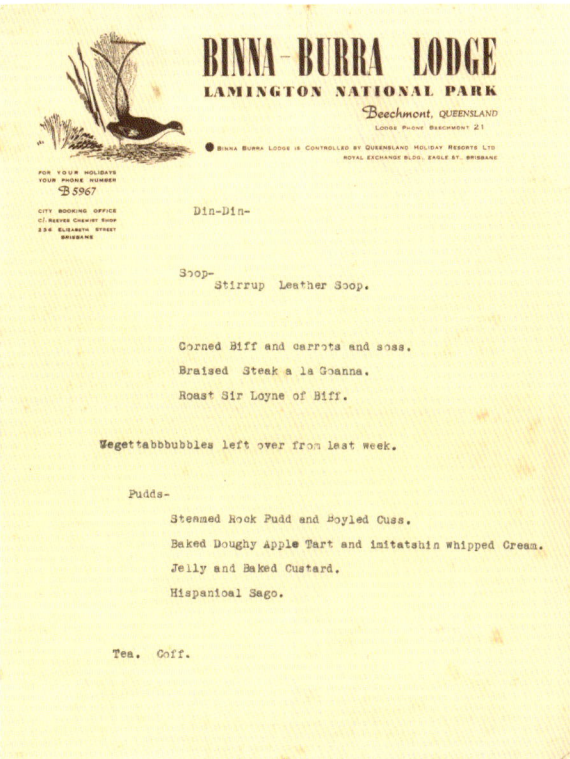

Above Lecture slides produced by Romeo Watkins Lahey which he used in his campaign for the preservation of the area that in 1915 was gazetted as Lamington National Park. In pursuit of this goal, Romeo Lahey went around the district lecturing and obtaining signatures which successfully influenced the Queensland Government to act for the park's creation.
[ACC 6177]

Far left Romeo Lahey and Arthur Groom enjoying a bush breakfast, 1938. Together they established Binna Burra Lodge in 1933 on the last freehold title on the boundary of Lamington National Park.
[Image No. 196158]

Left Comic "menu" for Binna-Burra Lodge, c. 1940.
[Ephemera Collection]

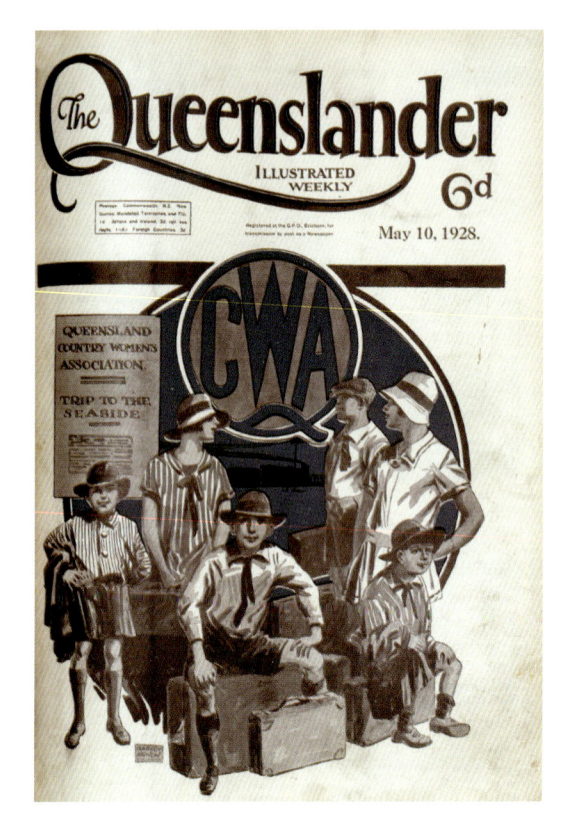

Above left Front cover for the *Queenslander*, 10 May 1928, illustrated by artist Garnet Agnew. School children are depicted preparing for a trip to the seaside sponsored by the Queensland Country Women's Association. [Image No. 191969] Above centre Alexandra Headland Surf Lifesaving Club rescue practice, c. 1926. The club was formed in 1924 by "Woombye Boys" at a time when holiday-makers were visiting the North Coast in significant numbers for the first time. The club grew to prominence in the 1950s and 1960s, including amongst its later members father and son, Hayden and Grant Kenny. [Image No. 8662] Above right The site of the Stinson crash in the deep rainforest of the McPherson Range, February 1937. The wreckage of the Stinson airliner was located after nine days of searching, and the rescue of survivors, Binstead and Proud, transfixed the nation. It was a reminder of how the bush could swallow up those who found themselves within its grasp, despite the wonders of modern technology. [Image No. 36983]

In February 1937, this deep jungle area was again the site of high drama when a Stinson plane carrying five men crashed near Point Lookout. Two survivors were found ten days later by the experienced bushman Bernard O'Reilly, the proprietor of a small guesthouse. The Chauvel film, *Sons of Matthew* immortalised the extraordinary feat of the O'Reilly family in establishing themselves on the Lamington Plateau by subduing the bush. O'Reilly's lodge remains one of Queensland's most notable ecotourism ventures. Just as the bush became a revered site for conservation, the beach was transformed into a pleasure ground. The Country Women's Association (CWA) provided holidays at the seaside for bush children from the 1920s. The lifesaving movement, first formed at Kirra in 1916, was established to provide public safety, particularly for country people who were unable to swim and unfamiliar with the beach. This volunteer movement had some elements in common with the Anzacs. Men offered their services to defend a way of life. Anonymous in their bathing costumes, they marched in military formations in the surf carnivals. Women did form their own clubs, such as the Neptunes, in the mid 1920s. Intense hostility by the male clubs prevented their enduring success until a lack of male volunteers in the 1970s made women lifesavers a necessity. Danger was ever present. Tragedy could strike, as it did in 1937, when two lifesavers were killed in a shark attack.

The bush and the beach were the scene of another common danger. Queensland is currently the melanoma capital of the world. Feminist Zina Cumbrae-Stewart, a supporter of the Cancer Trust, alerted the public to the dangers as early as the 1930s when she pointed out

The lifesaving movement, first formed at Kirra in 1916, was established to provide public safety, particularly for country people who were unable to swim.

Above Italian promotional poster for Charles Chauvel's 1949 film *Sons of Matthew*, the epic struggle of man against bush, filmed on the Lamington Plateau. [ACC 2911]

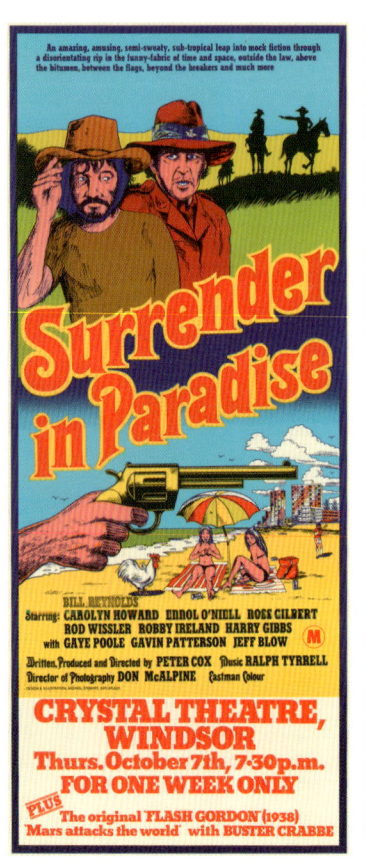

Above left Lorna Foley, Miss Surf Queensland 1948, photographed by Dorothy Coleman. The link between the natural beauty of the beach and Queensland girlhood was established early. The first beauty pageants were held at the South Coast in the 1920s, however, they were fiercely denounced by Catholic Archbishop James Duhig. [Image No. BC 887]

Above centre Poster for the film *Surrender in paradise*, designed and illustrated by Michael Stewart. [HPT FIL 010]

Above right Advertisement for the Rio Vista canal development, at Surfers Paradise, *Courier-Mail*, 23 December 1957. [Image No. 191443]

that the new fashion of "sun-hatching" made men look like "… niggers, and one could see they were really white men, when they turned up the soles of their feet". Despite its racist language, she identified the danger of sunbaking. Both work and play had their dark and deadly side.

The war gave an impetus to development of the beach. A souvenir fan produced to promote the Grand Hotel at Coolangatta around 1949, with a pin-up bathing beauty, suggests the commencement of a strong American influence on the Gold Coast. This was not a complete process even at the end of the decade. Lorna Foley, Miss Surf Queensland 1948, presented a wholesome natural beauty far from American glamour. The bush and the beach were again united in the 1950s when large wool cheques were invested into the development of the Gold Coast as a holiday destination. Other money came from southern entrepreneurs like Bruce Small who, having made his fortune in bicycles, needed new challenges. The Rio Vista Canal Development from 1957, invokes this transformation.

> **The bush and the beach were again united in the 1950s when large wool cheques were invested into the development of the Gold Coast as a holiday destination.**

Soon a process of "Americanisation" occurred as the Gold Coast became the Miami of the Antipodes with beach shacks being overtaken by American motels and high-rises. David Malouf in *Johnno* (1975) describes the coast "only sixty miles from staid, old-fashioned Brisbane, but already in those days the centre of a wickedly alternative life. Among its harlequin motels, Florida, El Dorado, Las Vegas … a fast crowd from the South was continuously at play." The film *Surrender in paradise* satirises this lifestyle.

Beach and bush 63

This page Souvenir fan produced for Ailsa and Bill Gollan, mine hosts at the Grand Hotel at Coolangatta, c. 1949. [Ephemera Collection]

64 Between the covers

> American popular culture began penetrating the bush from the 1920s. Rodeos provided the Australian bushmen with an avenue to display their fine horsemanship.

Above Sheet music for *Song of Cooloola*, with words and music by Nambour composer Keith Bartholomew, printed under the auspices of the Caloundra branch of the Wildlife Preservation Society of Queensland. [Image No. BC 890]

Above right Beach beauty riding on the back of a turtle at Mon Repos, east of Bundaberg, c. 1930. [Image No. API-100-23]

Queensland beaches initially became the winter home for wealthy Melbournians. Bernard Dowd, the owner of the Hickory franchise in Australia and the force behind the Miss Australia Quest from 1954 to 1969, owned a magnificent mansion on Sunshine Beach where he entertained lavishly. Wimbledon star Ashley Cooper and Miss Australia 1957 Helen Wood spent part of their honeymoon at his beach home in 1959.

Soon the Gold and Sunshine Coasts became retirement options for the less affluent. Annette Kellermann in her last years, far from her days of fame and fortune, retired in some obscurity on the Gold Coast. Suburbanisation took over the landscape. Centres like Bundaberg became destinations for whale and turtle watching and as a gateway to Fraser Island ecotourism. *Song of Cooloola* gives expression to this movement.

American popular culture began penetrating the bush from the 1920s. Rodeos provided the Australian bushmen with an avenue to display their fine horsemanship. In World War II the American Army held an impressive rodeo at the Exhibition Grounds in Brisbane to a packed audience. The State Library has a rare poster of a rodeo held on Cherbourg Settlement. Country and Western music, both in its American and Australian styles, has attracted a loyal following. Artists like Slim Dusty have been positive forces for Reconciliation. The Gympie Muster, running since 1987, features country and blues music and is a premier event in the national cultural calendar.

Just as the beach was changed by the influx of American popular culture in the 1950s, so too the bush experienced another form of American influence. The King Ranch of Texas began investment in Queensland properties after a visit by Sir Rupert and Lady Clarke there in 1951. The beautifully illustrated book *In the crucible of the sun* (1974) by Tom Lea gives a full account of initial operations.

The bush and beach remain entrenched in our psyche of how we see and express ourselves to the outside world even into the twenty-first century. The State Library's collections give us a window into these changes.

Chapter four
Queenslanders
Author Kay Saunders   Research Librarian Dianne Byrne

> "Queensland's 'monstrous distances' alongside the decentralised and widespread population, nurtured individuals with big ambitions to pursue their destinies."

Queensland novelist Thea Astley recalled a poem her father kept on his sub-editor's desk at the *Courier-Mail* in the 1940s:

The people of Melbourne are frightfully well-born.
Of much the same kidney
Is the beau monde of Sydney.
But in Queensland the people insult yer
And don't 'ardly know they've been rude
They're that ignorant common and crude …

This mistaken belief that Queensland produced nothing but "cockroaches, white ants and bananas" and later, in the Bjelke-Petersen years, that it was the "Deep North", have remained persistent stereotypes in the national imagination.

"The monstrous distances", alongside the decentralised and widespread population, nurtured individuals with big ambitions to pursue their destinies. Entrepreneurs like Thomas McIlwraith, Robert Christison, Hudson Fysh, Edward Theodore and Leslie Thiess developed industry; Reginald Murray Williams promoted distinctive masculine attire and Samuel Griffith provided the workable basis for the new Commonwealth of Australia. Rather than producing a people simply "ignorant common and crude", Queensland produced some genuine heroes such as Major Bertram Bell, and educated individuals like Eric Partridge

Opening image Queensland pianist Eddie Cahill, seated in the front row, with Queen Victoria's granddaughter, Princess Marie Louise to his right, at a private recital at the London home of the Dowager Lady Swaythling, 1935. [Image No. 188433]

Above left Sir George Bowen's ceremonial sword. It has a brass handle and hilt and is stamped "H. Poole & Co/Savile Row/London". [ACC 4837]

Right Pastel portrait of Queensland's first governor, Sir George Ferguson Bowen (1821–99), by English artist Henry Fanner, 1882. It is likely that this work was executed during Bowen's term as governor of Hong Kong. [ACC 4593]

Right Danish-born emigrant Poul C Poulsen arrived in Queensland in 1882, where he became a prominent photographer. [Image No. 123080]

Below In 1897, Poulsen was awarded this collection of medals for work displayed at the Royal National Association and Queensland International Exhibitions. [TR 1877]

Below right Queensland architect Andrea Stombuco was responsible for Brisbane's Her Majesty's Theatre and a portion of All Hallows Convent. This portrait bust was executed by sculptor Horace Broadhurst and was presented to the State Library, together with a collection of Stombuco's architectural plans, by his granddaughter Miss Venetia Stombuco. [TR 2099]

who wrote the standard text *A guide to good English* (1942). Many artists and writers like Partridge, Percy Stephenson, Rosa Praed, Margaret Olley, PL (Pamela Lyndon) Travers, Gwen Harwood and Jack Lindsay, found the cultural milieu far too small and stifling for their talents. Other personalities resisted the lure of metropolitan civilisation and realised their ambitions in the harder, pragmatic immensity of Queensland.

Sir George Ferguson Bowen, the first governor, set the tone for good administration and has left his mark in numerous Queensland place names. Italian architect Andrea Stombuco built houses and churches and public buildings in the spirit and style of his homeland, and Danish-born photographer Poul Poulsen documented the colony's people and their progress.

Sir Anthony Musgrave arrived in Queensland in 1883 during a period of prosperity and expansion. Born in the sugar colony of Antigua in 1828, Musgrave was a career administrator. Unlike many imperial governors, Musgrave was also an intellectual and author of *Studies in political economy* (1875). The State Library of Queensland holds a series of beautifully worked silk programs commemorating events that he and his American wife, Lucinda, attended. The toast list for the Townsville banquet where representatives of the sugar, mining and pastoral industries feted him, captures his role of vice-regal representative in a wealthy expanding colony. His interests were wide: he attended a benefit where *Trial by jury* was performed in June 1884 to raise money for Mary McConnel's initiative, the Sick Children's Hospital, as well as melodramas, circus performances and a benefit for the Commercial Rowing Club.

Like his close friend Samuel Griffith, Musgrave was an advocate of Indigenous rights. He clashed with McIlwraith over the

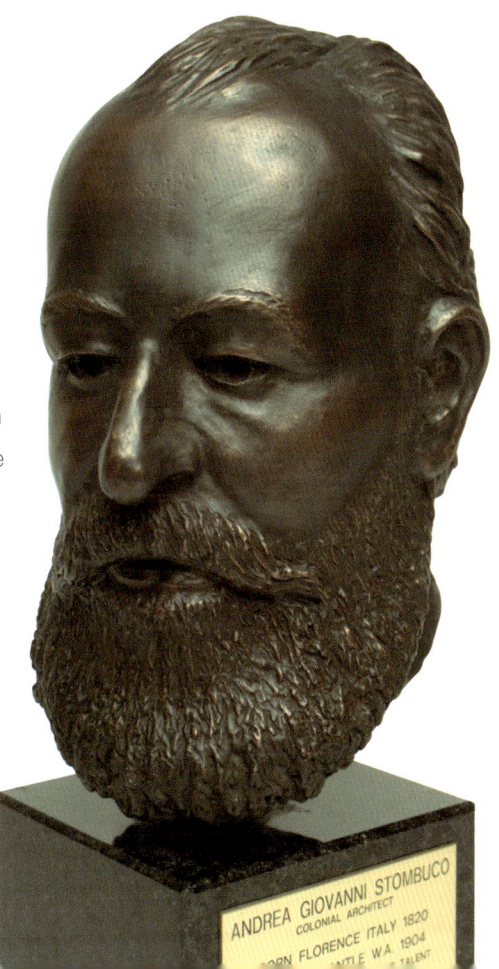

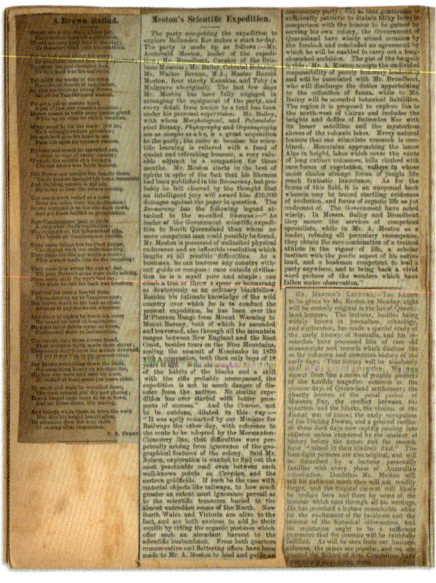

> Meston exemplified a particular type of intellectual man of action who literally embodied superior masculinity, curiosity and refined culture.

Above left Meston carried his interest in natural history into the larger world, studying the habits, customs and languages of Queensland's Indigenous people. [Image No. 8890]

Above right In April 1904 Archibald Meston, journalist, poet, botanist, historian and amateur ethnologist, undertook an expedition to the summit of Bellenden Ker Range. (top) The account of his climb is included in the Meston Papers, held by the State Library. (below) [OM 90-63/6/2]

governor's right to exercise the prerogative of mercy in the case of Benjamin Kidd, convicted of kidnapping Pacific Islanders for the sugar industry. McIlwraith insisted that the governor abide by the advice of his ministers. The conflict was so intense that Musgrave died suddenly in October 1888.

Other notable Queensland personalities were equally enthusiastic about Indigenous rights. A classical scholar, Archibald Meston was a scion of the Scottish gentry. In 1874 he managed the Pearlwell plantation on the Brisbane River before embarking on a career as a journalist with the *Ipswich Observer* and later in 1881, the *Townsville Bulletin*. A fitness fanatic and body builder, Meston climbed Mount Kosciusko in 1860. Like Thomas Welsby, another naturalist, parliamentarian and sportsman, Meston exemplified a particular type of intellectual man of action who literally embodied superior masculinity, curiosity and refined culture. An amateur ethnologist, natural scientist and linguist, Meston led an expedition to the Bellenden Ker Range in 1889.

Five years later, Home Secretary Horace Tozer commissioned a report on the condition of the Indigenous peoples. His well-researched report resulted in the *Aboriginals Protection and the Restriction of the Sale of Opium Act* (1897). Whatever his humanitarian intention, this legislation was disastrous, for it forcibly despatched fringe-dwellers across the colony on to reserves. This system endured into the 1980s, depriving Indigenous people of their fundamental rights.

Other notable men of action did not possess Meston's initial opportunities. John (Jackie) Howe was born in Killarney soon after Queensland separated from New South Wales. He was the son of a circus acrobat and of the companion to the wife of the wealthy Scottish-born squatter Patrick Leslie. As a shearer, young John Howe was notably successful, shearing 237 sheep by the new shearing machines on Barcaldine Downs in October 1892, and 321 in one day on nearby Alice Downs. Lady Lamington, on her visit to these properties, later remarked on Howe's feat. He won two gold medals for his shearing records.

Queenslanders | 69

This page A selection of silk theatre programs and menus presented to Sir Anthony Musgrave, governor of Queensland 1883–88. The entire collection includes personal notes, Sir Anthony's despatch box and Lady Musgrave's hymn book and Bible. [ACC 2812]

Above left Scrapbook kept by Jackie Howe containing clippings relating to prize winning merino breeds. [TR 2001]

Above right Queensland's most famous shearer, Jack Howe (second from right), on the footpath outside the Universal Hotel in Blackall, c. 1914. [Image No. BC 917]

These pastoral properties were the sites for intense class warfare in the Shearers' Strike in 1891, which saw union leaders jailed on charges of conspiracy rescinded decades previously in England. Howe was a union stalwart. As the president of the Blackall Workers' Political Organization in 1909, he supported the candidature of TJ Ryan, later Queensland's eminent Labor premier. Today he is remembered for the flannel shirt, named in his honour. The State Library holds his scrapbooks.

By the 1920s, with the rise of advertising, photography in newspapers, cinema, newsreels and radio, the nature of celebrity began to change rapidly. Heroes and stars could be created by the media with extraordinary rapidity. Queensland was part of this modern communication and cultural revolution, producing new celebrities, some acquiring national reputations. Others attained international recognition.

Bert Hinkler exemplified this new construction of celebrity. Born in Bundaberg in 1892 with a German father, young Hinkler began his career working in the local sugar industry. An early enthusiast for aviation, he joined the Queensland Aero Club in 1910. In 1913, he travelled to England and worked for the Sopwith aircraft factory before enlisting in the Royal Naval Air Service in 1914. A talented inventor, he improved the dual-control system that allowed the pilot to be relieved from flying continuously. He saw active service, flying night raids in a Handley-Page bomber as the gunner.

Hinkler's postwar career was initially beset with disappointment. Sopwith did not choose him as their representative on the first air race to Australia in 1919. He decided to undertake the feat alone, although he had to abandon his flight near the Italian Alps. He did, however, win the Britannia Trophy for this accomplishment. Hinkler returned to Australia briefly, making the first non-stop flight from Sydney to Bundaberg in 1921. In 1928 he was the first person to fly solo from England to Australia. His international fame was established, commemorated with a song *Hustling Hinkler* written in New York. The Depression hampered his career then, while attempting a global flight, he perished in Italy in January 1933. His death caused

Queenslanders

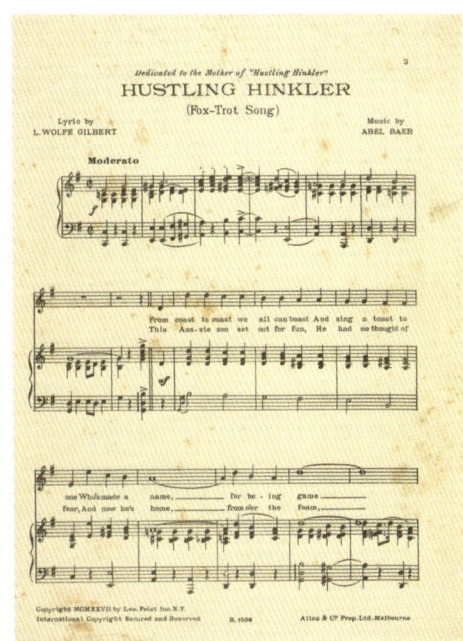

Right Sheet music for the song *Hustling Hinkler*, published in New York in 1927. [Sheet Music Collection]

Below Newspaper clippings, correspondence, cutting books and certificates spanning the flying career of Herbert (Bert) Hinkler, c. 1909–32, including 52 telegrams of congratulation on his flight from England to Darwin in 1928 and letters from his family. [OM 68-24]

Above Sixteen letters received by Matron Barron relating to Sister Kenny and the Townsville Polio Clinic, 1934–35. [OMR 15; TR 1829]

immense grief in his homeland where Hinkler is still revered as an aviation pioneer.

Other Queenslanders from this era also battled officialdom for recognition. Elizabeth Kenny, born in 1880, trained as a nurse but had no formal qualifications. After successfully treating patients suffering from infantile paralysis with hot cloth fomentations, Kenny opened her own cottage hospital at Clifton. During the First World War she served as a staff nurse overseas where she acquired the title of "Sister".

In Townsville in 1932 she established a clinic to treat poliomyelitis and cerebral palsied patients with her regime of hot baths and massage. Her new methods were bitterly opposed by the medical establishment, most particularly by Dr Harold Crawford, an orthopaedic surgeon who was instrumental in establishing the discipline of physiotherapy at the University of Queensland in 1936. He later established the multidisciplinary training schedule at the new Spastic Centre in Brisbane in 1948. The State Library holds the records of this organisation.

Kenny had some medical authorities on her side. Herbert Wilkinson, professor of anatomy at the University of Queensland, wrote the foreword to her book *Infantile paralysis and cerebral diplegia* (1937). Her methods faced condemnation at a royal commission. Despite this setback, Kenny was allowed to operate in a ward of the Brisbane General Hospital. In 1940 the Queensland Government paid Kenny's fare to the United States where she demonstrated her methods at the Minneapolis General Hospital. With notable improvement of many of her patients, she began teaching doctors and physiotherapists. In recognition of her endeavours the Sister Kenny Institute was established in Minneapolis in 1942.

Sister Kenny's autobiography *And they shall walk*, followed by the film *Sister Kenny* (1946) starring the glamorous Rosalind Russell, ensured her celebrity was international. Her trips back to Australia, however, were not greeted with enthusiasm. Her unfeminine combativeness was regarded as a liability and her lack

The postwar years produced many Queensland women with high-profile international careers. They included 'Sister' Elizabeth Kenny, who successfully but controversially treated patients worldwide suffering from infantile paralysis, and the Hollywood actor Mary Maguire.

of formal training tarnished her image. The State Library also holds the records of Queensland's first female medical graduate, Dr Eleanor Bourne, whose career took a more conventional path.

Another notable Queensland woman, actor Mary Maguire, achieved popular fame in the 1930s and 1940s. The daughter of the licensee of the exclusive Bellevue Hotel (across the road from the Queensland Club and Parliament House in Brisbane) Mary Maguire (born Helene Maguire) was discovered at the age of fifteen in 1934 by Charles and Elsa Chauvel, the prominent filmmakers. (Chauvel's family had strong links to Canning Downs where Jackie Howe was born.) After a stint in Hollywood, Chauvel began making films in Australia in 1926. Maguire (billed as Peggy Maguire) starred as the young Irish colleen Biddy O'Shea in *Heritage* (1936).

Going to Hollywood she starred in B-grade films such as *Alcatraz Island* (1937), *Mysterious Mr Moto* (1938) with Peter Lorre, and *Sergeant Murphy* (1938). Transferring her

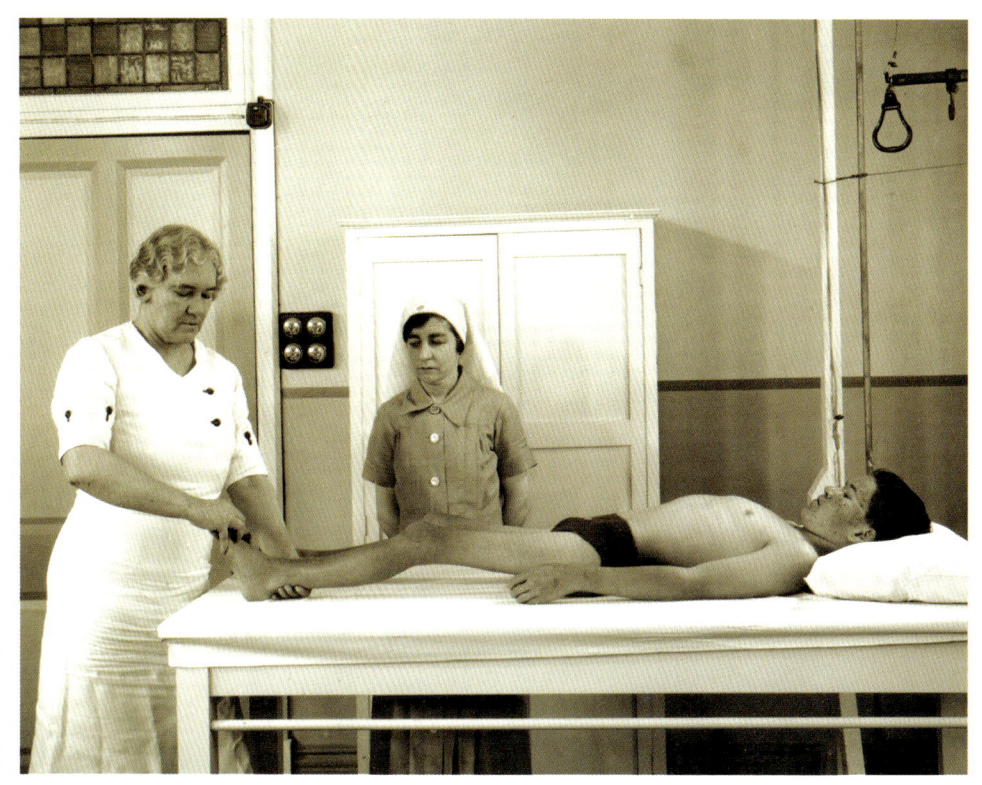

Top Sister Elizabeth Kenny demonstrating her therapy for polio patients, c. 1939. [Image No. 54002]

Above left For years after leaving Brisbane, actress Mary Maguire continued to make local headlines. [Image No. BC 959]

Above right Mary Maguire is welcomed home to Brisbane by family and friends after completing work on the film *The Flying Doctor* in 1936. [Image No. 150013]

Below left Aboriginal tenor, teacher and activist Harold Blair photographed in the 1940s with Melbourne-born soprano Marjorie Lawrence, who retired at the height of her fame after contracting polio.
[Image No. 144141]

Below right Queensland pianist Eddie Cahill, seated in the front row, with Queen Victoria's granddaughter, Princess Marie Louise to his right, at a private recital at the London home of the Dowager Lady Swaythling, 1935.
[Image No. 188433]

career to England, she married Captain Robert Gordon-Canning. *Truth* newspaper of 13 August 1939 reported on the Catholic wedding service with the seriously ill bride, in pale blue, resplendent in a wheelchair. Her mother attended the ceremony attired inappropriately in the middle of summer in a sable fur and a hat of birds. Marie Neyman from Jack Hylton's band sang.

Maguire made several films in England including a spy drama, *This Was Paris* (1942). Her life took an unusual turn when her husband was interned for his support of British Fascist Sir Oswald Mosley. After the war she married an American officer and retired to California where she died in 1974. Her sisters all made spectacular marriages and could be dubbed the Antipodean Gabors.

Other Queensland artists made careers overseas with varying degrees of success. Pianist Eddie Cahill from Beenleigh began his career at the Cremorne Theatre in Brisbane in 1917. Like Bundaberg-born Gladys Moncrieff, who was also encouraged by Dame Nellie Melba, Cahill and his partner, tenor George Brooke, went to London in 1923.

Good-looking and charming, he became a favourite of society hostesses like the Dowager Lady Swaythling and Viscountess Elibank. His career never reached the heights of an Arthur Rubinstein and he retired to Switzerland during the war. He was, however, notable for his fundraising for the British Red Cross and various refugee organisations.

Though a modest talent, Cahill fared far better than Cherbourg-born tenor Harold Blair, who was promoted by pianist Marjorie Lawrence. He appeared on the Australian Broadcasting Commission's Jubilee tour of Australia. Thereafter, Blair's career languished and he ended up running a milk bar.

Another Queenslander attained an extraordinary international career during these years. Lydia Ellen (Nelle) Tritton, the socialite daughter of the owners of the well-known furniture firm, might have had the charmed life of a privileged young woman. After dancing with the Prince of Wales during his visit in 1920, she rejected a conventional path. After commencing as a poet writing lamentable verses, she began a career as a journalist in Sydney before

Left Poems by Lydia Ellen (Nelle) Tritton, published in Brisbane c. 1920. The author inscribed this copy for Queensland governor Sir Matthew Nathan. [NAT A821.2 tri]

Below left Beverley Hylton wearing Balenciaga at the New York premiere of *My Fair Lady*, 1964. [TR 1818]

Below right Nelle Tritton created great interest when she returned to Brisbane with her second husband, former Russian Premier Alexander Kerensky, *Courier-Mail,* 14 November 1945. [Image No. BC 956]

transferring to London in 1925. Interested in international relations, especially Russian issues, she married the former White Russian officer and tenor Nicholas Nadejine. Divorced, she returned to Brisbane in 1939 where she undertook Russian lessons with Nina Maximoff – who later married the founder of *Meanjin*, Clem Christensen.

Tritton had met the exiled Russian leader Alexander Kerensky, for whom she initially worked as a secretary. They were married in Pennsylvania in late 1939. They went to live in Paris, leaving for the United States in 1940 on a British naval vessel. They returned to Brisbane in 1945 where she died a year later.

Brisbane had nurtured another famous Russian on the international stage: Peter Simonoff was a founder of the Communist Party of Australia and a later member of the Soviet Comintern. He promoted Bolshevik causes in World War I from Merivale Street in Brisbane.

The postwar years produced another Queensland woman with an international career. Born in Mackay in 1932, Beverley Prowse became Miss Victoria in 1954. A successful mannequin in London, she worked for

Norman Hartnell. In 1963 she married the English impresario, band leader and theatre owner Jack Hylton, taking her further into the world of glamour and celebrity. Widowed two years later, she went on to pursue an interesting and active life, marrying distinguished Australian newspaper executive Alex McKay in 1973. Rupert Murdoch acted as best man. Among her papers held in the State Library there is a photograph of Beverley Hylton, at the height of her beauty in 1964, wearing a Balenciaga evening gown, the same style as that displayed in a major exhibition in the National Design Museum within the Smithsonian Museum in 2005–06.

Beverley Prowse was a strong advocate of all things Australian and joked when her husband was knighted in 1981 that she was "McKay of Mackay." She was instrumental in raising the funds for the travelling Sir Robert Menzies scholarship and for the establishment of the Menzies Centre for Australian Studies in London in 1988. She was appointed a Member of the Order of Australia in 1991 for her advocacy of Australian studies. Unfortunately her autobiography, *A view from Camelot*, remained unfinished at her death.

Many Queensland personalities did not gain international recognition; their talents remained devoted to the national scene. Eddie Gilbert was Queensland's most notable cricketer in the 1930s. Born on Durundur Aboriginal reserve around 1905, his life initially represented the fate of those Indigenous people despatched to Meston's reserves. Separated from his brother, he was sent to Barambah (later Cherbourg). His talent as a cricketer was recognised by his schoolteacher, Robert Crawford. He was selected for the Queensland team in 1930.

From the outset his bowling wrist movement was controversial. On 6 November 1931, in the first match of the Sheffield Shield Season at the 'Gabba', Gilbert had the rare distinction of knocking the bat from Donald Bradman's hands and making him lose his balance. The match was heard by the Barambah community on Crawford's radio. Bradman recalled later: "[Gilbert] sent down the fastest bowling I can remember of that time, he was much faster than Larwood or anyone else".

Gilbert was dropped from the Queensland team on the grounds he threw the ball. He was not selected for the Australian team in the infamous Bodyline series in 1932–33.

Below Scrapbooks documenting the life of Queensland-born beauty Beverley Prowse. Originally from Mackay, she became a model, winning the title of Miss Victoria in 1954. Two years later, she moved to London to pursue an acting career and in 1963 married English impresario Jack Hylton, entering into the world of international society.
[TR 1818]

Queenslanders

> Many Queensland personalities did not gain international recognition; their talents remained devoted to the national scene.

With new rules from the Marylebone Cricket Club against "intimidatory" bowling, Gilbert's unique style was banned. This effectively terminated his public career. He was sent back to Barambah. His mental health deteriorated and he was admitted to Goodna Psychiatric Hospital in 1949. Years followed during which Eddie Gilbert lived on in obscurity. His funeral took place at Cherbourg in January 1978. The State Library holds many records documenting the career of one of Queensland's finest sportsmen.

Queensland also produced notable artists and gallery managers. James Wieneke, born in Bundaberg in 1906, was the grandson of German immigrants who arrived in Australia in the 1850s. His uncle Jack produced the famous Wieneke saddle. However, young James did not follow this path. After leaving school in the 1930s he visited Windorah where he produced many paintings and drawings of station life. Some of these works became covers for the *Queenslander* newspaper while others eventually became book illustrations. During World War II, Wieneke served with the Sixth Division in New Guinea where his drawings from the Wewak-Aitape (see page 78) campaigns captured the realities of jungle warfare.

On his return to civilian life he published a book of his New Guinea sketches and in 1951 became the owner and director of the Moreton Galleries in Brisbane's AMP Building, the former site of General MacArthur's wartime operations. He exhibited Lionel Lindsay's work in 1948 and later Margaret Olley's. A passionate advocate of Queensland excellence, he was a founding member of the Half Dozen Group of Artists with Lilian Pedersen. He was appointed as the Director of the Queensland Art Gallery in 1967 and held this position until 1974.

Queensland produced other notable gallery owners. Brian and Marjorie Johnstone's gallery was one of the most influential private galleries in Australia in the 1950s and 1960s. Their first gallery, the Marodian, opened in Edward Street in Brisbane in 1950 and was a modest affair. The second, which operated in the Brisbane Arcade from 1952

Above left (top) Eddie Gilbert with his cousins and a film producer at the Brisbane Exhibition Ground, November 1934. [Image No. 43482]

Above left (bottom) Fast Bowler Eddie Gilbert became a legend when he twice claimed Donald Bradman's wicket in Sheffield Shield matches. He was the first Aboriginal sportsman to play Sheffield Shield cricket for Queensland and represented Australia against South Africa, the West Indies and an English XI captained by Douglas Jardine. [Image No. 73614]

Above right (top) Brian and Marjorie Johnstone and their beloved dog Lindy in the garden of their Bowen Hills gallery with *Tripod Figure: Abstract Plant Form* by Queensland sculptor Kathleen Shillam. [Image No. BC 966]

Above right (bottom) The interior of the Johnstone Gallery, photographed by Arthur Davenport, c. 1976. [Image No. BC 965]

78 | Between the covers

Above Left Original drawings by Queensland artist James Wieneke for his book *Sixth Division sketches*, published in Sydney in 1946.
[Image Nos. BC 945, 946, 947]

Above right Wieneke photographed while serving with the Royal Australian Engineers at Wewak, c. 1942. He did numerous drawings and watercolours of people and events during the Aitape to Wewak Campaign and recorded the Japanese surrender at Cape Wom airstrip in September 1945.
[Image No. 59085]

Right Scrapbook containing articles, invitations and catalogues relating to the exhibitions and events held at the Johnstone Gallery in Brisbane from 1950 until 1972.
[RB HARC 7/1/1-7]

> In the postwar era, as Australian culture absorbed new American influences, the role of television in creating new forms of entertainment and new identities cannot be underestimated.

until 1957, was far more expansive, showing Sidney Nolan, Arthur Boyd, Donald Friend, John Brack, Margaret Olley, Clifton Pugh and Jon Molvig.

The Johnstones were not simply concerned with the business side of gallery management, they also showed young artists' works in a salon setting at their house, Wyandra in Cintra Road at Bowen Hills.

In 1958 they made the connection between art and life complete when they opened the new Johnstone Gallery at their home, where the local Twelfth Night Theatre gave performances in the tropical garden. Over the years, until they retired in 1972, the Johnstones continued to hold groundbreaking exhibitions including Charles Blackman's Alice in Wonderland series, a debut collection of paintings by Ray Crooke (1960) works by Lawrence Daws and Keith Looby (1969) and sculpture by Len and Kathleen Shillam. The State Library holds the extensive archive of this remarkable couple.

In the postwar era, as Australian culture absorbed new American influences, the role of television in creating new forms of entertainment and new identities cannot be underestimated. Hugh Cornish had a remarkable career in both radio and television in Queensland, immortalised by his opening words on the new medium in Brisbane on 16 August 1959, "Good evening and welcome to television". The son of an Anglican priest, Cornish was a well-educated, thoughtful man whose career was nurtured through the Ipswich Eisteddfod, where his mother was a notable contributor, and through amateur theatricals. He decided employment as a sugar chemist was not suited to his more artistic talents, opting for a career in radio

Above QTQ 9's Hugh Cornish makes an appearance on a 1967 telethon along with Graham Kennedy and Tommy Hanlon Jnr.
[Image No. BC 955]

Right Hugh Cornish's early television career saw him involved in some unusual activities, including this debate at the Brisbane City Hall in 1961.
[ACC 298, TR2110]

Between the covers

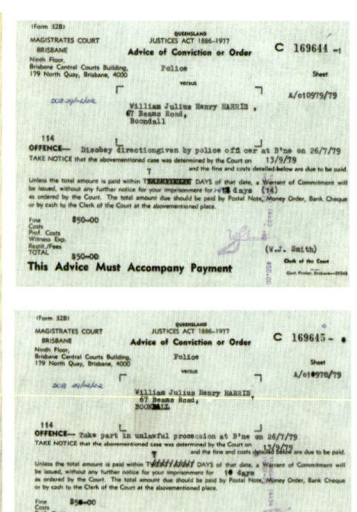

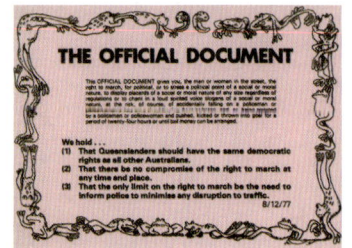

Above left William Julius Henry (Joe) Harris, Queensland trade unionist (centre) marching for peace as a BWIU delegate. [ACC 3251]

Above right Some of Joe Harris' bail notices and convictions, including advice for "unlawful procession" and disobeying a police direction, 1979. [ACC 3151]

where he promoted in-depth programs on Mel Torme, Winifred Attwell and The Platters. His interests extended beyond popular culture; for he reported on the savage mass killing in Cannon Hill in 1957. He also chaired a public debate on life in outer space at the height of interest in space exploration.

As the program director for QTQ 9, Cornish was a fearless advocate for journalistic integrity, exposing questionable personalities and plans favoured by premier Bjelke-Petersen and the drink-driving scandal involving Sir Edward Lyons, the chairman of the TAB. The channel's owner, Alan Bond, was alarmed that the current affairs program *Today Tonight* was not sufficiently sympathetic to the Bjelke-Petersen Government. When Lyons was appointed chairman of QTQ 9, more conflict arose over the station's reportage of the SEQEB strike. Bond dismissed Cornish personally on 10 March 1985.

Other notable Queensland personalities also dedicated themselves to "fighting the good fight". One of these was Joe Harris, who was born in Vladivostok in Russia in 1922 and moved to Australia in 1940. He served in the Australian Army in New Guinea and Darwin where his wartime experiences of combat convinced him that both pacifism and communism were the only civilised options for society. He later joined the Australian Labor Party where he was a leader of the socialist left faction. By trade a carpenter, Harris was an organiser for the Building Workers Industrial Union. He was amongst the BWIU members who volunteered their services to rebuild Darwin after Cyclone Tracy in 1974.

His interests were wide and not confined to party politics or political action. His extensive archive in the collection of the State Library demonstrates his broad interests in human liberation, civil liberties and social justice. He took part in campaigns for land rights, women's issues, anti-nuclear and environmental campaigns. He also became involved in international issues relating to Timor and South Africa.

The State Library of Queensland holds many collections and materials documenting the lives and achievements of notable Queensland personalities who defy stereotypes.

Sponsored by
st.george
Good with people. Good with money.

Chapter five
Young Queensland

Author Kay Saunders   Research Librarian Dianne Byrne

> *Several themes recur throughout Queensland history. One was that physically and morally healthy children were seen as the basis of a progressive society and the cornerstone of a strong and resilient people, dedicated to hard work and able to cope with vast distances and a hot climate.*

In November 1940, amidst the anxiety of war, a call went out in Melbourne that Noel Coward was desperately seeking *Queensland cousins*. His search was not for long lost relatives, but for the novel by EL Haverfield which he had enjoyed as a boy in Edwardian London. Actor Robert Keable had brought this exciting tale of wild adventure and excitement back from his tour of Australia to a delighted young Noel. Within an hour of his request his beloved book was found. This copy is now in the State Library of Queensland with a pencil inscription reminding the reader that Noel Coward took it to Mooloolaba to rekindle his childhood pleasures.

The world that delighted a young Noel Coward was fiction, the tale of Eustace Orban, a British boy who, with his resourceful Queensland cousin Bob Cochrane, tested his powers of endurance in the bush. For young British children embarking on a life in Australia there were real adventures and hazards, remote from the safety of fiction.

The State Library owns several important old educational items for privileged children in Europe. The "Horn Book" with its beautiful silver and ivory offers a rare insight into educational practice. The French dictionary with "K" depicted as a kangaroo is the first recorded use of the new knowledge from the Antipodes.

Opening image Robert Louis Stevenson's *Treasure island* with illustrations by William Bustard, published by Jackson & O'Sullivan, Brisbane 1956. [RBQ 820.8 ste]

Right *Queensland cousins* by Eleanor Louisa Haverfield, originally published in London c. 1908. One of a number of books produced by this English author depicting young people in an Australian setting. [J 823.1 hav]

Young Queensland

Left An 18th century "Horn Book" used to teach children their alphabet and numbers. This rare item was produced in England and is composed of thin slates of silver and ivory, nailed together with 30 silver studs. The silver plates are engraved with upper and lower case alphabets and numbers. [RB 099 17—]

Right *Alphabet illustre du dictionnaire general et grammatical* by Napoleon Landais, published in Paris in 1837. [RBJ 440.03 lan]

In Queensland, life for most children was set on other trajectories. Several themes recur throughout Queensland history. One was that physically and morally healthy children were seen as the basis of a progressive society and the cornerstone of a strong and resilient people, dedicated to hard work and able to cope with vast distances and a hot climate.

A country's wealth is not simply measured in material possessions but in the strength of its children. How these ideas developed and adapted to changing circumstances is both complex and intriguing.

At the outset of non-convict settlement, Reverend Dr John Dunmore Lang put forth a bold proposal. In his polemical text entitled *Juvenile–pauper emigration: a letter* (1849) addressed to the Poor Laws Commissioner, Lang proposed that pauper children over 12, with equal numbers of males and females, should be despatched to the northern districts of New South Wales. Not only would England be relieved of "the raw material out of which the future pauperism, prostitution and crime are in due time to be extensively manufactured", the new district would solve labour shortages in the proposed cotton industry. The child workers would be uplifted by their life of labour.

For modern readers this is an unpalatable plan; at that time it appeared to be a practical solution reminiscent of the reasons for British settlement in 1788. Lang's proposal did not eventuate, as colonial authorities wanted morally upright immigrants. However this type of scheme held great appeal as it provided both a source of population growth and cheap labour. From the 1920s, thousands of neglected and orphaned English children from institutions were sent to Australia as unskilled workers under the Barnardo and Fairbridge schemes. These plans provide a ready indication of enduring attitudes to poor children. Their lives were to consist of regimentation, consistent toil and self reliance from an early age.

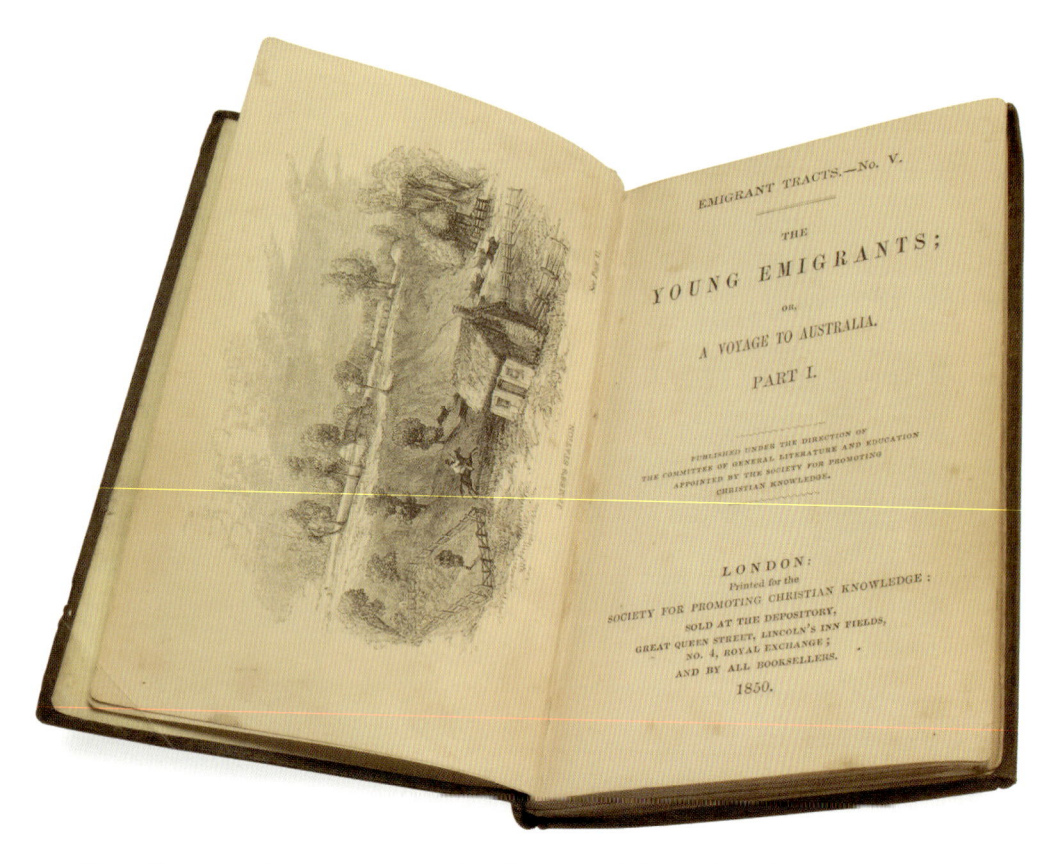

Between the covers

For early immigrant children from poor homes, life was also hard, as the religious tract, *The young emigrants or, a voyage to Australia* (1850) shows. Maria Steley's diary is a unique record of that world. She was born in South Wales in 1848, emigrating with her parents and five siblings on the *Ariadne* to the new colony in 1863. Her diary is addressed to her friend, Elenor with acute observations about the poor food (consisting of black pudding, cabbage and salt pork) served to the passengers in cramped steerage. Quarantined on Stradbroke Island because of an outbreak of measles, the Steleys eventually moved to Rockhampton and then to Maryborough where her father worked at the Burrum coal mine. Tragically, her life in the new colony was brief, as she died in a horse-riding accident near Agnes Vale station on 14 November 1869.

One published account of the life of young Queenslanders, both British and Indigenous, is contained in a remarkable autobiography, *My Australian girlhood: sketches and impressions of bush life* (1902), by the daughter of the prominent pastoralist and parliamentarian Thomas Lodge

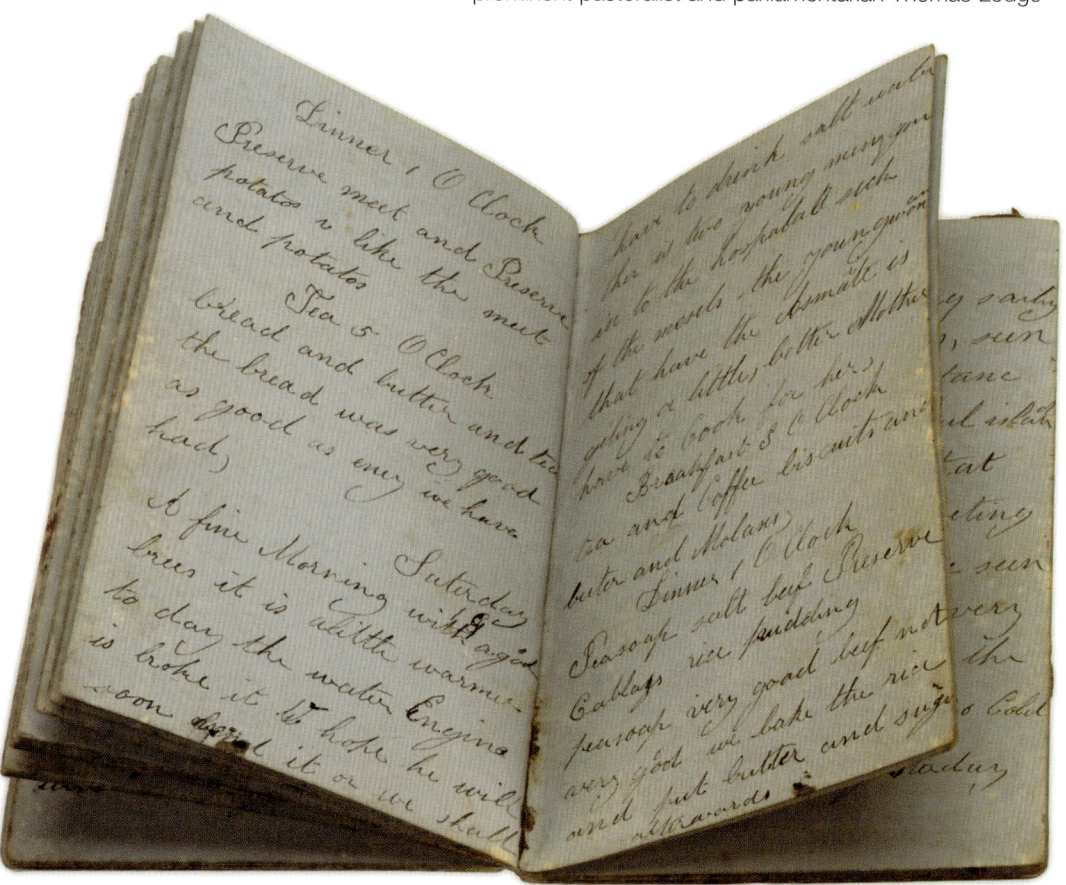

Above *The young emigrants or, a voyage to Australia*, published in London by the Society for Promoting Christian Knowledge, 1850. It was a thinly disguised tract about a little Cornish girl who left her "cottage on the down" for a "station in the bush." [RBJ 919.4 you] **Below** Diary kept by 15-year-old Maria Steley during her voyage from England to Australia aboard the *Ariadne*, 1863–64. [OM 71-14]

Young Queensland

This page Three sketches illustrating the antics of Charles Junior (Paddy) and Lionel ("Plum Bun"), the children of Charles and Winifred Rawson, wealthy and well-connected pioneers who resided at The Hollow, near Mackay, 1877. Rawson Archive. [ACC 2967]

> **Children in some privileged families could enjoy the pleasures now seen as the right of all children. Colonial family life, though often harsh and difficult, was not always dictated by purely utilitarian views.**

Murray-Prior. Rosa Praed relentlessly chronicled the view of the outside world around her and the violent realities of the frontier which witnessed the dispossession of the Indigenous peoples. "Men travelled with their flocks and herds, and, like Abraham and Lot, fought the tribes for land and water …"

Children in some privileged families could enjoy the pleasures now seen as the right of all children. Colonial family life, though often harsh and difficult, was not always dictated by purely utilitarian views. In wonderfully evocative drawings the Rawson family in Mackay documented the daily lives of the boys, Charles (Paddy) and Lionel "Plum Bun". The first steps of Lionel, created through a series titled *"Fancy portrait of Mr P Bun"* on 26 January 1877, as well as the boys playing with their toys and pets in numerous photographs in the albums, depict a world of carefree childhood in affluent and affectionate circumstances.

A young mother, Lady Lamington had a modern empathy for children. One of the first entries in her record of her stay in Queensland concerns a baby suffering from extreme prickly heat when she first arrived on Thursday Island in 1895. She arranged for ice to be sent from the vice-regal steamer, for "in that terrible heat they have no ice works". She later made a point of visiting the children of Indigenous peoples from all over southern Queensland who had been forcibly sent to Fraser Island Reserve.

Education in the vast territories was always a concern. Private education came in various forms. For Scotswoman Mary McConnel of Cressbrook station in the Brisbane Valley in the 1850s, education and religious instruction were

Above Lady Lamington and her baby daughter, the Hon Grizel Annabella Gem Cochrane Baillie, photographed by Frederick Whitehead at Government House, Brisbane, 1898. [Image. No. 108976]

School (interior) Mapoon Mission.

important features for the children of her husband's employees. Many were emigrants brought out by Dr Lang in 1849. As hard working, skilled and religious Protestants, these families valued education and moral instruction.

She helped found the Brisbane Children's Hospital to assist "the suffering little ones" in 1878. As the death rate among colonial babies and children was much higher than in England, these facilities were vital. The registrar general in 1878, when childhood deaths from diarrhoea alone accounted for 18 per cent of all deaths in the colony, identified "the absence of drainage, the accumulation of filth, bad ventilation, impure water, uncleanly personal habits, unwholesome foods …" as the major causes of child deaths. The Rawson Archive shows the need for medical resources. There is a drawing of Mackay children being inoculated, presumably against smallpox, in 1877.

Other privileged women supported early educational and medical endeavours. Diamantina Bowen, the wife of the first Governor Sir George Bowen, was an enthusiastic patron of All Hallows Convent School, the first girls boarding school, established in 1863 and run by the Irish Sisters of Mercy.

The first provision of state-funded education was for grammar schools on the English model, whereby privileged boys received both a classical education and one to ensure they could run the enterprises of the British Empire. Ipswich Grammar School was established in 1861.

For young Queenslanders, until the first Education Act was passed in 1875, the right to even a basic education was not a foregone conclusion. For working class and farm children the emphasis was always on labour to support themselves and contribute to the family income. Once established, schools reached from Thursday Island to Quilpie. The album

Above Children at school at Mapoon Mission, photographed in their classroom during a visit by the Home Secretary, the Hon JFG Foxton, 1899. [ACC 6538][Album APA 50]

> **There was ongoing concern when mass education was established on the basis of being 'free, compulsory and secular' that this was dangerous and immoral.**

of photographs by HW Mobsby, documenting an official visit to the Torres Strait in 1899 offers a rare insight into the place of children in this world.

There was ongoing concern when mass education was established on the basis of being "free, compulsory and secular" that this was dangerous and immoral. The Bible in State Schools League successfully lobbied for some religious instruction in state schools from 1910. William O Lilley's pamphlet, *Why are our Queensland children bitterly wronged* (1913) asked "What kind of nation are we rearing? Clever, doubtless; smart and keen, but without much conscience, and GODLESS …"

Just as Irish Roman Catholics were able to receive both religious and secular education within their extensive parochial school system, so too did other ethnic and religious groups seek to maintain their identity. A charming photograph in the State Library's collection shows Mrs Blundell's dancing school in Charters Towers in 1900 offering Scottish dancing for both boys and girls. On a more formal level, the German Lutheran community arranged instruction in language, culture and faith at the church in South Brisbane.

Another form of German education later spread through the society. In 1907, only a few years after its establishment in Europe, the Crèche and Kindergarten Movement was established in Brisbane under the patronage of Lady Chelmsford, the wife of the Governor, offering high-quality education for pre-schoolers. Emphasis was on creative play, positive self-esteem and a love of the arts. This was a different view of the child as a unique individual rather than a miniature adult.

Above Students at the German School at South Brisbane, 1901. This photograph was taken about the time of the death of Queen Victoria, an event which inspired great demonstrations of loyalty and tributes among German immigrants in Queensland. [Image No. 10122]

Below Children at Thargomindah dressed in diggers costumes, Anzac Day 1919. Patriotic "uniforms" of this kind were offered for sale by drapers all over Queensland. [Image No. 170843]

Young Queensland

Above left Souvenir programme for the Children's Coronation Pageant held in aid of the Queensland Art Society at the Brisbane Exhibition Grounds, 17 June 1911. [Ephemera Collection]
Above right *Queensland march song and chorus*, produced by a composer identified only as "D Davis", published at Sandgate, c. 1895. Music collection [ASM PVM QUE]

When the Australian colonies federated in 1901, the people saw themselves as a strong, virile European nation within the British Empire. The sheet music, *Queensland march song and chorus* captures the tone of this era. This view was radically transformed as Britain went to war with Germany in 1914. The rapid change in attitude to the Germans can be contrasted by looking at Queensland children's re-enactment of the coronation of George V in 1911, when the Anglo–German heritage of the British Royal family was acknowledged. Only three years later this pride was submerged under a hatred of all things German. Young Queenslanders were enlisted into a militaristic derision of the enemy at the front which affected relations with once-valued German neighbours. Often girls appeared in patriotic pageants as Britannia.

After the death and injury of so many young men in the war and the Spanish flu epidemic, the health of the new generation became paramount. With far smaller families by the 1920s and new ideas on childhood coming through from the works of Freud, a new concern

WHOOPING COUGH

SEE YOUR DOCTOR ABOUT INJECTIONS

WHOOPING COUGH is spread by germs — ISOLATION PREVENTS SPREAD OF INFECTION
don't give them a chance
CALL YOUR DOCTOR

AUTHORISED BY HON. C.A. KELLY M.L.A. MINISTER FOR HEALTH

Above The eradication of global disease was a great dream of the post World War II era. In Australia, the introduction of the Salk vaccine in 1956 dramatically reduced the incidence of polio epidemics and, in the wake of this success, immunisation was seen as the way forward to protecting Australian children. [ACC 6586]

> "The establishment of the Queensland public health system in 1936, with its emphasis on maternal and child health, was a national and international innovation."

for the health, rights and welfare of children gathered momentum. In 1918 the Baby and Child Health Clinics were established to monitor the growth and fitness of young white Queenslanders. The Mothercraft Association led by women physicians also was founded.

Especially after the Depression, the State Government began public awareness campaigns on good nutrition, fitness, dental health and recreation. In a foreword to a landmark pamphlet entitled *Health, food and fitness campaign*, the Minister for Health, Ned Hanlon, stressed the health of children for the nation's progress.

Dr Phyllis Cilento was a pioneer in family public health, with her newspaper column as "Medical mother", and her books such as *Square meals for the family* (containing the economical recipe, "hazlet ragout" using the lungs, heart and liver of the sheep). Sir Raphael Cilento, as Director General of Health, implemented widespread public health campaigns for children's wellbeing.

The private Bush Children's Health Scheme allowed poor sick children from the bush to receive free quality medical care in Brisbane, followed by recuperating beach holidays in Redcliffe. Despite its generosity, this scheme could hardly meet the widespread demand. The establishment of the Queensland public health system in 1936, with its emphasis on maternal and child health, was a national and international innovation. Scarlet fever, diphtheria, poliomyelitis, whooping cough and measles continued to devastate young children with vaccination programs becoming more widespread.

Life for young Queenslanders increasingly allowed for play and leisure. The State Library owns an extremely rare

Young Queensland

The Nursery.

The little child on cushion white
Should surely sleep in peace;
So nursie rocks with all her might
Nor will she ever cease.

The little boy with stick in hand
The raven black doth beat,
While pussie cannot understand
That bird is not to eat.

Above and below *Look at me! A new movable toybook* by Lothar Meggendorfer, printed in Germany and published in London in 1891. Munich-born Meggendorfer (1847–1925) was a sophisticated and imaginative artist who, beginning in the 1880s, created a number of ingenious childrens books using stand-up panoramas and pull-out tabs. [RB 741 1891]

Above Certificate awarded by the Anzac Committee of the Queensland War Council to Herbert Von Dohren for his contribution to the support of Queensland's war widows and orphaned children. [ACC 6559]

Above *The pop-up Mickey Mouse*, with story and illustrations by the staff of the Walt Disney Studios, published in New York by Blue Ribbon Books, c. 1933. [RB 813.06 1933]

English-language childrens illustrated book, *Look at me!* printed in Germany in 1891 with pull-out sections that make the characters move. Children enjoyed a wide range of popular culture. Photographs in the State Library's collection show two older girls around 1900 reading the English comic, *Sunny hours*. By the late 1920s, children enjoyed Australian comics such as *Ginger Meggs* and *Cobbers* as well as American imports. Children delighted in films and cartoons especially the new Walt Disney productions seen in suburban and travelling tent cinemas. Toys of beloved characters such as Mickey Mouse were prized possessions. Shirley Temple dolls were esteemed by Queensland girls. A new brochure from the Cairns Toy Works shows the limited nature of Australian-produced childrens wooden toys.

Despite the pleasures of toys and cartoons, life was often grim for many children whose lives were caught up in the wider dramas of war and Depression. The opening of the Story Bridge in 1940 was a vote of confidence by the government that huge public works like those advocated by President Roosevelt in the United States could get the economy kick-started. The symbolism of the faith in the future of the state, represented by children holding the Queensland flag, would not have been lost on a contemporary audience.

The love affair with American culture became even more pervasive after the presence of so many American personnel in Queensland during World War II. Some groups, such as the Communist Party, were alarmed by the new American post-war dominance. Most specifically the dangers of nuclear warfare and the threat of a third world war endangering all life on the planet, and taking money away from the development of health, education and housing programs were expressed. The State Library possesses photographs of the families of veterans so destitute after the war that they were living in tents in Victoria Park near the Exhibition Grounds in Brisbane.

Yet these years saw remarkable advances in opportunities for children. The establishment of the Spastic Children's Welfare League's facilities for treatment, initially in Brisbane in 1948, witnessed an innovative world-class holistic method to assist children with cerebral palsy. Dr Harold Crawford's methods gave hope to many disabled children formerly relegated to a back room in the family home. The records of

Young Queensland 93

Above Commemorative flag presented to the school children of Queensland to mark the completion and opening of the Story Bridge, 1940. [ACC 3296] **Below** Corinda Cub Scouts wearing the latest "sensation", Mickey Mouse ears, October 1959. [Image No. BC 480]

> **The advent of television in Queensland in 1959 saw an intensification of Americanisation. In the first few weeks some families, with children wearing their pyjamas, took up spots in front of stores selling televisions.**

the League, as well as material from Sister Elizabeth Kenny's methods of treating children with poliomyelitis, show how Queensland was in the forefront of treatment of childhood illness and disability.

The visit of Queen Elizabeth in February 1954 again reinforced the importance of youth and the pursuit of a secure future. The Queen visited the New Farm facilities for cerebral-palsied children. With the British Commonwealth led by a beautiful young monarch with two charming children, optimism in the new, more affluent, world of the 1950s began to take shape after the traumas of world wars and Depression that had marred public life for four decades. Publicity around the large wealthy Cronin family gave insight into a life far removed from the world of most people.

Australian life in the 1950s attempted to reconcile its British heritage, its unique Australian features and emerging new multiculturalism with pervasive forms of attractive American popular culture. The beautiful illustrations by William Bustard demonstrate the resilience of British culture here. The advent of television in Queensland in 1959 saw an intensification of Americanisation. In the first few weeks some families, with children wearing their pyjamas, took up spots in front of stores selling televisions. Watching the new medium was a public community event. Neighbours with television found themselves suddenly popular. BTQ 7's *The Mickey Mouse Club* was a much-loved program. The photograph of a group of boy scouts, the symbol of developing British manliness and public spiritedness, wearing Mickey Mouse

Above Original illustrations by artist William Bustard for Robert Louis Stevenson's *Treasure island*, published by Jackson & O'Sullivan Pty Ltd, Brisbane, 1956. [ACC 5683]

Left Australian Communist Party campaign leaflet with promises aimed at the welfare of the coming generation of Australian children, late 1950s. [Ephemera Collection]

Above Queenslanders Mr and Mrs Kevin Cronin with their family of eight daughters on a visit to Washington DC, June 1958. [Image No. BC 482]

ears shows how Australian culture was caught between the older British forms and the new American culture of consumerism and celebrity. Boys and girls also wore the coon-skin hats of Daniel Boone, a marketing craze from the popular film. High-quality, locally produced shows featured stars like Captain Jim Iliffe and Dick McCann, who had made their names in children's radio, and Nancy Knudsen, Miss Queensland 1959. These programs retained a loyal following. The State Library's collection of the magazine *TV Times* contains valuable insights into the penetration of television.

Some educationalists were worried that children were watching far too much television. Lynn Barrow's landmark book of 1966 on children's consumption of television showed that for some, the new technology was addictive. However, the records of the Australian Children's Theatre, a non-profit travelling company founded in 1948 and patronised by Lady (Elisabeth) Murdoch, had a loyal following. Over two million children saw performances. Its founders, Betty and Joan Rayner, believed television made "the children more appreciative of live theatre than ever before." Their emphasis on Australia's place in the

Above Children performing at a concert at Cherbourg Mission in the late 1950s. This photograph was used on a poster for NAIDOC Week, July 2000. [Poster Collection]

Below The first appearance of the Bee Gees on QTQ 9's *Teen Beat*, 1960. [Image No. BC 481]

Asia-Pacific region, their trips to rural Indigenous communities and their belief that the arts could assist underprivileged children were ahead of their time.

For children in remote areas, however, all these issues were far from their daily lives. The School of the Air provided correspondence lessons through radio, initially provided by the Royal Flying Doctor Service, but was not established until 1959. Limited television in the form of the ABC had to wait for decades until repeater station technology broke the tyranny of distance. One country mother wrote to the Rayner sisters in 1966: "Australians have a far-flung country and few people think of the children who live in its loneliness. But you and your artists travel thousands of miles to bring light and colour to the children's world …"

American popular culture was pervasive, as this poster showing lads from Cherbourg playing American guitars attests. The market for the new affluent consumer group, the teenager, allowed shows like Channel 9's *Teen beat* to gain a large audience with emerging stars like the Bee Gees finding an avenue for exposure. As working-class English immigrants, the Gibb Brothers' story is an outstanding success among those who came from the United Kingdom and places that were newer mass-migration sources such as Italy, Yugoslavia, Greece, Cyprus, Finland and Holland. Redcliffe boy, Colin Petersen starred in the internationally popular film *Smiley* before embarking on a career in pop music.

Concerns about strong and healthy young Queenslanders with varied interests and balanced lives endured throughout the twentieth century. Colonial settlement faced challenges of heat, unsanitary conditions and infectious diseases; in our affluent post-industrialised society there are major issues of child obesity due to a diet of fast foods and a sedentary lifestyle. What is most striking is the relevance today of the Cilentos' message for "commonsense [and] a balanced moderated diet … rather than food faddism … to raise a generation to its pride."

The State Library of Queensland contains a veritable storehouse of material concerned with the lives of children.

Chapter six
Life and love

Author Kay Saunders   Research Librarian Dianne Byrne

❝ In the early 1880s a male cattle drover in the Barcoo could expect 100 shillings per week whilst a female domestic servant earned just 10 shillings ... The prospect of spinsterhood, regardless of the legal and economic inequalities within marriage, was not attractive. ❞

Queensland's most admired colonial poet, George Essex Evans, possessed a rare ability to capture the new national mood in poems such as "Ode for Commonwealth Day". His poems also expressed the emotional bonds of loyalty and duty that bound together men and women. In his most enduring poem, "The Women of the West", he poignantly intoned:

Well have we held our father's creed. No call
Has passed us by.
We faced and fought the wilderness, we sent our
sons to die.
And we have hearts to do and dare, and yet, o'er
All the rest,
The hearts that made the Nation were the Women of
the West.

Steele Rudd also captured these bonds. In *On our selection* he commented that "With our combined male and female forces … we rolled the thundering big logs together in the face of Hell's own fires …" There were no romantic longings, rather a realisation that shared enterprise was the basis of any enduring pact between Queensland men and women. Incipient frontier violence, intense competition in the workplace and later participation in wars, made tough men who often displayed little capacity for domestic life and tenderness.

The high ratio of settler men to women, encouraged by the economic base of pastoralism, sugar production and mining, made life for colonial women extraordinarily harsh and potentially life threatening. For many colonial women, marriage was the most favoured option as a life choice. With few opportunities for well-paid work, marriage became a necessity. In the early 1880s a male cattle drover in the

Opening image *R & R Girls* by Frank William Smith, oil on board, c. 1945. Smith worked as an artist and draftsman for the Postmaster General's Department, and his painting captures the wilder side of wartime Brisbane nightlife, as described in the diaries of Donald Friend. [ACC 4840]

Above *Australian etiquette or the rules and usages of the best society in the Australasian colonies*, published in Sydney and Melbourne in 1885. [RBJ 395 aus]

A Mackay Ball — Manners & customs of the natives.

Barcoo could expect 100 shillings per week whilst a female domestic servant earned just 10 shillings. In 1896 a young female shop assistant might expect 2 shillings and 6 pence per week. Thus, most women willingly sought to make a 'good' marriage. The prospect of spinsterhood, regardless of the legal and economic inequalities within marriage, was not attractive. The Rawson Archive contains amusing drawings illustrating the continuing male–female social divide. Decades later, a function at the exclusive Tattersall's Club in Brisbane, amongst people of similar social standing, shows how the male-only domain of leisure had been formalised.

The comprehensive treatise, *Australian etiquette* (1885) has a long section on courtship, engagement and weddings. The basis of a happy marriage, it intoned from the comforts of Sydney, was "Respect … social equality, intellectual sympathy, and sufficient means…" These are "very important matters to be considered by those who contemplate matrimony …" In a rougher frontier society these refinements may have been a luxury for most settlers. Margaret McIlwraith, the wife of a future premier, found life on a western station in summer intolerable and fled back to Melbourne in September 1869.

Above A ball at Mackay, showing the divide between male and female guests, with the "wallflowers" sitting in a row and the men drinking at the bar, June 1871. From an album recording the lives and activities of the Rawson Family of The Hollow, near Mackay. Rawson Archive. [OMR 98; ACC 2967][Image No. 00078]

Below The annual Governor's Dinner at Brisbane's Tattersall's Club, c. 1970. [R 503][Image No. BC 1042]

> *Having no doctor or no nurse, and knowing I might die [in childbirth] before there was any hope of medical assistance, I endeavoured to prepare my mind for leaving this world.*

This page Queensland sugar planter Claudius Buchanan Whish and his wife Ann, depicted in portrait miniatures by an unknown artist, c. 1887. The pair married in Bombay in 1858 and settled in Australia where Whish established the Oaklands sugar plantation at Caboolture. Ann perished with her husband aboard the *Quetta*, when it sank in Torres Strait on 28 February 1890.
[Colour Images BC 1064; 1065]

Few commentators suggested any choice for women other than perpetual motherhood. If men provided either the capital or hard labour to forge the new prosperous society, women ensured the next generation. Matilda Murray-Prior, the first wife of the proprietor of Bromelton station near Beaudesert, recorded in her diary in 1848: "Having no doctor or no nurse, and knowing I might die [in childbirth] before there was any hope of medical assistance, I endeavoured to prepare my mind for leaving this world". Her daughter, Rosa Praed, later commented "Poor little bride of nineteen!" Jane Collins remarked to her husband William Collins in a letter dated 30 August 1867 that passing strangers often assisted women in childbirth in the bush. With families consisting of nine to 12 children living into adolescence, the burdens of motherhood were high for many settler women.

There were strong social conventions about relations between the roles of men and women, which added further pressure to life in the harsh land. An interesting pamphlet entitled *Marriage and the social evil* (1890) in the State Library's collection by Mrs Harrison Lee, proclaimed that "Marriage makes man the protector and leader; it makes the woman the gentle loving helpmate. Unholy desires, impure affections, degrading appetites have no place here …" She invoked the Christian marriage service that proclaimed the centrality of the procreation of children. Any other sexual acts between spouses she deemed "sensual sin". She held a particular repugnance for double beds though she was a young married woman of only 28.

Other forms of sin stalked the colonial landscape. Lady Lamington visited a "private Rescue Home" for unmarried mothers in the early 1900s in Brisbane. She commented that "… in a country where there naturally is a mixture of all races, good and bad, there is a good opening for sin". She was particularly distressed to see "a child of twelve being brought to me dressed in pinafores, and she was going to have a baby … I think if men saw more of these Homes and the sadness in them, it might help try to make them live better."

The rapaciousness and predatory character of many men towards both working-class white young women and

> There were strong social conventions about relations between the roles of men and women, which added further pressure to life in the harsh land. An interesting pamphlet entitled *Marriage and the social evil* (1890) in the State Library's collection by Mrs Harrison Lee, proclaimed that 'Marriage makes man the protector and leader; it makes the woman the gentle loving helpmate …'

Indigenous women was endemic. Mary Bennett in her father's biography, *Christison of Lammermoor* (1927) noted that: "In every camp of blacks, while there are young men as well as old men there are only old women, for the young women and girls are taken by white men 'at will and unchecked', retained a while, then discarded". Figures like Pastor Schwarz of Hope Vale Mission in Cooktown and the Hon John Douglas, Government Resident at Thursday Island, campaigned strenuously against these practices. In 1901 the Welsh priest, Aneurin Williams in Herberton established the Anglican itinerant Bush Brotherhood of St Barnabas to bring Christian morality to the bush regions. "O for a band of men that will preach like apostles, [and] ride like cowboys …" intoned Bishop Frodsham in 1908. Yet as *Aunty Rita* (1994) by Rita and Jackie Huggins attests, labour and sexual exploitation of Aboriginal girls continued into the mid-twentieth century. In some cases conventional European marriages were an option. The weddings of Gallipoli veterans, Jim Lingwoodock and Johnny Geary demonstrate how European practices occurred in some Indigenous families.

Other members of society reacted in a different way to their circumstances. Charles Eden in his eccentric book *My wife and I in Queensland* (1872) tried to keep up the standards of bourgeois England as he insisted that men always wear their coats when his wife was present. He believed that even educated men went downhill without the civilising influence of ladies. Keeping their acknowledged status as ladies when going into the public realm was often difficult. In one incident, young Irish larrikins in Kangaroo Point in Brisbane described as "low, lascivious foul-mouthed hooligans", shouted out to passing middle class women "you're the one!!" much to the women's embarrassment.

Some privileged men were, however, always gentlemen. The Rawson Archive, with its inimitable drawings giving a rare vibrancy and immediacy to daily life, contains a superb drawing of Winifred Rawson attempting to use a sewing machine and exclaiming "Ah! Now, if they could only see me at home! Quite the dressmaker". This drawing illustrates two points. First, a genteel woman in England would not sew clothes. Second, and even more interesting, is the

Above Aboriginal serviceman James Lingwoodock and a friend, with their brides at St Luke's Anglican Church, Brisbane, c. 1914. [Image. No. 157092]

Above and opposite (top) Letter written by Helen Mitchell (the future Dame Nellie Melba) from the Rawson's property, The Hollow, near Mackay, to her former singing teacher Signor Pietro Cecchi, c. 1884. [TR 1797/6; ACC 348]

Opposite page (below) Melba, the opera diva, photographed in costume in London in 1921. By this time, her life as a struggling young wife in Queensland was far behind her. [Image No. BC 1037]

assistance of her husband, Charles, with a lathe joined to the machine to make it go faster. In the domain of separate spheres when men's and women's work rarely intersected, this is an astonishing and undoubtedly rare depiction of the claims that colonial life made on well-born settlers.

Wilhelmina (Mina) Rawson, the wife of Lance Rawson, did not find marriage as congenial as her sisters-in-law who were married to more affluent sympathetic men. At first the Australian born Mina lived at The Hollow cattle station before moving to the Kircubbin sugar plantation in 1877. Going bankrupt in 1880 they moved to Boonooroo near Wide Bay. With several children to support, she published comprehensive advice books such as *The Australian enquiry book of household and general information* (1894). Her recipe for flying fox with breadcrumbs has not become a household favourite. Her wish for women to be able to exchange hints through a newspaper points to the isolation of women and their inventiveness. This was realised by Louisa Lawson, mother of writer Henry Lawson, in the periodical *The Dawn*.

With its resident aristocrats like Sir John Lawes and the Hon Henry Stormont Finch-Hatton (later Earl of Winchelsea and Nottingham), Mackay contained a sophisticated upper stratum within a crude frontier multiracial town in the 1870s and 1880s. The intricacy of relationships that the Rawsons enjoyed as scions of the English gentry was extraordinary. The State Library possesses two remarkable letters written by Nellie Armstrong, later to become the heralded diva Dame Nellie Melba, from the Rawson residence, The Hollow, to her former singing teacher Signor Pietro Cecchi in Melbourne. She confides to her teacher: "My husband is quite agreeable for me to adopt music as a profession. I do not mind telling you that times are very bad here and we are very poor as it is possible for anyone to be … I am anxious to leave Queensland as soon as possible. I must make some money …" She made £750 the following year in Melbourne, a small fortune when a domestic servant earned £26 annually. Despite her not living

ery day,(3) so you will understand that I am anxious to leave Queensland as soon as possible. I _must_ make some money. Could you not form a small company & let us go touring through the Colonies for of course I should like to study for the Opera, but would have to be earning money at the same time. My husband will accompany me, & my baby will be quite big enough to leave in Melbourne with my sisters.(4) Madame Elmblad would join us, I am sure. Do you think we could make money? I shall wait anxiously for a letter from you, for I am very unhappy here where there is no music, no nothing. We spoke of August next year, let it be much earlier than that if you can possibly arrange it, for I believe I should be dead by then. Mr Noble I daresay would gladly help you. I shall be advised by what you say in this. I hope what I say will be agreeable to you—

A few colonial women did not have to go so far afield to find satisfying and lucrative careers. Mareeba photographer Harriet Brims used the location around her husband's sawmill to capture the beauty of the rainforest and its peoples.

Above Henry Tippler and his wife in front of their hut at Currigee on South Stradbroke Island, watercolour by Robert Rayment, 1889. The Tipplers were a well-known local family who held leases granted by the Queensland Government to "collect, preserve, fatten and sell oysters of every description". [Colour Image 66351]

a humble life, Melba's letter shows her expectations of the standard of living of a privileged women and, unusually for her time, her ambition to ensure she would attain it from her own endeavours.

A few colonial women did not have to go so far afield to find satisfying and lucrative careers. Mareeba photographer Harriet Brims used the location around her husband's sawmill to capture the beauty of the rainforest and its peoples. The Lynch sisters remained unmarried, running a successful business as timber cutters. Occasionally a woman took over her husband's business on his death. Mrs Gladys Chick Tong ran the Brisbane Joss House after her husband died. This interracial marriage was unusual in a class – and racially – structured society. The careers of these women were remarkable given the gender demarcations that ruled the labour market.

Many women found domestic life debilitating and often soul destroying. Steele Rudd, commenting on the selectors at Stanthorpe, pondered: "I often wonder how the women stood it in the first few years ... Mother, when she was alone, used to sit on a log ... and cry for hours." Joan Colebrook in *The northerner* (1948), set amongst affluent dairy farmers in the 1920s, captures this despair: "[The wife] was dimly aware, from behind the welter of ceaseless activity, that part of herself had never lived, that it had been buried beneath the needs of her children and her husband, that it had died from inanition and loneliness so that like a continually lopped tree, she could grow no other way now than the way she had grown ..."

For many men, life was an enduring round of hard work for little reward. JJ Hilder's painting, *Ploughing* (1910) shows an anonymous farmer bent by his lonely toil.

In the colonial period, with a small, educated middle class concentrated in Brisbane and Toowoomba, the feminist movement was not large, however it was vocal. The Women's Christian Temperance Union, the largest international women's organisation, lobbied to raise the age of consent from twelve years, for more opportunity for

In the colonial period, with a small, educated middle class concentrated in Brisbane and Toowoomba, the feminist movement was not large, however it was vocal.

Left Mr and Mrs Chick Tong. Chick Tong managed the Brisbane Joss House at Newstead. After he died, his wife Gladys took over his responsibilities. [Image No. 150952]

Below left Professional photographer Harriett Pettifore Brims (1864–1939) on location in the Queensland bush, c. 1895. The daughter of prominent settlers from the Barcoo district, she married and moved to Ingham where she opened the Britannia Studios, before moving operations to Mareeba, Chillagoe, Irvinebank and the Herberton district.
[Album GL 59/1; Image No. 147022]

Below right Lady pine cutters, the Lynch Sisters, who worked in the Kingaroy district. Their expertise with the axe enabled these women to earn better wage contracts than most men. [Image No. 64649]

Above Edward, Prince of Wales with Miss Aileen Bell during his weekend visit to Coochin Coochin station near Boonah, 31 July to 2 August 1920. [Image No. 150384]

Left Steamy cover for Charles Chauvel's novel *Uncivilised*, published in 1936. It told an erotic tale of a white ruler of an Indigenous community and a society journalist sold into slavery. [J A823.2 cha]

women to escape violent marriages and for infant custody rights. They campaigned against the discriminatory practices of the *Prevention of Contagious Diseases Act* (1868), which saw prostitutes gaoled in lock hospitals. These liberal-minded Protestant churchwomen left their homes to campaign on behalf of white women's rights. Under her pseudonym Lucinda Sharpe in the newspaper *The Worker*, Annie Lane, the Chicago journalist living in Australia, proposed even more radical rights for workers and women.

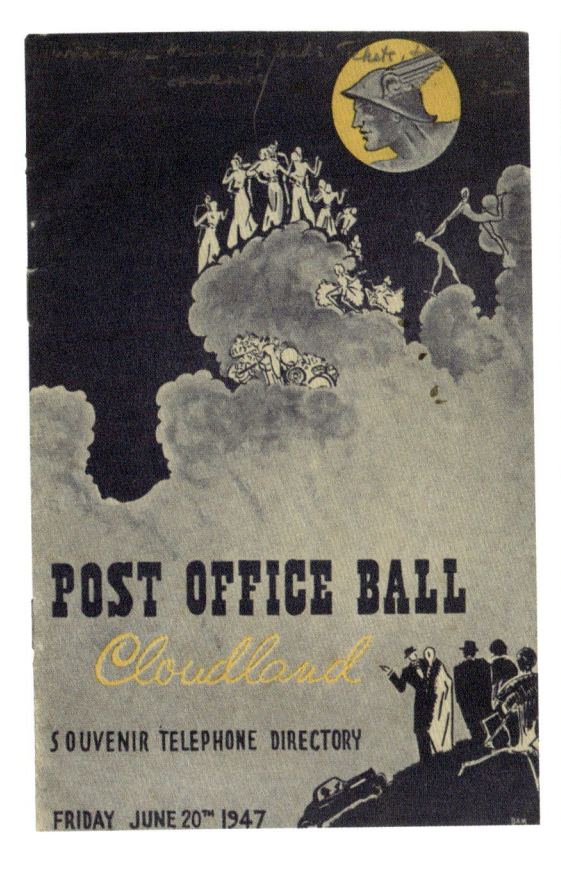

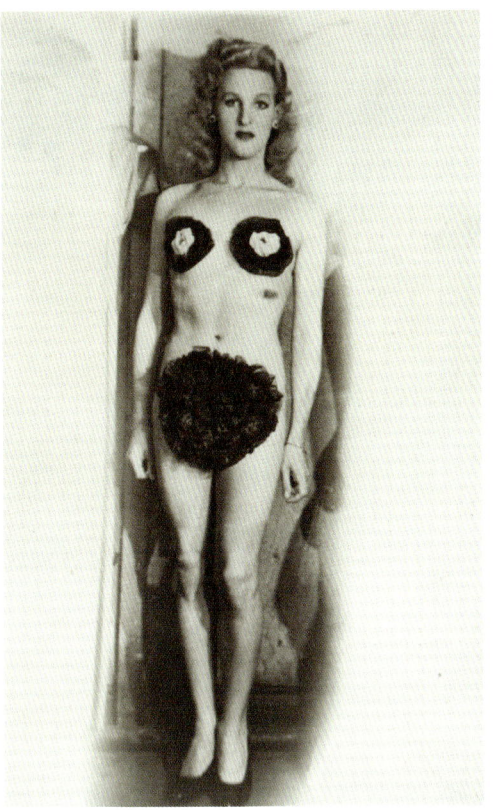

For rare wealthy privileged women, life on the land was gracious. The Bell sisters of Coochin Coochin station remained single and resisted the definition of a "spinster". Aileen Bell danced with Edward the Prince of Wales in Sydney and the family entertained him at the station in 1920. Later, other English dignitaries like Agatha Christie, Laurence Olivier and Vivien Leigh enjoyed the Bells' hospitality. This was a world away from the steamy sexuality portrayed on the book cover and the poster for Charles Chauvel's film, *Uncivilised* (1936).

However, it was privileged women who had the education and time to devote to social reforms and improvement, if only with the help of domestic servants. When Lady Lamington visited Talgai station around 1900 she commented that she was "waited on by a neat little maid (a difficult thing to have in Queensland)." Getting reliable domestic assistance was a constant theme for middle-class women. A resident in Queensland from 1906 to 1936, Zina Cumbrae-Stewart lamented the rise in domestic servants' wages under the Labor government of EG Theodore. Active in various patriotic activities to support the war effort from 1914–18, she told the premier that future generations of community-minded women would not marry if they had no servants. As president of the National Council of Women from 1926–35, the Anglican Mothers' Union, and a founder of the Queensland Social Service League in 1930 to counteract the effects of the depression, Cumbrae-Stewart was a remarkable force for social reform, albeit within a conservative framework.

Above left Souvenir program for the Post Office Ball at Cloudland, Friday 20 June 1947. The booklet includes a telephone directory used by male and female guests to contact one another at different tables. [Ephemera Collection]

Above middle Female impersonator Peter Moselle performing in an army Les Girls revue in England during World War II. [Image No. 56538]

Above right *R & R Girls* by Frank William Smith, oil on board, c. 1945. Smith worked as an artist and draftsman for the Postmaster General's Department, and his painting captures the wilder side of wartime Brisbane nightlife, as described in the diaries of Donald Friend. [ACC 4840]

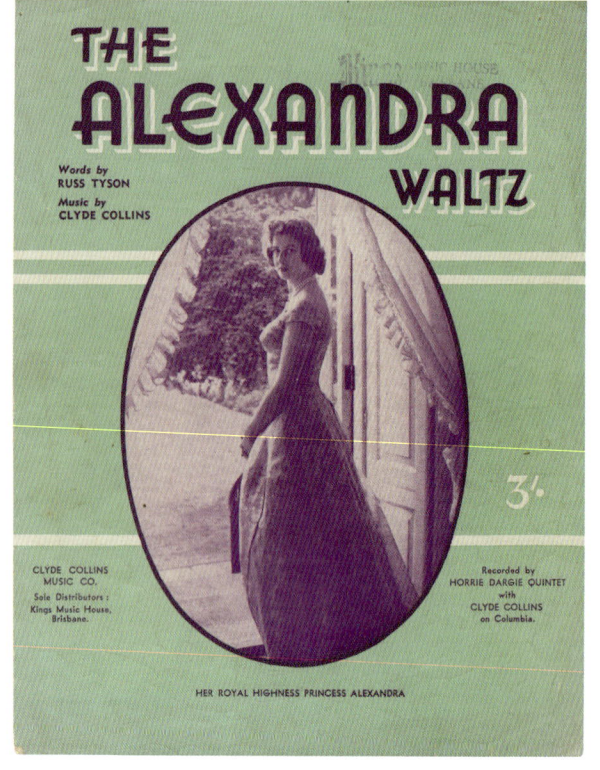

Left Role reversal: Television personalities Jim Iliffe and his wife Melody pose for a *TV Week* photographer, c. 1967. [Image No. BC 1043]

Right *The Alexandra waltz*, words by Russ Tyson, music by Clyde Collins, 1959. [Sheet Music Collection]

Below Local pastrycooks with cakes produced in honour of the March 1954 royal visit to Queensland. [Image No. 147621]

> "Queenslanders' love affair with the new monarch Queen Elizabeth was genuine."

The Second World War disrupted the gender order in Queensland. With nearly one million American troops passing through the largely provincial state, Australian men were anxious, however women were delighted. Well-dressed, affluent and charming Americans made a stark contrast to local men more intent on drinking in public bars and betting on the horses. Maureen Meadows' memoir, *I loved those Yanks* (1948), is a poignant tale of romance and love lost in wartime. Not all Americans were respectful and romantic. William Dargie's watercolour, *The Brothel, Brisbane* and Frank Smith's *R and R Girls* give a picture of the rougher, sexually charged atmosphere of wartime.

The war was also liberating for men like Peter Moselle, offering extraordinary professional and personal opportunities. As a female impersonator he toured in the successful Les Girls review for the British Army.

Australian men who had seen battle in the Middle East and then were sent to Papua were hardly impressed by their countrywomen's attraction for those "over-paid, over-sexed and over-here" Yanks. Many Queensland women married Americans and relocated overseas; others were disappointed that their American suitors were already married or engaged. For many Queensland men the war years "sorted out" the women into potential mothers and wives, and "goodtime girls".

Coming to terms with the new peace in 1945 was not easy, with currents of optimism and regeneration vying with the fissures left by dislocation of death, grief and political upheaval. Ruth Park in *Fishing in the Styx* captures the mood of those "restless, often irascible and disillusioned servicemen … It was as though a tsunami had swept across society …" The emerging affluence, stability and consumerism saw a reconfiguration of the relations between men and women. Decorous courtship rituals like the Post Office Ball at Cloudland in Brisbane show the moves towards normalcy—Queensland Style.

The State Library contains another fascinating artefact from this period concerned with marriage and domesticity. The recording of the marriage service between Jean Pettigrew and Jack Carney is an unusual treasure from this era. The wedding of Wimbledon star Ashley Cooper to Helen Wood, Miss Australia 1957, in January 1958 caused a riot in Ann Street when thousands of people converged to see the bridal party.

The staged photograph of television and radio personality Jim Iliffe and his wife Melody Iliffe is an amusing commentary on domestic life in the 1950s. The audience knows that this is a joke. Frilly aprons were not the normal attire of the successful man, nor were kitchens his domain. The image of the two pastry cooks looking a little embarrassed over their creation of a cake in the shape of the Crown of State demonstrates their expertise in a somewhat eccentric homage to the forthcoming royal visit.

Queenslanders' love affair with Australia's new monarch was genuine. More than three-quarters of the entire nation made sure they saw Queen Elizabeth and Prince Philip on their tour in early 1954. The visit of her cousin, Princess Alexandra, five years later to mark the centenary of the

This page The first Queensland marriage to be captured on record was between Jack Carney and Jean Pettigrew. It took place at the Mobraytown Presbyterian Church, 25 November 1950. [ACC 6567]

Between the covers

Above Brochure produced by the Family Planning Association of Queensland, 1992. [Ephemera Collection]

Left *You Don't Have to be a Queenie to get Aids*, a poster created by Redback Graphix for the Federal Department of Community Services and Health, Aboriginal Health Workers of Australia (Queensland), 1988. [Image No. Zoo00061]

> The development of more professional training and employment sharply contrasted with the class-ridden prewar society where privilege and education were the prerogatives of a tiny minority.

colony's formation was also a highpoint of public events in Queensland. Alexandra held a particular fascination for many Queensland schoolgirls. This adoration extended wider as the charming music, *The Alexandra waltz* shows.

The more liberal attitudes expressed by Dr Norman Haire in his *Sex problems of today* (1943), where he discusses abortion (using his own relatives as examples), homosexuality and the woeful sexual ignorance of the young, was swept away in the conservative postwar era. Reverend Arthur Preston, who later established the Blue Nurses, in his pamphlet, *The sacredness of sex* (c. 1955) reinforces traditional moral precepts about chastity and marriage. Unlike Mrs Lee in the 1890s, Preston abhors chastity within marriage. He also saw danger in "perverted sex" such as "orgies in New Zealand among satanic cults". "Unchastity is the enemy of society … It leads to venereal disease, prostitution, illegitimacy, abortion, divorce and other social evils." Attempts at sex education by the "Father and Son Movement" and films like the one shown in Bundaberg in 1950 were hardly effective, given the delicate manner in which the topic was discussed. Mothercraft lessons in state high schools in the 1960s informed girls about routine baby care but never mentioned reproduction.

By the late 1960s, attitudes about what constituted appropriate behaviour amongst the young changed rapidly. The photograph of the young farmer's social hop at Finch Hatton in 1958 where they jived and enjoyed the dangerous new music, rock'n'roll now appears innocent.

Above left *The sacredness of sex* by Arthur Preston, published in Brisbane, 1950. [P 241.66 pre]

Above right Crowd outside the Paramount Theatre, Bundaberg, at a screening of the sex education film *Secrets of Life* c. 1950. [Image No. 64547]

112 Between the covers

Above left Queensland debutantes and their junior attendants, c. 1948. [Image No. BC 1041]

Above right "If you want to even the score, first even the numbers", a silkscreen poster produced by the Melbourne community-based print workshop Red Planet. [Image No. BC 913]

Debutante Balls were suddenly passé as new freedoms were explored. For young women they proved hazardous as loss of reputation and a potential pregnancy initially loomed in any consideration of sexual experimentation before marriage. Pamphlets produced in popular formats, such as the comic book style *Too great a risk* issued by the Family Planning Association began to change this double standard.

The development of more professional training and employment sharply contrasted with the class-ridden prewar society where privilege and education were the prerogatives of a tiny minority. Some, like Nobel Laureate Peter Doherty, received an excellent education at Indooroopilly State High School and then university training in veterinary surgery in the 1960s. With better education and the rise in places for a university education from 1973, new possibilities presented themselves for young Queenslanders. Women began entering "male" professions, with Governor Quentin Bryce the first female lecturer in law at the University of Queensland. Notable women achieved power with Joan Sheldon, the first woman in Queensland to lead a political party, becoming state treasurer in 1996 and Jackie Huggins, becoming co-chair of Reconciliation Australia in 2002. In 2006 Professor Ian Fraser, renowned for his work on cervical cancer, became Australian of the Year. *If you want to even the score* marks this shift in attitudes to women in parliament. The lives of men and women in Queensland had undergone a transformation from the hazards and uncertainties of the time when Matilda Murray-Prior sent prayers to heaven.

The collections of the State Library of Queensland are particularly rich in material that depicts the lives of men and women. Often surprising, sometimes whimsical and occasionally shocking, these records survey a wide terrain of human experience.

Chapter seven
The greatest game under the sun

Author Kay Saunders   Research Librarian Dianne Byrne

> "... the warm climate, abundant playing fields and healthier population encouraged the development of sports, particularly outdoor team sports."

Sport took a strong hold in the new society from the convict period. As Gordon Inglis points out in his important book, *Sport and pastime in Australia* (1912), the warm climate, abundant playing fields and healthier population encouraged the development of sports, particularly outdoor team sports. Australians' fascination with sport and our excellence in international competitions, made more remarkable by our small population, is a theme which dominates the history of sport. Though some sports such as rowing and yachting have largely remained for the privileged, postwar sport has increasingly cut across class, ethnic and gender boundaries.

Extensive public and corporate sponsorship ensures excellent venues for players and spectators. Suncorp Stadium in Brisbane, redeveloped in 2003, is a world-class venue enjoyed by Queenslanders from all walks of life. Match attendance often becomes a family occasion where men and women, boys and girls, enjoy watching both Rugby League and Rugby Union.

Jules Guerassimoff's career as a Wallaby in the 1960s exemplifies the development of sport. His background as the son of white Russian émigrés who settled in Queensland made him an unusual representative for Australia at that time. His collection in the State Library of Queensland captures both his career in Rugby Union as well as his later achievements as an environmentalist.

Emerging from private schools in the past 50 years, Rugby Union has been in the forefront of social change.

Below Press cuttings and photographs documenting the Rugby Union career of Jules Guerassimoff, including the Wallaby tours to South Africa (1963), New Zealand (1964), British Ireland, France and Canada (1966–67). [ACC 1750]

Australian Rugby Union and the Qantas Wallabies, with players coming from diverse backgrounds such as Zimbabwe, Fiji, Samoa and Tonga, as well as Aborigines, has been a positive force in making Australia a more tolerant society. The sport promotes "the common values that bind us all including national pride, understanding, inclusion, respect, teamwork and tradition". Its extensive programs in schools advocate good health, fitness and racial tolerance.

The State Library's collection documents the development of horse racing, the first organised sport in Queensland. Racing was always a sport that enjoyed patronage from across the social spectrum. A race meeting was first recorded behind the old convict female factory (now the Brisbane GPO). In May 1852 a fashionable race meeting was held in New Farm, where "[a]mong the company on the course was observed a number of ladies on horseback …" A dozen Aborigines held a foot race "for such encouragement is calculated to assimilate their customs to our own". In July 1843, the Moreton Bay Racing Club held a meeting at Cooper's Plains. Regular meetings were held at Drayton, Ipswich and Warwick by the end of the decade. In 1852 pastoralists established the North Australia Jockey Club in Ipswich, then the most affluent town in the northern district.

Wealthy squatter Thomas White's *Rules and regulations of the Queensland jockey club* (1861) is one of the earliest books printed in Queensland. *Racehorses in Australia* (1922), with magnificent equine portraits by Martin Stainforth, details the early bloodlines commencing with "Young Rockingham" in 1799. Racing always attracted an appreciative crowd, whether on a station property, a country race meet or at Eagle Farm Racecourse. Vice-regal patronage was frequent, with Lady Lamington presenting a cup at the beginning of the twentieth century.

Other sports kept their exclusive status. To celebrate the third anniversary of Separation in December 1862, an Oxford–Cambridge match was held, with Attorney-General John Bramston (Wadham) leading against Cambridge, headed by WP Townson (St John's). The Hon RGW Herbert (All Souls) added lustre to the Oxford team. *Athletic Queensland* (1900) outlined the developments of rowing

Above Lady Lamington decorating the winner of the St Ledger at the Queensland Turf Club, Eagle Farm, Brisbane, May 1900. [ACC 6228; Album APO-35]

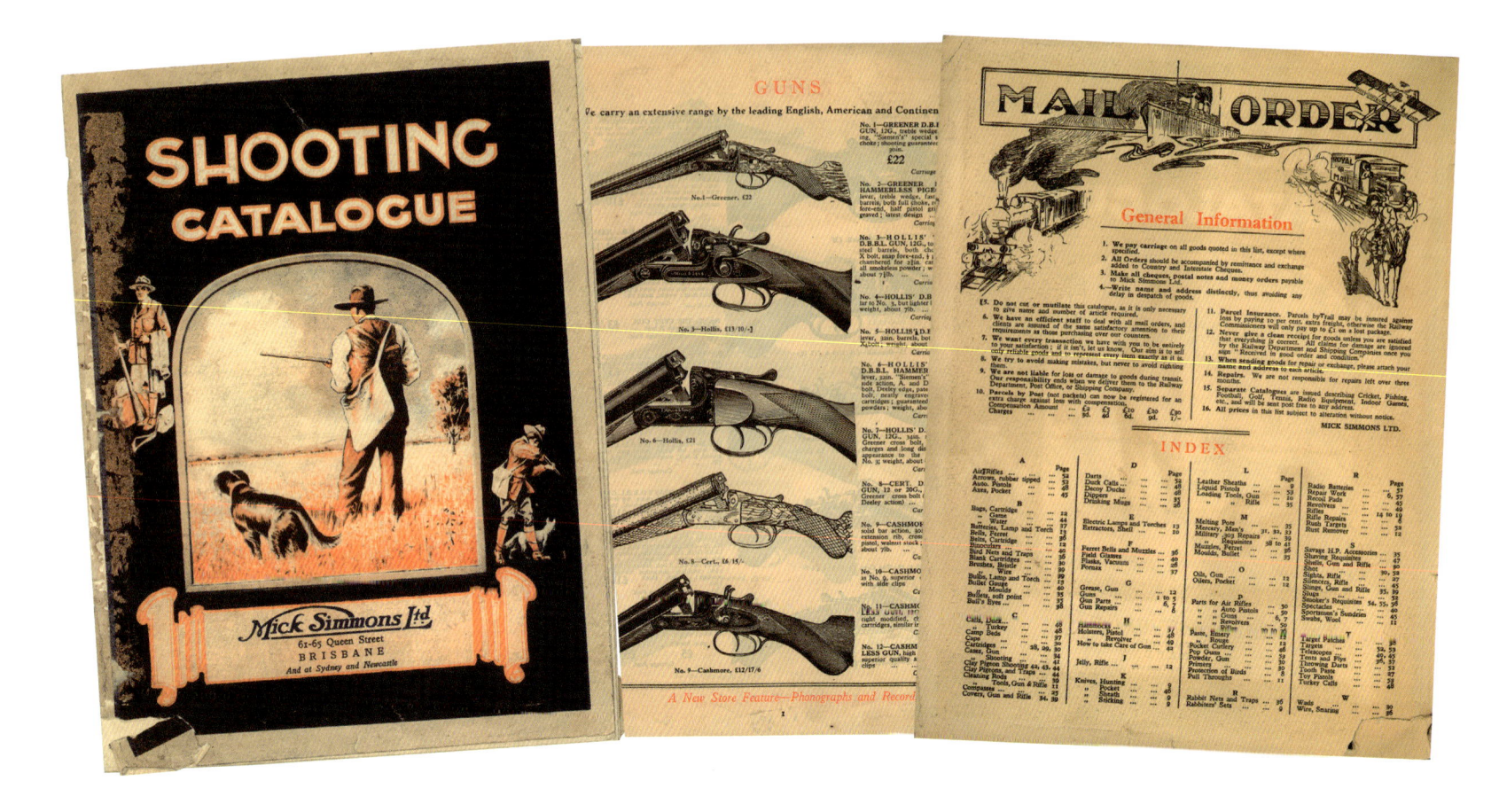

> **Some colonial sports contributed directly to national development. Shooting was aligned closely to defence, with each colony possessing its own defence force until 1901.**

Above Catalogue for the sporting goods firm of Mick Simmons Limited, founded in Sydney in 1877 and still in operation. [Ephemera Collection]

with sections demonstrated by Tate Hilder and composed by Brisbane Grammar School Headmaster Reginald Heber Roe, who had been a member of the Balliol College crew — Head of the River at Oxford in 1873. The exclusivity of the sport of rowing is preserved today in the GPS Carnival, begun in 1918.

Some colonial sports contributed directly to national development. Shooting was aligned closely to the military, with each colony possessing its own defence force until 1901. The Queensland Volunteer Corps was formed in 1864, with the Queensland Rifle Association established in 1877 attracting militia volunteers. In 1886, the Australian Military Rifle Team visited England with two Queenslanders among the players. From the 1907 Empire Match, Australia began a series of wins until 1948. The Mick Simmons catalogue allows us to see the connection between the defence and sporting aspects of shooting. On the other hand, fencing, with its chivalrous military overtones, never took off even among the upper echelons of Queensland society. One exception was champion Sir Raphael Cilento, the Director-General of Health in Queensland.

Boxing and wrestling were initially sports for the colonial elite. Emerging out of the ancient Olympic tradition, they also feature in *Athletic Queensland*. Dame Nellie Melba's husband "Kangaroo" Armstrong, was a champion middleweight boxer. Thomas Welsby was the inaugural president of the Queensland Amateur Boxing and Wrestling Union, establishing the Brisbane Gymnasium.

Governor Norman and his family attended displays at this venue. In 1894, the first colonial championship was held here.

Boxing became a way for non-European sportsmen to excel. The West Indian pugilist Peter Jackson is featured in WJ Doherty's *In the days of the giants* (1931). He is buried in Toowong Cemetery. Aboriginal boxers came to the fore when the Marquis of Queensberry rules superseded the brutal bare-knuckle contests. Beginning in 1907, an Aboriginal fighter from Jimbour station, middleweight Jerry Jerome, rose to prominence. He took part in over 50 professional bouts, the majority won by knockout.

Before retiring in 1945, Ron Richards from Ipswich captured the Australian middleweight, light-heavy and heavyweight titles. The *Pink-un's* souvenir of the Bradley versus Godfrey match at the Brisbane Stadium in 1921 reflects this shift in the appeal of boxing to a wider audience. David Malouf in his evocative novel *Johnno* (1975) takes his protagonist Dante and his father to the stadium where fights assume the character of "an Aristotelian tragedy". "They had a brutal simplicity … The fight itself was a ritual in which the loser fought heroically against his own weakness, against a fate that was already decided, and to the expert visible from the start …" he writes, capturing the visceral physicality of the sport.

Cricket also promoted the concept of "gentlemen and players" alongside advocacy of Indigenous excellence. The exclusive Moreton Bay Cricket Club was formed in 1857, with the first inter-colonial match against New South Wales played in Brisbane in 1864. The first Australian cricket team to tour England in 1868 was composed exclusively of Aborigines from Victoria. That same year saw the foundation of the Albert Cricket Club in Brisbane, the records, up to 1892, are housed in the State Library. In 1877 an Australian XI defeated England by 45 runs in Melbourne, creating a tremendous surge of nationalism, a recurrent theme in Australian sporting achievement. Five years later Australia struck even harder by defeating England on their home soil. From this victory arose the Ashes, still keenly followed as a premier sporting event.

The State Library possesses many rare mementos of cricket. These include official programs from the Campbell

Above Champion Boxer Jerry Jerome became the first Indigenous Australian to win a national boxing title, the National Middleweight Championship. He died at Cherbourg settlement in 1950. [Image No. BC 216]

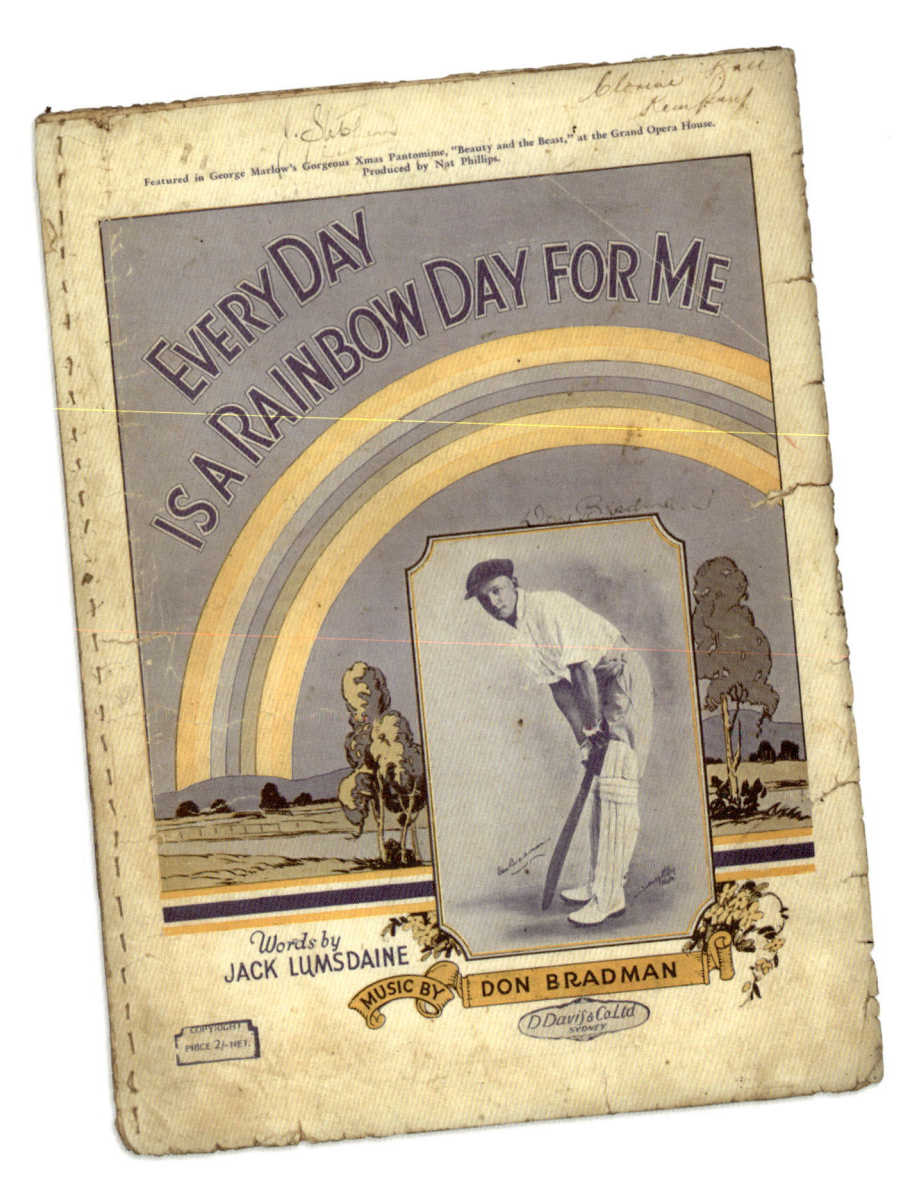

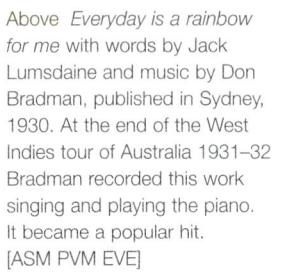

Above Everyday is a rainbow for me with words by Jack Lumsdaine and music by Don Bradman, published in Sydney, 1930. At the end of the West Indies tour of Australia 1931–32 Bradman recorded this work singing and playing the piano. It became a popular hit. [ASM PVM EVE]

Opposite page "The Second Knot" is a wry comment by cartoonist Hal Eyre on the cricket rivalry between England and Australia, reproduced in the *Daily Mail*, 1928. [Image No. 58073]

Challenge Cup in 1888–89; the first Sheffield Shield match between Queensland and South Australia in 1926; the First Test of England versus Australia held at the Brisbane Cricket Ground in 1948; and a pamphlet titled *Kings of cricket – Australia or the West Indies. Guide for the 1951–52 series*. Extensive material on Wally Grout, the West Indian Tour of 1961 and Eddie Gilbert add lustre to the collection. Lady Lamington's superb memoir mentions with some enthusiasm the visit from India of Prince Ranjit Singh to play cricket in Brisbane.

Perhaps one of the treasures of the State Library's collection is a rare piece of sheet music, *Every day is a rainbow for me*, with music composed by our national sports hero cricketer Don Bradman. No item of this nature is held by the National Library of Australia or the Bradman Museum. The cartoons of Hal Eyre documenting the tussles between England and Australia, particularly the "Bodyline" series of 1932–33 are further important gems that are also held by the State Library.

Cricket was played across all groups in Queensland. The Cherbourg Cricket Team, from the government reserve, produced cricketers of the calibre of Eddie Gilbert. They toured extensively within the state. Social cricket matches were often played between teams of gentlemen and ladies in the colonial period. The State Library holds a photograph of the Cooktown Endeavour Social Club's "mixed" 1911 match. In 1934, when the outrage against "leg theory" was still fresh in Australian minds, an English women's cricket

THE SECOND KNOT

Above Cherbourg Cricket Team and administrators in Townsville, 1930s. The most famous cricketer to come out of the Cherbourg (originally Barambah) Aboriginal reserve near Murgon was Eddie Gilbert. A cricket club was formed there around 1917 under the guidance of Jack Daylight.
[Image No. BC 207]

team led by Betty Archdale, successfully toured Australia where they played a conventional game before appreciative crowds.

The State Library's collections are particularly rich in material on the various codes of football. Along with New South Wales, Queensland remains the bastion of both Rugby Union and Rugby League in Australia. This is reflected in material such as the 1909 program souvenir of the visit of the New South Wales Rugby Football team to Brisbane, the official programs of the "Mighty Springboks" Tour of 1937, the 1908–09 Wallabies Tour of England, Wales, the United States of America and British Colombia, and an AIF (Australian Imperial Force) versus Australia game held in Brisbane in 1919.

Football emerged from the great English public schools. Eton played a type of soccer, but Rugby and Marlborough played what later became Rugby Union. Rules were fluid. Australian National Football was initially played at Queensland's private boys schools. Rules were formalised after the Rugby Football Union was formed in England in 1871. Five years later, this code began in Queensland's grammar and church schools. In 1878, Englishman Fred C Lea, in a match of Australian National Football held in the Botanical Gardens, suggested players "try a hand at rugby". From this time it took off as a major force, initially with four clubs: Brisbane, Wallaroo, Excelsior and Ipswich. Dressed in on-field knickerbockers, in 1882 a Queensland side led by Arthur Feez and with half-back Thomas Welsby,

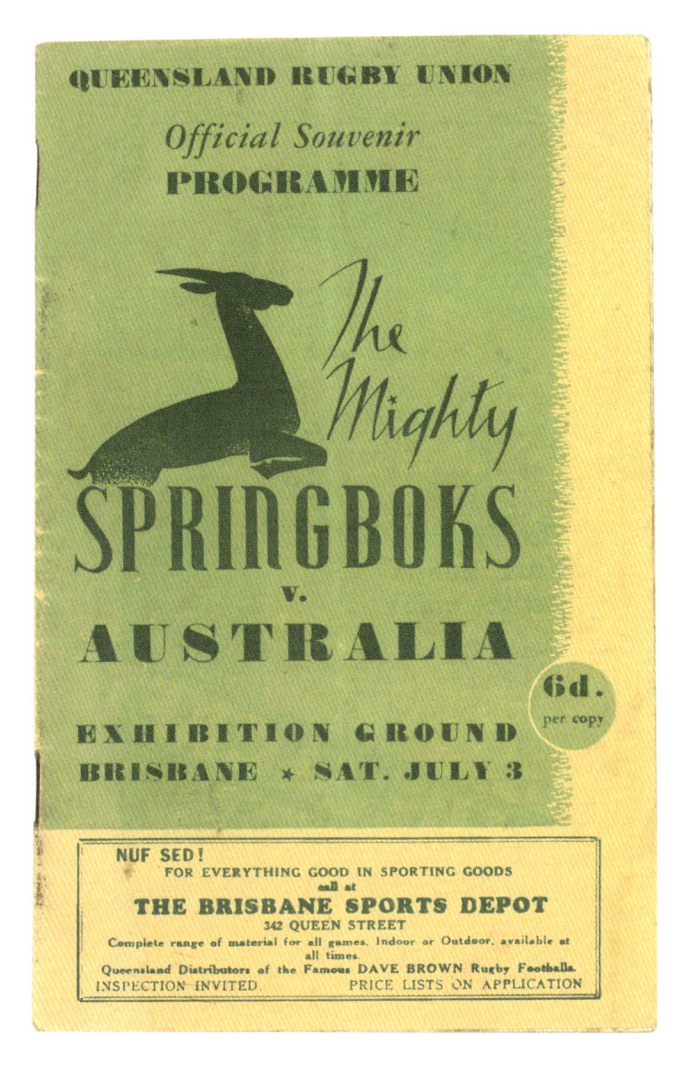

Above left Official souvenir program for the Springboks' tour of Australia 1937. This was one of their most successful tours. The members of the visiting squad, led by Philip Nel, were dubbed "the Invincibles". [P 796.333 MIG] **Above right and below** Visit of English Women Cricketers to Queensland, 1934–35. Captain Betty Archdale went on to become one of England's first women barristers and, later, one of Australia's most respected educators. [Ephemera Collection]

played New South Wales. Though defeated, the enthusiasm generated ensured a commitment to the code. Formally constituted in 1883 as Northern Rugby Union, the first inter-colonial match here was held at the Albert Sports Ground at Toowong, an enclosure formerly occupied by Chinese market gardeners.

Rugby Union took hold across the colony. Charters Towers was fortunate when, in 1892, Harry Speakman, who had played for England and captained Queensland, developed the sport. Other mining towns like Ravenswood produced excellent teams such as the Imperial Premiers Rugby Union team.

Early international games were featured with a match against the Maoris in 1889. A name change to Queensland Rugby Union in 1893 coincided with considerable expansion.

Below left Northern Rugby Union Junior Challenge Cup, presented to the Pirates, who were runners up to the Sandgate Football Club in the 1890 season. [ACC 6416]

Below right Imperial Minor Junior Premiers Rugby Union Team at Ravenswood, 1907. [Image No. BC 208]

The first international match against Great Britain occurred in 1899. The following year Queensland defeated its rivals New South Wales 11 times with three draws. In the jubilee publication, *Fifty years of football* (1932), the seemingly ubiquitous Thomas Welsby took the limelight again. Welsby remained a stalwart of Queensland Rugby Union for half a century, with his name commemorated by the Welsby Cup.

From 1899, the premier clubs contested the Hospital Cup. The original donor is believed to be Dr James O'Neil Mayne, a Brisbane Grammar School old boy and colleague of Thomas Welsby in the Queensland Amateur Fishermen's Association. The impact of Rugby League and World War I adversely affected the sport; it was not until 1928 that Queensland Rugby Union was re-formed with the major clubs, including the GPS, returning to the traditional fold. Nearly 40 years elapsed before Queensland Rugby finally found a more permanent home at Ballymore in 1966.

When the Springboks arrived in Brisbane in 1971 sport and politics converged, producing violent scenes when police attacked anti-apartheid protesters including future Queensland Premier Peter Beattie. The Bjelke-Petersen government declared a "state of emergency". Fortunately, these confrontations did not reflect on local Rugby Union, which continued gaining strength. In 1992 the Queensland Reds won the Super 6 competition, the Super 10 in 1994 and 1995, and the Super 12 in 1996, the year that Rugby Union turned professional. A totally new direction occurred the following decade with corporate sponsorship by

Suncorp. Major development of the old home of Queensland Rugby League, Lang Park, transformed it into a world-class sporting venue. When it opened in 2003 as Suncorp Stadium, it finally provided a site that could be shared by both football codes without conflict.

In 1895, Rugby split when some northern players in England turned professional. This was the beginning of the code that became Rugby League. The State Library owns important material on this sport, including souvenirs of the Great Britain versus Central Queensland match at Browne Park in June 1962; the France versus Ipswich match held at the North Ipswich Reserve in July 1955; and the program for the Queen's Birthday match, France versus New Zealand, in June 1957. The Duke of Edinburgh was the official patron of the sport in Australia in the 1950s.

In 1906 the Queensland Amateur Rugby League was formed, followed two years later by an interstate game against New South Wales. The professionalising of sport would become a contentious issue decades later. Governor Sir John Lavarack in the foreword to *Cavalcade of Queensland sport, 1901–51* deplored "commercialism [which] tends to produce teams composed entirely of professional players, turning them into a kind of gladiator". He advocated widespread participation in amateur sport. He did acknowledge, however, that international and interstate teams required a high degree of professionalism.

Professional games attracted loyal followers. Australia's Kangaroo team have achieved notable international success. The State Library has a rare memento of the 1937 series, an invitation in the shape of a kangaroo. When the Rugby League World Cup was established in 1954, Australia was a foundation member with France, New Zealand and Great Britain. Australia won ten of the 13 series.

A high point of the game occurred in 1980, when Arthur Beetson led Queensland to victory against New South Wales in the first State of Origin match. Since then,

Above Photographs and papers of sportsman, administrator and newspaper commentator Harry Sunderland, 1890–1940. Harry Sunderland's lifelong sporting involvement covered cricket, boxing, wrestling, Rugby League and amateur athletics. He managed a record three Kangaroo tours, introduced the code into France and staged exhibition matches in California. His legacy lives on in the Harry Sunderland Medal awarded to the Man of the Series in Anglo-Australian tests.
[ACC 5486]

Left and below Invitation to the "Hop Off Ball" at the Brisbane City Hall, a farewell to the 1937 Rugby League Kangaroos who were leaving for a tour of New Zealand, France and England, June 1937. [Ephemera Collection] **Right** Cut-out head of Allan 'Alfie' Langer, legendary State of Origin half-back. [Ephemera Collection]

this annual encounter has perhaps surpassed test matches in the intensity displayed by both sides. The calibre of players such as Alfie Langer and former Queensland captain Wally Lewis, "The Emperor of Lang Park", has certainly made the State of Origin one of the highlights on the Queensland sporting calendar.

Between 1987 and 1991, the entry of the Brisbane Bears into the VFL/AFL competition was responsible for generating a surge of interest in Australian Rules among Queenslanders. Their successors from 1996, the Brisbane Lions, have taken the game in Queensland to unprecedented heights, especially since winning their first premiership in 2001.

Soccer, now the most international football code, had reached Brisbane by 1882. The strangely titled Dinmore Bush Rats toured New South Wales in 1890. There has been a dramatic upsurge in popularity during recent decades. The State Library possesses two interesting programs, one from the 1939 tour of the Palestine Team (composed of many Jewish players fleeing Austria) and the other from the Hungary versus China match played in Brisbane in July 1957.

Like golf and croquet, tennis was initially seen as women's sport in Queensland, although Brisbane Boys' College maintained one of the first courts. In 1898, a New South Wales team came to Brisbane for an interstate match. What is fascinating is how quickly the game took off: by 1907 the Australasian team defeated the British Isles at Wimbledon. The State Library owns a program from the Australia versus United States match held in Brisbane in November 1932. The Lawn Tennis Association of Australia brought the world's top players to celebrate the Victorian Centenary celebrations in 1934. A souvenir program of these international squads' visit to Brisbane provides an interesting insight into the game's development: "Back in the prewar days, tennis was generally considered an effeminate sort of game, which could be played by wealthy people. Masculine fancy tended

The greatest game under the sun

In 1906 the Queensland Amateur Rugby League was formed, followed two years later by an interstate game against New South Wales.

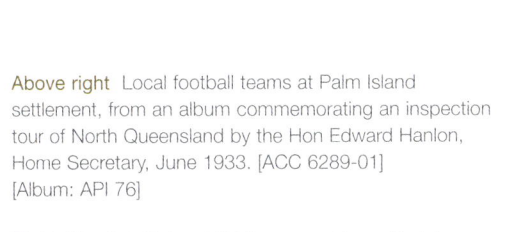

Above right Local football teams at Palm Island settlement, from an album commemorating an inspection tour of North Queensland by the Hon Edward Hanlon, Home Secretary, June 1933. [ACC 6289-01] [Album: API 76]

Right The first State of Origin game at Lang Park in Brisbane on 8 July 1980 was greeted with enthusiasm by the Rugby League community of Queensland. Over 35,000 Maroon supporters filed through the gate instead of an expected 5,000. The game looked to be within reach of New South Wales until star of the night Chris 'Choppy' Close scored a try which brought Queensland over the victory line. [Image No. BC 217]

126 Between the covers

This page Program for Jack Kramer's World Championship Tennis, Australian tour 1961–62. [Ephemera Collection]

towards football and cricket … after the war, people turned to sport as a kind of reaction from the years of storm and stress …" Social tennis, with male and female players, took off after the establishment of the Church Tennis Association in 1920 centred on the non-conformist churches.

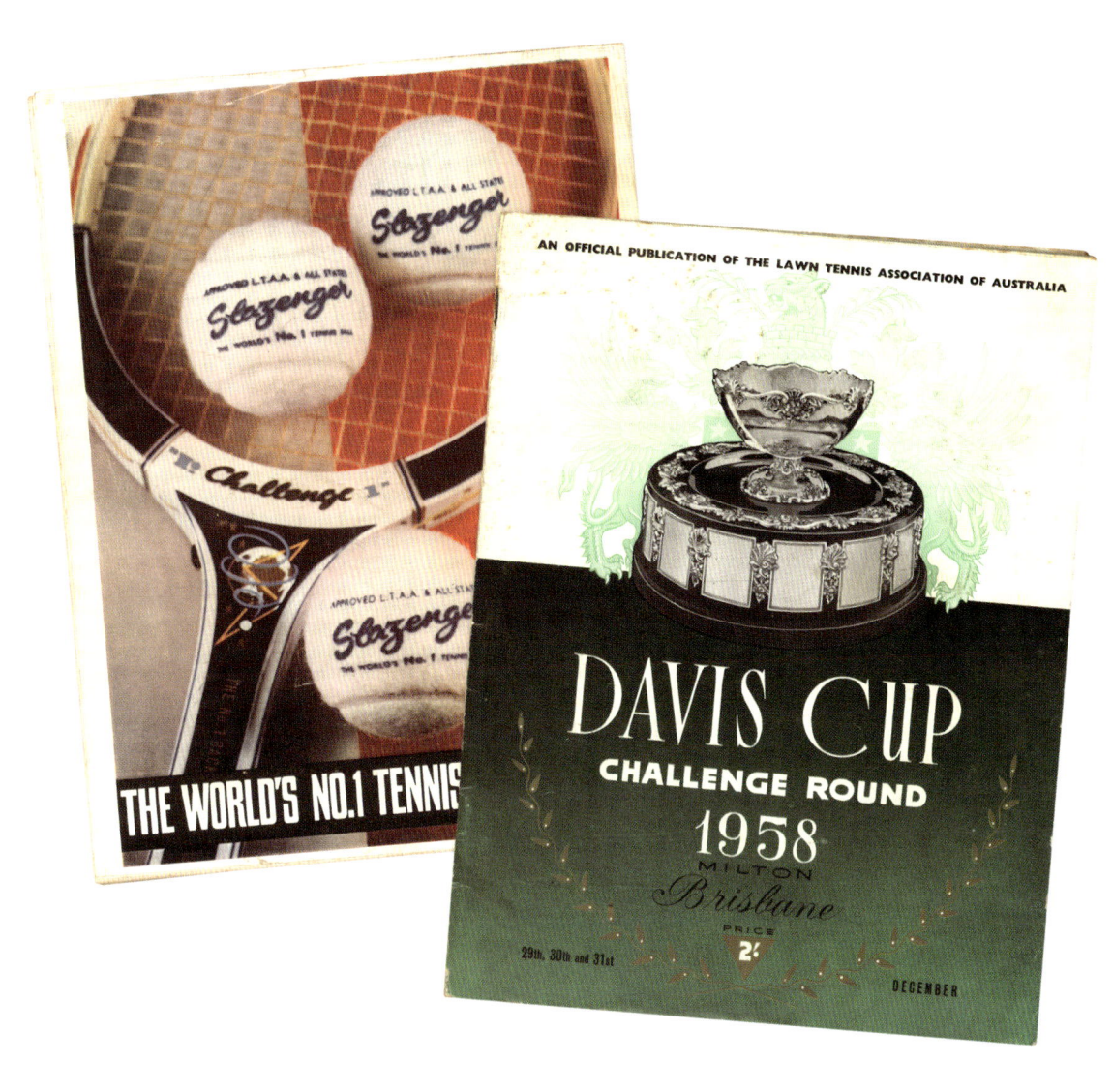

The State Library's collection of tennis material is particularly rich and this is not surprising when considering the number of champions the state has produced, including Edgar Moon, Margaret Molesworth, Rod Laver, Roy Emerson, Neale Fraser, Mal Anderson and, later, Pat Cash. Three tickets for seat 78, row T, section 10, accompany the official program for the famous 1958 Davis Cup Challenge held at Milton Tennis Courts, where the Australian team of Neale Fraser, Ashley Cooper and Mal Anderson was defeated. Australia had convincingly defeated the United States at Kooyong the previous year and this was regarded as a "grudge match". The program for one of the first major professional matches, Jack Kramer's World Championship Tennis, which toured Australia in 1961–62 is a fascinating insight into how a gentleman's game turned professional.

Under the guiding hand of veteran Harry Hopman, the 1960 Australian Davis Cup squad — consisting of Laver, Fraser and Emerson — carried off a stunning victory over Italy. Two years later, Laver capped off his amateur grand slam title by again figuring prominently in Australia's Davis Cup win over Mexico. Turning professional, Laver was prevented from playing in the major tournaments until 1968 when tennis authorities finally allowed professionals to play alongside amateurs. Laver responded by winning the Wimbledon crown and in 1969 took his second grand slam title — the only male player ever to do so.

Unlike tennis, a number of sports have achieved only limited popularity. From *Cavalcade of Queensland sport* (1951), we

Above Program and tickets for the Davis Cup Challenge at Milton Tennis Centre in Brisbane, December 1958. At the final, a capacity crowd saw the United States team defeat Australia's Neale Fraser, Ashley Cooper and Mal Anderson 3-2.
[Ephemera Collection]

> **The intensive program of sports played from primary school onwards has largely determined which sports remained popular.**

Left Programme for the Queensland Motor Sporting Club's Cavalcade of Motoring, held at Albion Park Racecourse in October 1948. This amateur sporting body was affiliated with the RACQ and had been reformed after a recess during the war. [Ephemera Collection]

Below Baseball used by some of the first American servicemen to be stationed in north Queensland during World War II and used at a game in Townsville in Christmas 1942. It is signed by several of the participants. [ACC 6495]

know that sports director Walter Greenwood introduced American men's basketball to the Queensland Young Men's Christian Association premises in Brisbane in 1908. He had studied with the game's inventor, Dr James Naismith, at Springfield College. By 1946, men's basketball was played at the University of Queensland. However, basketball was generally regarded as a woman's sport.

In some respects this is surprising, for Australian culture has been receptive to American popular culture from the early twentieth century. In sport, however, British heritage continues to dominate. The well-attended baseball matches held during World War II at the Brisbane Exhibition Ground and in Townsville did not translate into an acceptance of American sports. Later, fundraising to support the Centaur War Memorial Nurses Appeal (to honour those women who died at the hands of a Japanese submarine off Moreton Bay in May 1943) remained within Queensland's British sporting traditions. In October 1948 a Cavalcade of Motoring featuring many British cars, including a 1926 Rolls-Royce as well as JR Petrie's 1933 Jaguar, raised funds for this cause.

The intensive program of sports played from primary school onwards has largely determined which sports remained popular. For example, hurling, from Ireland — the precursor to hockey — did not take off, despite its promotion by the Queensland Irish Association. Many British games including tennis, lawn bowls and golf have become internationalised. Foxtel, with its coverage of American football and baseball, has yet to deter Queenslanders from their love of British-derived sports. The State Library of Queensland can be proud of its unrivalled role in the collection and preservation of the records of so many sporting achievements.

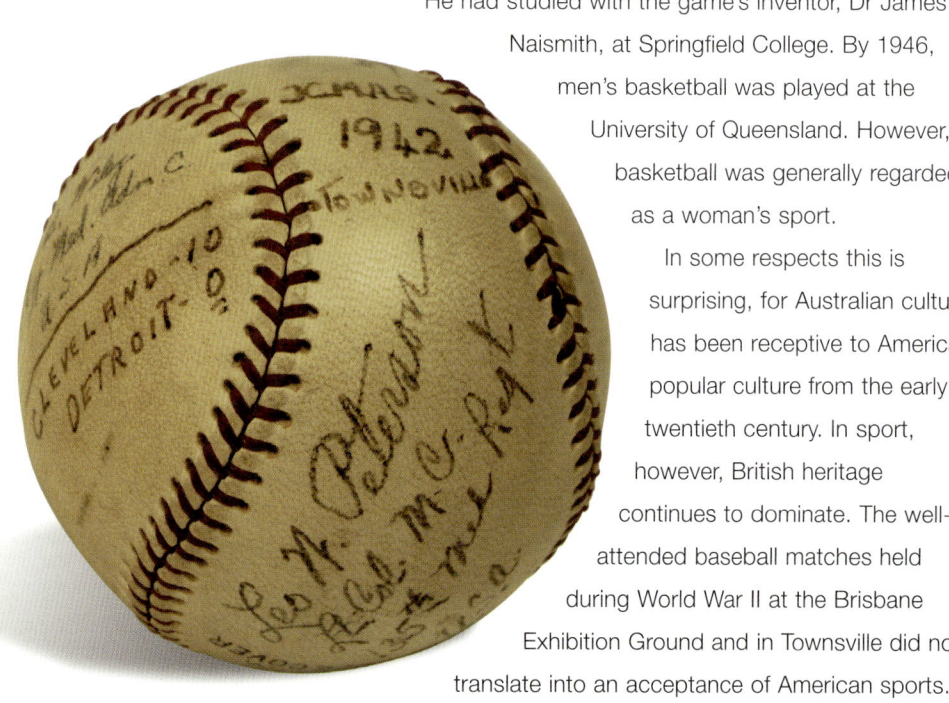

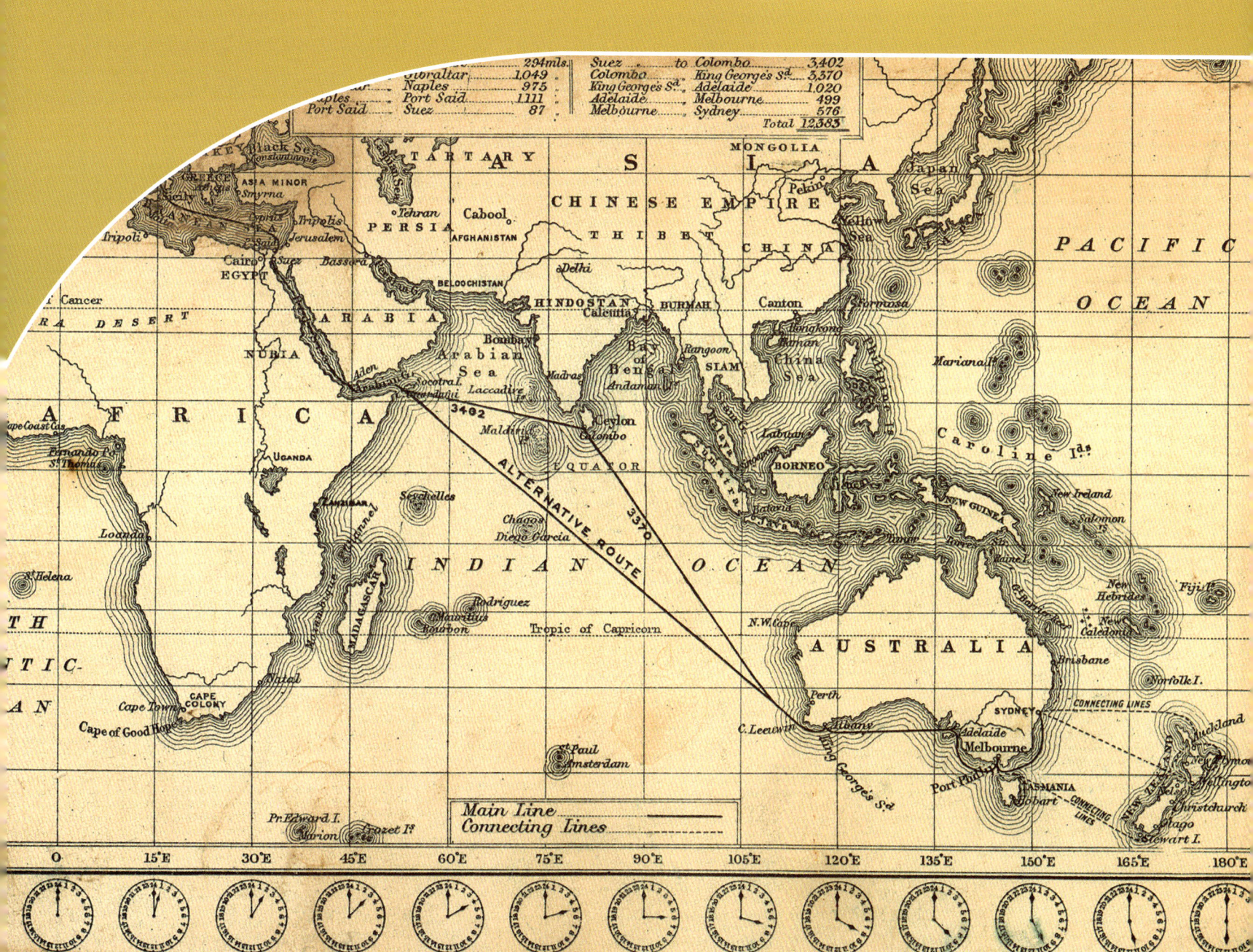

Chapter eight
The great escape 8

Author Kay Saunders   Research Librarian Dianne Byrne

Between the covers

> *These images of escaping poverty, cramped circumstances, poor health and securing a new Eden in a new land recur throughout Queensland's history.*

On New Year's Eve 1848, the *Chaseley* left Britain bound for the northern districts of New South Wales. Mostly Scottish artisans recruited by the Reverend Dr Lang, they each paid £200 for land grants hoping to improve their prospects in a distant land. One passenger, a gentlewoman from Edinburgh, Mary McConnel, came from more privileged circumstances and her marriage to the wealthy young grazier David McConnel, suggested a far different life. She later recalled the momentous departure: "That evening before sailing Dr Lang came on board, met with his emigrants, and addressed them in a faithful, fatherly manner, reminding them of their responsibilities in making their home in a new land, and bidding them to be true to their religious principles. They were all of one faith [Presbyterians], and he trusted that brotherly-kindness would bind them together as fellow passengers. A hymn was sung; he earnestly prayed for the safety of the ship and all on board …"

On the berthing of fellow Langites on the *Fortitude* in February 1849, the *Moreton Bay Courier* published a poem commemorating the arrival of these worthy people:

Hail! Strangers, hail! Right welcome to our shore,
We wish you joy, – Eden could yield no more.
We bid you welcome to Australia wide,
Land of the sunny clime, – the ocean's pride,
Land of the azure heaven, – the gorgeous sky,
Of wide-spread fertile plains, and mountains high;

… That loathsome sight, England's New Poor Law prison,
Where poverty is punished more than treason …
Welcome, then, strangers, to our Eden shore, –
And for its joys indulgent heaven adore.

These images of escaping poverty, cramped circumstances, poor health and securing a new Eden in a new land recur throughout Queensland's history. The State Library of Queensland's collection is rich in accounts of those travelling for pleasure, curiosity or necessity, in, through, and out of Australia.

The State Library owns a series of travel diaries of immigrants, most notably those of Rosamond D'Ouseley (1869), James Lee (1883), Richard Hews (1865), and Maria Steley (1863–64). Apart from capturing the flavour of the conditions on board, potential emigrants all held high expectations of their rejuvenation in a new land where opportunity seemed limitless. For both men and

Opening image Printed passenger list for RMS *Orizaba*, an Orient Line steamer which operated between England and Australia, February 1895. [Ephemera Collection]

Right 18-ct gold railway travel passes presented to Sir Samuel Walker Griffith (1845–1920), Chief Justice and Premier [ACC 6568] and Joseph Henry Turley (1859–1929), Member for Brisbane South. [ACC 6569]

women, Queensland offered a prospect of regeneration of health, fortune and material prosperity. Francis Adams in his travel book, *The Australians: a social sketch* (1893) noted that success for those escaping Britain's limited opportunities came at the cost of "over-work".

The shipboard diary by William Smith on the *Young Australia* (1864) is an unusual addition to travel diaries. Along with fellow middle cabin passenger Richard Watt, Smith produced an elaborate journal, *Etches and sketches*, which was later published by William Fairfax in Brisbane. Smith went on to work for the American Glace Photographic Company producing images of Charters Towers, Gympie and Maryborough.

This theme of new opportunities continued through the next century. During the Depression, Prime Minister Scullin in a travel brochure simply called "Australia" extolled the virtues of "A White Settlers' Country". He stated that: "A career in the professions offers less attraction and opportunity than it did, perhaps, in the past. Circumstances are cramped, and by contrast, the open spaces of Britain's Dominions suggest bigger things". Like Dr Lang almost a century before, Scullin stressed the opportunity for those with resources who could work: "To the man who is prepared to work and make initial sacrifice, there is assurance, not necessarily of a quick fortune … but of comfort, of plenty, of a good living, of independence, of the finest career of all — a man's job".

Above left Diary kept by Mildred Howell while a passenger aboard the *Larg's Bay*, from England to Australia, May–July 1947. [M 786]

Above right After enduring the German raids in Birmingham during World War II, Mildred Alice Howell emigrated to Australia with her husband and two children in 1947. The family were in the first batch of 22 postwar immigrants to travel on assisted passage from England.
[Image No. SD 069a]

Between the covers

Above Diaries kept by Sir James Dickson, auctioneeer, estate agent, and Premier of Queensland (1898–99). When not involved in business or politics, Dickson travelled widely in Europe. His diaries for the years 1886, 1890 and 1891, record his visits to England, France and Italy and contain press clippings, letters, souvenir menus and invitations. [OM 67-13]

The diary of Mildred Howell captured the hopes of a new life. During World War II she worked for Imperial Chemical Industries in Birmingham. Though she lost two children to German air raids in 1940, Howell remained positive, reading to her remaining children by the light of candles and hurricane lamps through the blackouts. In 1947, the worst winter in Britain for decades, she and her family left on the *Larg's Bay* bound for Australia, arriving as some of the first postwar assisted immigrants. (This vessel had repatriated Australian prisoners of war from Singapore to Australia in 1945.) Newspaper commentary stressed the new immigrants' "long[ing] for our sunshine". Mostly skilled tradespeople, like Lang's immigrants a century before, "[a]ll agreed that there was a better future in Australia than England".

Some earlier immigrants rose to prominence through their intelligence and talents. Queensland politics and public life in the 1880s and 1890s were dominated by Sir Samuel Griffith and Sir Thomas McIlwraith. The State Library owns two gold railway travel passes belonging to Griffith. He had come from

> To the man who is prepared to work and make initial sacrifice, there is assurance, not necessarily of a quick fortune ... but of comfort, of plenty, of a good living, of independence, of the finest career of all – a man's job

humble circumstances in Merthyr Tydfil in Wales and he was constantly reminded of his rise to fame and fortune. When Griffith was Chief Justice of Queensland, Francis Adams wrote that Griffiths' "father … [is] an aggressive, fanatical, little dissenting minister – the immortal religious log-roller". Scotsman McIlwraith, educated in mathematics at the University of Glasgow and fired by the vision for large-scale development in Queensland, never encountered such public acrimony over his lower-middle class origins.

Cornishman Sir James Dickson, who also studied in Glasgow, became Brisbane's leading auctioneer and property developer in the 1870s. Elected a member of parliament in 1873, he resigned in 1887 intent upon a grand tour of Europe. His diaries are detailed records of his well-informed travels to purchase luxury items and they illustrate the strong personal and professional connections between Queensland and Great Britain. While on his tour, on 26 June 1890, Dickson received an invitation to meet Lady (Lucinda) Musgrave, Griffith's confidante and advisor, to "show you pictures and gifts of my kind Brisbane friends". Her husband, Governor Sir Anthony Musgrave had died suddenly in Brisbane in 1888. The State Library holds an extensive collection of commemorative programs presented to Sir Anthony.

Other notable Queenslanders in the next century continued this tradition of grand tours. Vida Lahey, the sister of environmentalist Romeo Lahey, departed in some ways from this pattern by her years of work for the Allied war effort in France. She studied art in Paris and her correspondence about her demanding and exasperating instructor is amusing.

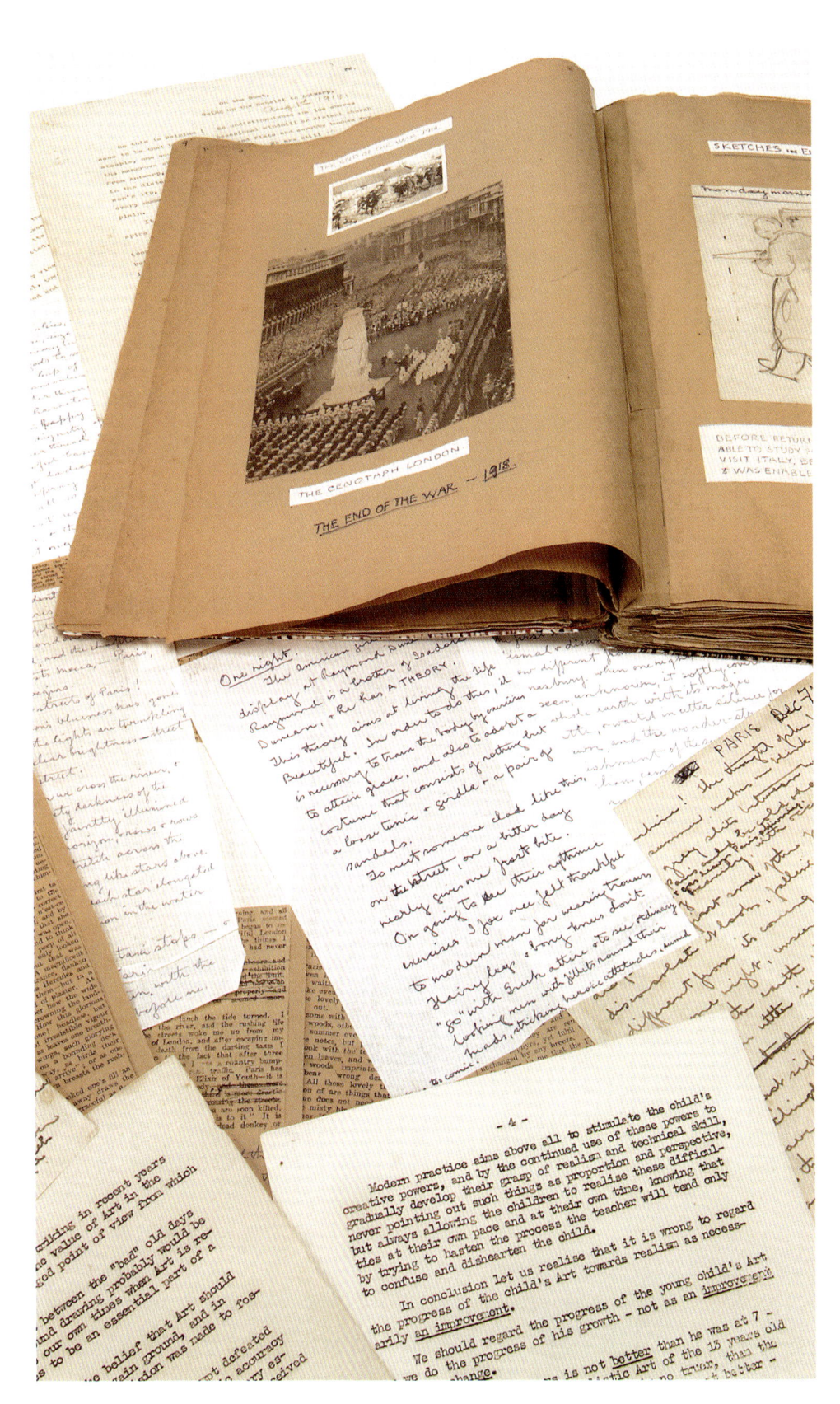

Above Scrapbook containing photographs, sketches and watercolours produced by artist Vida Lahey during her travels in Europe and art studies in Paris after the First World War. [OM 67-30/3]

Above and opposite (below)
Diary of journalist and adventurer Henri Gilbert. Entries in French and English record the people whom Gilbert met in the course of his travels. Press cuttings and photographs are pasted in the diary. The Queensland section covers about a dozen localities. [OM 67-15]

Opposite (above)
French journalist Henri Gilbert photographed at Barcaldine, 9 April 1900. [ACC 6154] [Album API-13]

She visited the studio of Isadora Duncan's brother Raymond with a young American woman friend. He had, she noted:

"A THEORY [sic]. [Which] aims at living the Life Beautiful. In order to do this, it is necessary to train the body by exercises to attain grace, and also adopt a costume that consists of nothing but a loose tunic, a girdle and a pair of sandals. To meet someone clad like this, on the street, on a bitter day nearly gives me frost bite … I for once, felt thankful to modern man for wearing trousers. Hairy legs and bony knees don't "go" with Greek attire …"

Lahey was not caught up with the decadence of post-war Paris and she did not meet other notable women expatriates such as Gertrude Stein, Sylvia Beach or Natalie Barney. Her war work kept her within a far more conservative mould. She wrote movingly of the Armistice Day commemorations in 1920 in Trafalgar Square: "the Unknown Warrior is borne down the Mall and Whitehall on his way from an obscure grave in France to his last place in Westminster Abbey … [It is for] the unknown heroism of the 'Digger', the 'Tommy' and 'Jack Tar' that we all gathered here …"

The grand tour was a two-way process. Few were like the intrepid and eccentric French pedestrian Henri Gilbert who walked across Spain and the Middle East on his way to Australia, arriving in Fremantle in 1897. On the second morning of his walk he was drugged and robbed. This did not deter his march across the Nullarbor. The State Library possesses his diary for the Australian leg, written in French, with entries of those he encountered in English.

Many curious visitors, like Lord Henry John Montagu-Douglas-Scott, visited the colonies initially for their health. He came to New South Wales after time in Italy, Egypt and the Caribbean. Studying art under Conrad Martens, Montagu-Douglas-Scott came to Moreton Bay and the Darling Downs to collect fossils, ferns and shells in 1853. His sketches of the Glasshouse Mountains and the Kangaroo Point ferry are among the treasures of the State Library. The State Library also owns the 1846–47 diary of W Layton Lowndes recording his voyage up the coast to Port Curtis

Many curious visitors, like Lord Henry John Montagu-Douglas-Scott, visited the colonies initially for their health. He came to New South Wales after time in Italy, Egypt and the Caribbean.

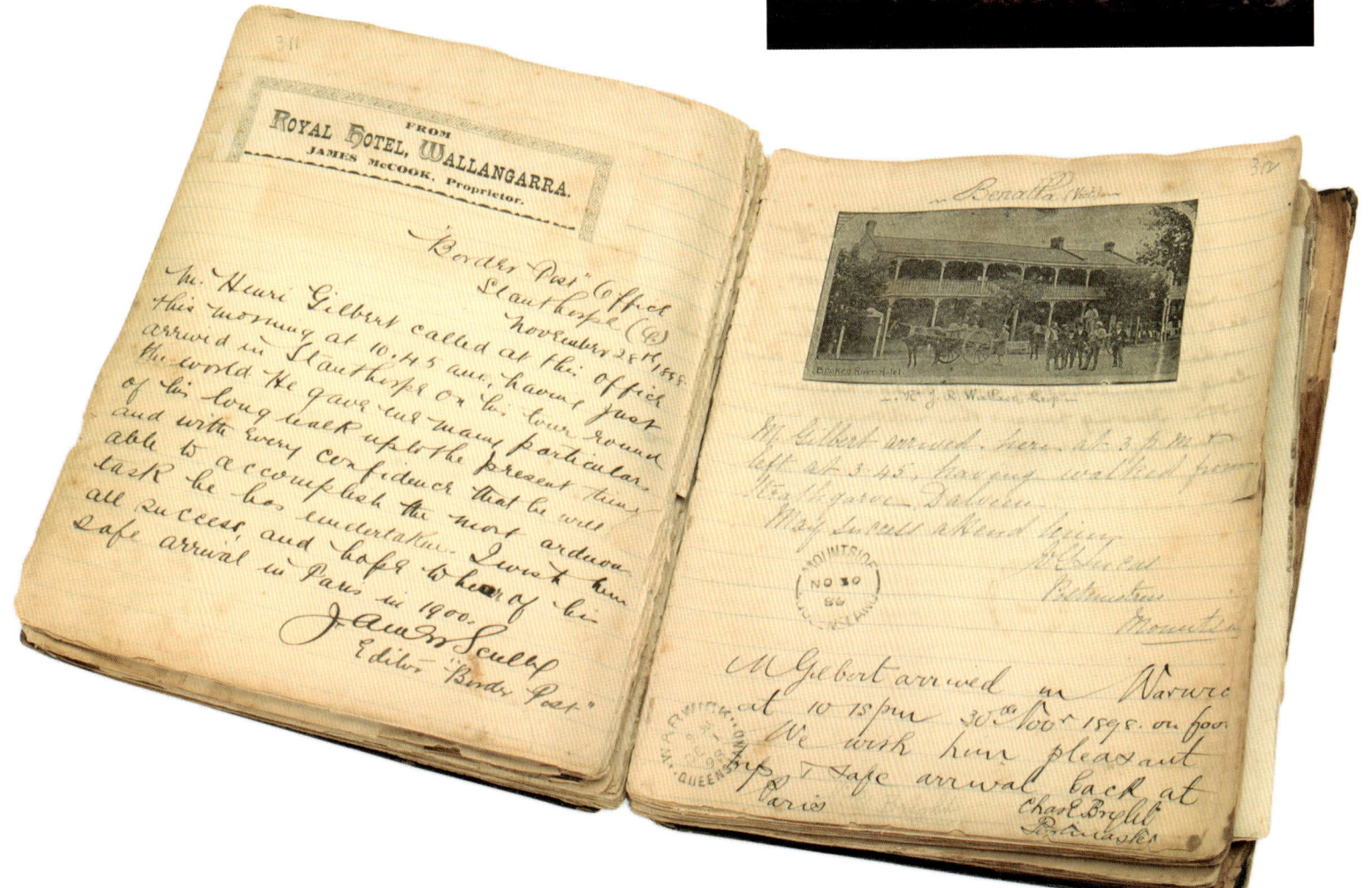

Above Printed passenger list for RMS *Orizaba*, an Orient Line steamer which operated between England and Australia, February 1895. [Ephemera Collection]

where a new colony of North Australia under Colonel Barney was gazetted in May 1846. JF Hogan's book, *The Gladstone colony* (1898) charted the history of this doomed experiment that might have solved north Queenslanders' longing for independence from the control of Brisbane interests.

For visitors arriving by boat, such as those aboard the Orient Line's RMS *Orizaba* in 1895, the voyage was filled with exotic sights and adventures. The diary of the well-connected Alice Heber-Percy details her travels through the Orient and later staying on large pastoral stations like Waverely, Gracemere and Brighton Downs. Others with less resources and connections also enjoyed their escape to the Antipodes. Miss B Gandy from West Kensington in London undertook a voyage out to Queensland with her aunt Emily Salisbury in 1899–1901. Her album contains many fine watercolours of flora, vistas and people along the way through the Suez Canal to Australia. Her sketches of Southport, Main Beach and Magnetic Island capture the wild lushness of these environments. On the way home, wool bales in the Queensland Royal steamship, *Jumna* caught fire. Her cool, calm demeanour in the face of an emergency showed an admirable strength of character. The State Library also owns the diary of Annie Stubbs, an immigrant on the *Jumna* in late 1900.

Enterprising reporters started coming to Queensland from the 1870s. In 1872 the celebrated novelist Anthony Trollope visited Queensland, reporting extensively on the wealth of various industries like mining, timber, cotton, pastoralism and

The great escape | 137

This page Leather-bound travel album kept by a young woman identified only as Miss Gandy, who accompanied her aunt on a voyage from England to Australia 1899–1901. The pair resided for a time at Southport and returned home on the SS *Jumna*, via Townsville, Thursday Island, Java and Ceylon. [OMR 43; TR1884]

sugar. Trollope was an advocate of the plantation system within the sugar industry. He also informed his readers of the curious system of leasing Crown land to wealthy graziers, a question that was later central to the Wik judgment in the High Court in 1996. Like his mother's celebrated book, *Domestic manners of the Americans* (1832), his acute eye charted the vagaries of class in a settler society. His discussion of the "nomad tribe of pastoral labourers" was a forerunner to *The Bulletin*'s idealisation of rural life in the following decade. His sympathy for the small selectors also sets the scene for Steele Rudd's *On our selection*.

Some notable travellers were not so fulsome in the praise of the wealthy. *The Times*' special correspondent Flora Shaw (Lady Lugard), in her *Letters from Queensland* (1893), surveyed the wealth of Mount Morgan, Chillagoe, and the pastoral industry where she also addressed the question of the "wandering tribe of workers". She realised how difficult their lives could be: "You learn in this country what dying like sheep may really mean, and more men actually do probably so die than are … [registered] … [left] to the scavenging birds wheeling overhead".

Other visitors later came to Queensland to further their professional expertise. The album of L Plass, a Texan engineer who in 1931 took a sea voyage to Australia over the Pacific, has some excellent photographs of his travels, as well as good representations of the early days of Mount Isa. His camera records residents adorned in body paints on Palm Island Reserve. The final image of a family of koalas belies the originality and freshness of his collection.

Unlike working crusaders such as Flora Shaw, some travel was purely for employment. Journalist Newton Barton's diary of his time as a government agent on board the recruiting vessel, *Rio Loge* from Bundaberg to the New Hebrides and the Solomons in 1894 gives a rare insight into the labour

Below Diary kept by able seaman Newton Barton on a voyage from Bundaberg to the Solomon Islands and Vanuatu, as helmsman aboard the "black-birding" vessel *Rio Loge*, October 1894–March 1895. [ACC 3299]
Right Newton Barton (1870–1935) was the son of a prominent journalist who became senior master at Maryborough Grammar School. [Image No. BC 068]

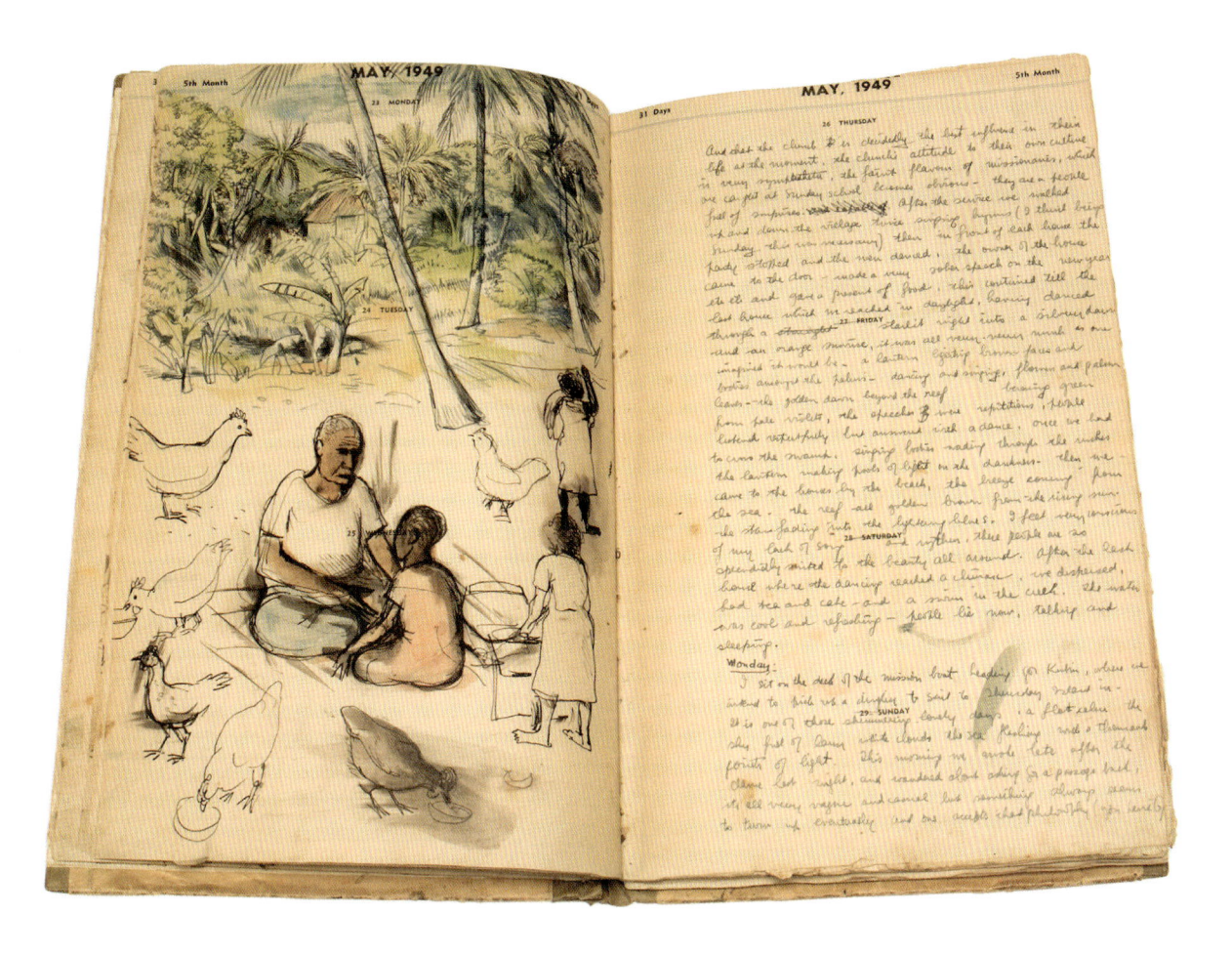

Following in the tradition of French painter Paul Gauguin in Tahiti, other Europeans sought a tropical island paradise in Queensland.

trade. The previous voyage had been crisis-ridden with five returning Islanders dying of dysentery and both crew members and Islanders dying when a large wave hit the small cover boat. Vessels took home those indentured Melanesians who had finished their contracts in Queensland and set about recruiting more workers under government regulations. After the previous scandals about kidnapping, government agents oversaw procedures. The work was neither well paid nor prestigious. Able Seaman Newton Barton summed up the quality of those who undertook the work, mostly remittance men "who would have made their mark but rum is the cause of their presence here". He invests his fellow British colleagues with grandiose titles such as "Fenwick Bart and the Right Honorable Henry-Gibbs … Sir George Hicks-Beach MLC, Sir John Franklin Lucemore KCB and Brigadier General TB Pearn … and Charles Wilson-Vetters RA". There were some enjoyable moments such as the concerts with "Gibbs leader of the orchestra". The son of a prominent educationist, Barton did not fit the mould of the remittance man reduced to this desperate work. He later established a pleasure launch business for tourists in Yeppoon.

Following in the tradition of French painter Paul Gauguin in Tahiti, other Europeans sought a tropical island paradise in Queensland. The eccentric recluse, artist Noel Wood, fled to Bedarra Island in 1936. Photographs show him barechested in sarongs. Later, artist Ian Fairweather used island solitude in order to paint his visions of antipodean Arcadia. Others sought to convey the joy of their Eden to the world.

Above left Diary produced by artist Ray Crooke during his stay in the Torres Strait, 1949. The work with its text, sketches and beautifully detailed watercolours suggests much of the inspiration for Crooke's early paintings. [RB HARC 6069]

Above right Edmund James Banfield (1852–1923), author and naturalist settled on Dunk Island in September 1897. Fleeing from ill health and life on the mainland, Banfield remained on Dunk for 30 years, growing vegetables and keeping a diary which became the basis of numerous articles and books. [Image No. 111290]

Between the covers

Above left Tourists aboard TSS *Katoomba*, which visited Long Island, Hayman Island and Brampton Island, Christmas 1933–New Year 1934. [ACC 6021] [Album APA 109]

Above right Hugo Brassey and his wife, the former Baroness Christa von Bodensen, at Dunk Island, September 1935. Brassey turned his island into an exclusive resort, patronised by his social friends. [Image No. 98540]

EJ Banfield, an English journalist on the *Townsville Daily Bulletin* published his first book *The Torres Straits route from Queensland to England* (1885) with backing from Burns Philp. He published widely on the North Queensland Separation Movement. In 1896 he took a 30-year lease on Dunk Island and went there to live when he was diagnosed with tuberculosis. He wrote articles under the name of "Rob Krusoe" and the "Beachcomber" for the *Lone Hand*. His life was hardly that of a beachcomber, for his hard work and his dedication to the environment and the Indigenous people became his life's mission. His *Confessions of a beachcomber* (1908) was dedicated to Robert Philp, the Townsville entrepreneur who established Burns Philp for the Pacific trade. The State Library holds a collection of Philp material.

The 1949 journal of artist Ray Crooke also documents a working life involved with exotic travel. The detailed sketches of the people and environment of the Torres Straits, with their influences from Gauguin, formed the basis of his later successful large-scale paintings, exhibited at the Johnstone Gallery in Brisbane. His *Island journal* (2000) was dedicated to Brian and Marjorie Johnstone.

Dunk Island was turned into an exclusive resort by the Irish aristocrat Hugo Brassey and his wife, the former Baroness Christa von Bodensen, in 1935. In May 1942 during World War II, the RAAF took over the island, which was central to operations for the Battle of the Coral Sea. The State Library owns an interesting photograph of the Mandalay Guest House, constructed like a Balinese house, on Magnetic Island in the early 1920s. Other island resorts took off after the Second World War. A signed souvenir menu from the 1948 Christmas Dinner at Nicolson's resort on Lindeman Island shows the new development. The menu was a strange mixture of English food such as haricot oxtail and kidney, and plum pudding and cognac sauce, alongside Queensland delicacies such as mackerel au gratin and tropical fruit salad.

After World War I, Australia was promoted as a healthy outdoor destination for tourists. A 1924 brochure, *Australia calls you!,* first used the motif of the bather at

The brochure *Discover Queensland* from the early 1960s contains a large map where each region is characterised by a robust Queensland man engaged in activities such as killing crocodiles or wild buffaloes, deep-sea fishing, travelling along desert roads in four-wheel drives or rounding up sheep on horseback.

Above English-born artist Eileen Mayo's famous poster featuring the long-spined butterfly fish and corals of the Great Barrier Reef, produced for the Australian National Travel Association, 1959. [HPT TOU 001]

Left Brochure prepared for visitors to Dunk Island, 1950. A kitchen garden and Jersey cows provided for the food needs of 40 guests and "excessive luggage" was discouraged. [P 919.436]

142 Between the covers

Above *La Grande Barriera*, a poster printed in Rome in 1956 for an Italian language film set on the Great Barrier Reef. [HPT TOU 021]

Above right Poster aimed at the new youth market of the 1960s. [HPT TOU 005] Right *Sunshine tours to Brisbane and Cairns*, a brochure produced by Pioneer Tours to attract the many southern visitors who began to follow the winter sunshine to Queensland in the early 1930s. [Ephemera Collection]

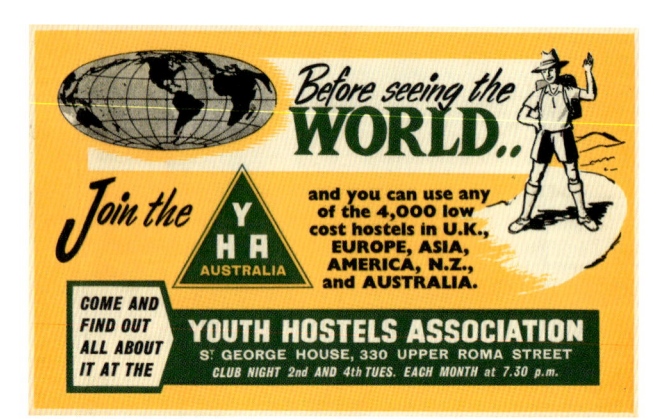

The great escape

After the initial experimentation with aircraft in the First World War, this new form of transport captured the emerging mood of optimism and limitless opportunity.

Bondi Beach with a lifesaver in the background. The map showed an elegant couple in a luxury yacht. By the 1930s the Great Barrier Reef had become a tourist destination for affluent visitors. Sylvia Glass's album demonstrates its pleasures. Eileen Mayo's poster captured the natural wonders. Despite the global Depression, the Federal Government heavily promoted travel to Australia. The State Library owns important brochures like *Australia — a place in the sun!*, and *Picturesque travel in Western Australia*. This central form of advertising continued through the postwar years, with sections on each state. The brochure designed for the French market, *L'Australie pays a surprises* (Australia — Land of surprises) featured a koala, kangaroo, surfboard rider, helicopter and Uluru on its back cover. Family barbeques, "un bifteck pour le petit déjeuner" (a steak for breakfast) demonstrated 'normal' Australian life.

Each state promoted its own scenic destinations through their tourist bureaux. In the 1940s, the Queensland Government Tourist Bureau promoted combined rail and road day tours to the Glasshouse Mountains. This was before most families owned a car. The brochure *Discover Queensland* from the early 1960s contains a large map where each region is characterised by a robust Queensland man engaged in activities such as killing crocodiles or wild buffaloes, deep-sea fishing, travelling along desert roads in four-wheel drives or rounding up sheep on horseback. The inside cover featured a woman sunbathing, and Lennon's Hotel in Brisbane. *Sunshine tours to Brisbane and Cairns* by bus operators Pioneer Coaches from the 1950s reiterated the theme that Queensland was a good winter destination. For more modest budgets and anticipating the later large youth market, the Youth Hostel Association (YHA) promoted its facilities around the same time.

After the initial experimentation with aircraft in the First World War, this new form of transport captured the emerging mood of optimism and limitless opportunity. The State Library owns the Aircraft Logbook dated 22 November 1921 to 14 February 1932 for an Avro 3 seater

Above left Queensland socialite Aileen Bell prepares to board a Qantas flight to Singapore in 1937. The plane, a Gipsy Six was introduced to the South East Asian run in 1935. [Image No. 13164]

Above right Logbook for the first aircraft of the Western Queensland Auto Aero Service Limited, the airline which later became Qantas, November 1921–32. [OMAN; ACC 4117]

Above left Australian Express Grand tour of the Americas, 1977. This Queensland-based company was founded by Cypriot migrant Constantine Philippides who had served in the British Army.
[Ephemera Collection]

Above right Queen Elizabeth II and Prince Philip board the "Royal Aeroplane" a Qantas Super Constellation at the end of their first visit to Queensland, 18 March 1954.
[Image No. 105618]

Above far right A selection of Qantas brochures, 1947–58.
[Ephemera Collection]

540K aircraft, the first logbook for the initial aircraft of the Western Queensland Auto Aero Service Ltd, which later became Qantas. It is signed by its co-founder Hudson Fysh who had joined the AIF before transferring to the new Australian Flying Corps. The logbook records the names and duties of pilots, dates of flights and details on cargo and passengers. The first service went from Sydney to Longreach where the Qantas Founders Outback Museum is now located.

The young airline's first run went from Charleville to Cloncurry. The State Library has a photograph of the first passenger, 87-year-old Alexander Kennedy, along with more glamorous images of socialite Aileen Bell, wearing then-daring trousers, in a 1937 trip to Singapore. In 1934 Qantas formed Qantas Empire Airways for overseas travel, with Fysh securing the lucrative airmail contract. His expertise was a vital part of the air war against the Japanese in World War II.

The postwar years produced extraordinary advances for the company. Queen Elizabeth and Prince Philip left their Queensland leg of the Royal visit on 18 March 1954 in a Qantas Super-Constellation. The State Library also owns a splendid collection of Qantas brochures from the period 1947–58.

Other Queenslanders later developed travel businesses to introduce Australians to overseas destinations. In 1958, Cypriot born Constantine Philippides established Australian Express, which went on to become one of the country's largest travel companies, escorting travellers by the new international jet services to exotic locations such as South America.

The State Library possesses an extraordinary range of valuable materials on travel, immigration and tourism. From the shipboard diaries of hopeful immigrants in the 1840s to the foundation records of Qantas, the state's iconic company and Australia's iconic airline, the collections tell us much about the lure of escape and adventure.

Chapter nine
Dreamers and yarners

Author Kay Saunders Research Librarian Dianne Byrne

> "The role of the "yarner" in describing life "as it is" created the much needed cohesion and connection between people in the new society, allowing them to accept the day-to-day challenges of life."

In his poem, *The fall of hyperion* (1819), the apothecary and poet John Keats captured the tension between literature and visionaries:

The poet and the dreamer are distinct,
Diverse, sheer opposite, antipodes.
The one pours out a balm upon the world,
The other vexes it.

The vast natural landscape presented European settlers with the new opportunity to envision how it should be developed. These visions needed to be practical and immediate to create the infrastructure and lifestyle. Only when material needs were satisfied could the idealistic and sometimes unrealistic dreamers also find a place.

The role of the "yarner" in describing life "as it is" created the much needed cohesion and connection between people in the new society, allowing them to accept the day-to-day challenges that came to them. Yarners portrayed ordinary people's aspirations and struggles in daily life. Periodicals like *The Bulletin*, established by JF Archibald, and *Steele Rudd's Magazine* published yarners who took on the essential human role of the storyteller. They defined the emerging vibrant Australian identity.

Indigenous cultures within Queensland operate upon entirely different material and spiritual foundations.

Opening image and below Two watercolour paintings by Torres Strait Islander artists illustrating traditional myths and legends. [TR 1791/345 and 349]

Above *In the beginning far off in the dreamtime*, by Helen Malone, 1993. This work (executed in gouache and gold leaf on vellum) takes the form of an *icosahedron*, a solid figure with twenty faces. Each face is decorated with the aboriginal myth of the rainbow serpent and excerpts from the Book of Genesis. The box of Japanese paper, which encloses the work, opens to form a cross. [RBH MON MAL]

In the 1960s and 1970s, Margaret Lawrie recorded many traditional stories and collected beautiful watercolours illustrating the myths and legends by Torres Strait Islander artists. This collection is one of the finest holdings within the State Library of Queensland. Brisbane artist Helen Malone's *In the beginning far off in the dreamtime* (1993) reconciles the traditional Rainbow Serpent creation story with the Christian account of creation in the Book of Genesis. The State Library also holds many traditional Indigenous artefacts from Lammermoor station at Hughenden. Robert Christison respected the Dalleburra people, insisting when he sold the property that its traditional custodians remain. His daughter Mary Bennett wrote in 1928: "The old Blacks never forgot that Lammermoor was their country, and they took pride in its triumphs in the show and at the races, so they shared in the work …" When poet Kath Walker (later Oodgeroo Noonuccal) stood as a Labor Party candidate in 1968 in the seat of Greenslopes, using the shape of an ochre boomerang for her election pamphlet, a century of Indigenous rights activism was realised. These collaborations between Indigenous and European-Australians herald a hope of reconciliation and mutual respect.

Some British settlers like Christison, held dreams for a better future for the rapidly displaced Indigenous peoples. In the early 1870s, the Scottish Catholic priest Father Duncan McNab saw a loophole in the *Crown Lands Alienation Act* (1868) and applied for land for the people around Mackay. His land rights advocacy was not successful, but his dream of a vibrant autonomous life for the original owners was a precursor to

Above Boomerang promotional flyer for Kath Walker who in 1969 stood unsuccessfully for the Queensland Parliament as ALP candidate for Greenslopes. In 1983 she again stood for the Democrats in Redlands. [Ephemera Collection]

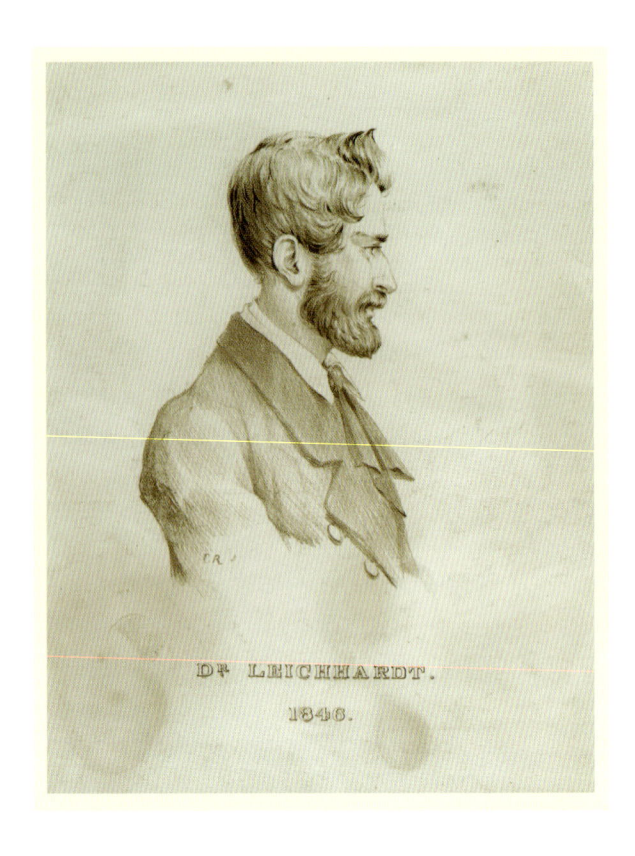

Above left *Leichhardt's grave*, an "elegiac ode", with words by Robert Lynd and music by Isaac Nathan, 1845. The work was composed at the time when Leichhardt was overdue from his first expedition and there was intense fear among the Australian public that he would never return. [RBQ 782 nat]

Above right Lithographed portrait of Ludwig Leichhardt by Charles Rodius, 1846. This rare image was produced in Sydney in March 1846 after the explorer's return from his first expedition. [ACC 6415]

the success of the Mabo claim in 1992. Lutheran pastor George Schwarz established the Hope Vale Mission near Cooktown among the Guugu Yimithirr in 1886 as a refuge from the frontier. He was a strong public opponent of the settlers' sexual exploitation of Indigenous women as well as the kidnapping of children to work in the pearl-shelling industry. Through the PANDORA initiative, the State Library has archived and is preserving a website on Mainland Missions and Communities, which contains information about this enterprise.

At the commencement of free European settlement, figures like Ludwig Leichhardt articulated his respect for the Indigenous peoples. However, as an explorer he was the harbinger for the development that irrevocably changed their traditional life. Leichhardt was a scientist with a passion and curiosity to explore where no European had been. Although he was a dreamer, he was also a man of action. His first expedition left from Jimbour station on 1 October 1844. Beset with difficulties of defections and the spearing of his colleague Gilbert, the expedition reached Port Essington in December 1845. Feted as a hero and as the "Prince of Explorers", poems and images of the young explorer, whose party had been feared dead, suddenly appeared. Charles Rodius's rare portrait produced immediately on Leichhardt's return in March 1846 was an unauthorised image. The "elegiac ode" composed by Robert Lynd and set to music by Isaac Nathan, at a time during 1845 when all the party was long overdue, captures the mood of public fear that he would not return. Leichhardt's book, *Journal of an overland expedition in Australia, from Moreton Bay to Port Essington, a distance of up to 3000 miles, during the years 1844–1845* published in London in 1847 secured his reputation.

Henry Stuart Russell in his *Genesis of Queensland* (1888) recalled his own dealings with Leichhardt in 1844 as he passed through Cecil Plains station. He concluded the explorer lacked "bushcraft" and the ability to manage men. WW Craig's 1925 assessment of his expeditions, especially his last ill-fated attempt to cross the continent from east to west in 1848, argued that "… fame of men like Leichhardt, Kennedy, Burke and Wills is, in a considerable measure, kept

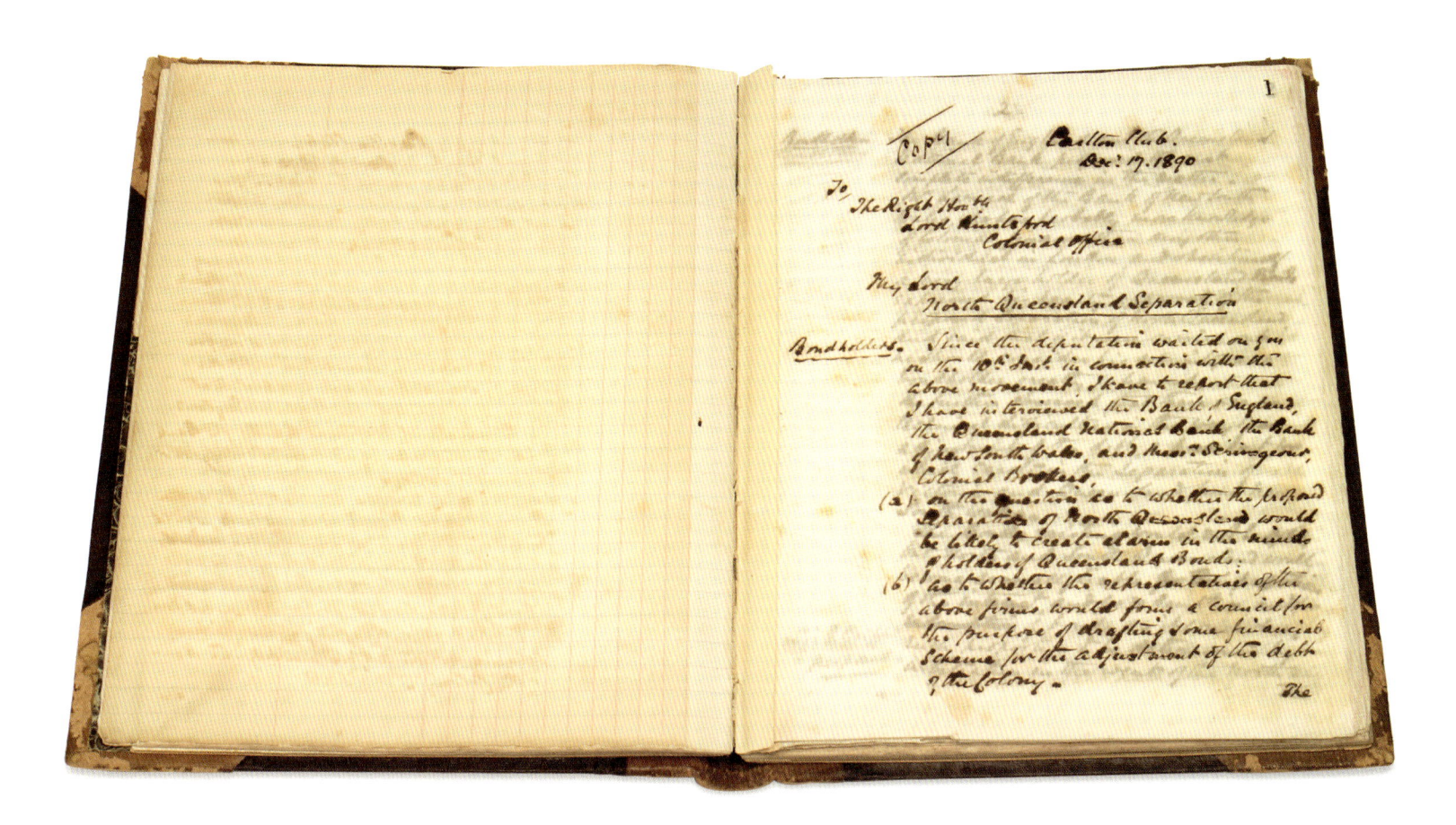

Above *Letterbook of the North Queensland Separation League*, 1890–93, recording the correspondence of Harold Finch-Hatton and Charles Rawson, two active figures in the movement. Rawson Archive [OMR 98; ACC 2967/4]

> The charting of the vast expanses of the continent was the first step towards the shifting of ownership from Indigenous peoples to the new settlers.

fresh in memory owing to the disastrous ending of their undertakings … in most cases, plainly due to mismanagement and errors of judgement …" The story held a profound fascination for later generations. Patrick White's novel, *Voss* (1957) and the opera libretto by David Malouf in 1986 capture Leichhardt's dream within biblical images of redemption and death.

The charting of the vast expanses of the continent was the first step towards the shifting of ownership from Indigenous peoples to the new settlers. The demarcation of territory took new meaning as colonies were established. The original colony of New South Wales was gradually amended as new settlements were envisaged. In June 1846, Colonial Secretary William Gladstone proposed a new colony of North Australia centred around Port Curtis, with Colonel Barney as administrator, as chronicled in JF Hogan's book, *The Gladstone colony* (1898). Reverend Dr Lang's *Cooksland in north-eastern Australia: the future cotton field of Great Britain* (1847) also dreamed of a new empire where tropical resources could be exploited.

The idea of a northern colony took hold. In 1853 Colonel O'Connel (later Governor Sir Maurice O'Connel) was appointed government resident at Gladstone. The discovery of gold in July 1858 revived hopes for the distant outpost. Surveyor Clarendon Stuart's 1861 pencil sketch of *Port Denison looking south east* held in the State Library is an early landscape of northern Queensland.

By the 1870s, with the establishment of the sugar, mining and pastoral industries ensuring great wealth to the new colony, there was growing resentment that distant decision makers in Brisbane did not appreciate the importance of the north. In 1882 a separation league was formed in Townsville,

Above Collar owned by Henry Lawson (1867–1922) Australia's greatest short story writer. It is signed by the author and bears an inscription in his hand which refers to the problems he experienced with alcohol in later life. [OM 90-42]

followed by similar organisations across the north. With the unprecedented wealth from the Charters Towers and Ravenswood goldfields and the Mackay sugar districts, the movement took on an urgency that did not diminish until Federation in 1901. The State Library holds extensive collections on the Separation movements. Most notably, the Rawson Archive contains material from the Honourable Harold Finch-Hatton, author of *Advance Australia!: an account of eight years' work, wandering and amusement in Queensland, New South Wales and Victoria* (1885), concerned with Northern Separation. A letter dated 17 December 1890, composed in the Carlton Club in London, outlined the claims of the movement. As the founding treasurer of the Imperial Federation League and later a chairman of the London Committee of the North Queensland Separation League, his assessment possessed an unassailable authority.

These dreams of political and economic autonomy, though glibly promised by Premier Sir Samuel Griffith, drove the Federation movement in north and central Queensland. The southern districts overwhelmingly voted "no" in the referendum proposing Federation of the six colonies, fearing that Queensland secondary industry and commerce would be destroyed by union. The northern and central districts saw the formation of the new Commonwealth as the opportunity to create new states, far from the domination of Brisbane. Their dreams were not realised. These concerns still resound today, however, as the more recent public declarations of far northern politicians like Bob Katter Junior demonstrate.

Acceptance of Federation was largely carried by the votes of the radical miners in Charters Towers, then the second city of Queensland. Public debate was fierce in this cosmopolitan centre with newspapers such as the *Australian Republican* operating in the early 1890s. There had been other notable republican texts like Dunmore Lang's *Freedom and independence for the golden lands of Australia* (1852) and Henry Lawson's first poem *A song of the republic* (1887). The woodcut by Sir Lionel Lindsay depicting Lawson (c. 1910) captured the disillusionment of this poet of new visions for

By the 1870s, with the establishment of the sugar, mining and pastoral industries ensuring great wealth to the new colony, there was growing resentment that distant decision makers in Brisbane did not appreciate the importance of the north.

a new land. Lawson understood what DH Lawrence later described as "that peculiar lost weary aloofness of Australia". The collar Lawson presented to the female cashier in an hotel who advanced him money for his drinking is a touching reminder of his unrealised visions. Lilian Pedersen's illuminated book *The lights of Cobb and Co* (1943) containing two Lawson poems showed how his dreams transcended his own tragic life.

The republican cause was not strong in late colonial Australia, with the exception of Charters Towers. The editor of the *Australian Republican*, Cornishman Frederick Vosper, was a strong advocate of Northern Separation along with many of the wealthy planters and mine owners. Where he parted company with them was over the issue of workers' rights. A dominant feature of the period was class warfare. During the 1891 Shearers' Strike, which saw the Liberal Griffith Government send in the colonial army and the Native Mounted Police against striking workers, Vosper wrote his famous "Bread or Blood" editorial which advocated revolution. This slogan had previously been the cry in the 1866 unemployment riots in Brisbane. Charged with seditious libel, he was convicted of inciting a miners' riot in 1892 and served three months imprisonment.

Other prominent supporters of the workers' struggles, like the Worker's editor William Lane, believed that the power of the ruling class would not be easily broken in Queensland. Lane was an admirer of Henry George, American author of *Progress and poverty* (1879) who visited Brisbane in 1890. Lane's novel, *The working man's paradise* (1892) was written

Left and below *The lights of Cobb & Co*, an illuminated book handwritten and illustrated by Lilian Pedersen containing two poems by Henry Lawson. The work was produced in Brisbane in 1943 and is hand-bound by the artist. [RBH MON PED]

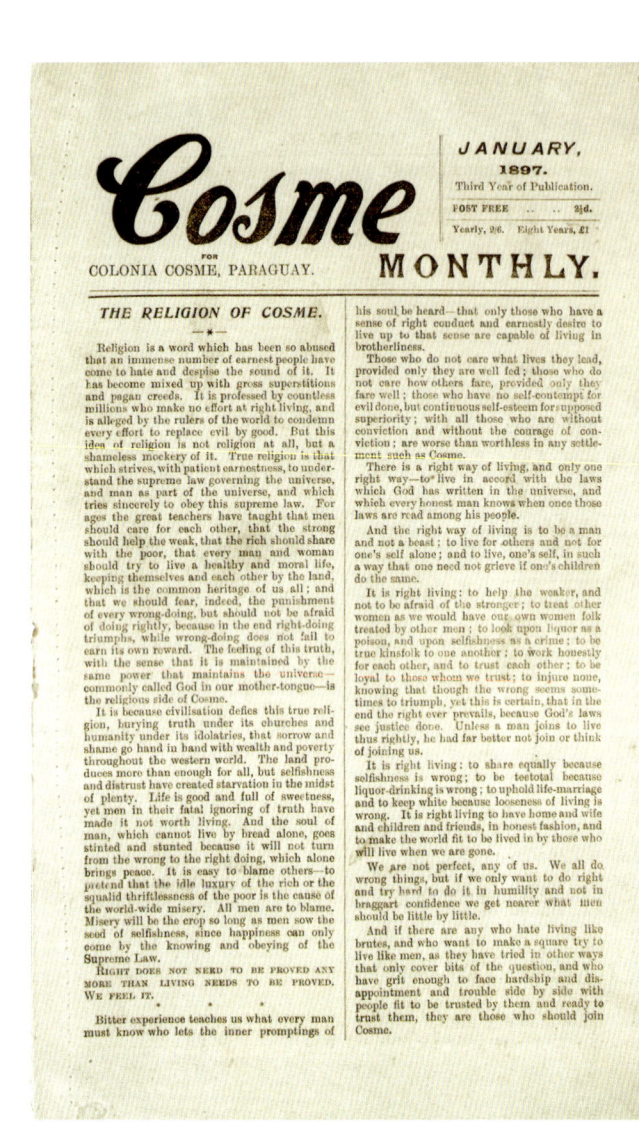

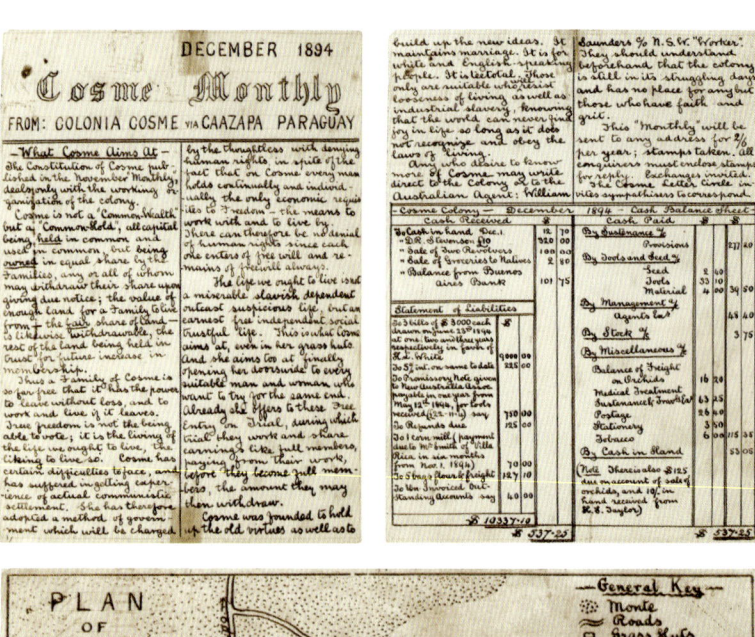

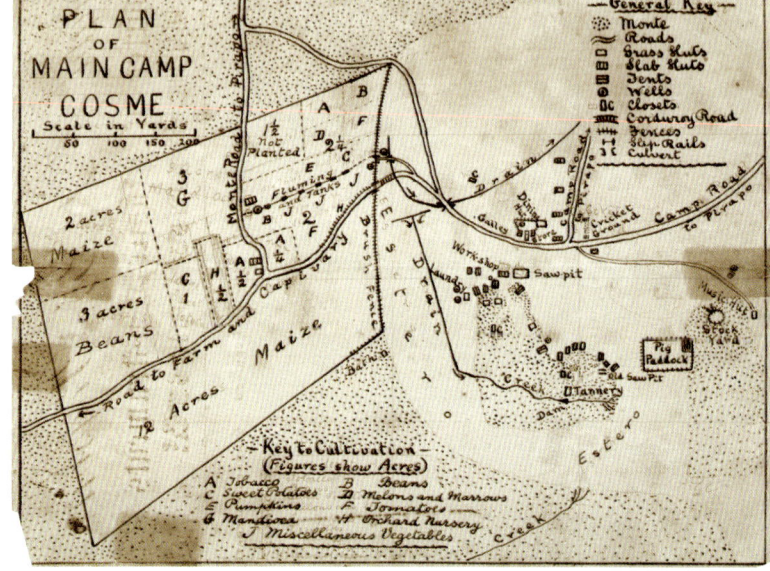

Above *Cosme Monthly*, 1894–1903. This journal was published by the Cosme Co-operative Colony in Caazapa, Paraguay, the utopian scheme founded by journalist and trade unionist William Lane. It was edited by May Cameron (later Dame Mary Gilmore). [RBS 307.7 COS]

hastily to raise money for the families of union leaders given harsh sentences in Saint Helena prison in Moreton Bay. Lane had earlier maintained an interest in utopian communities such as the communal settlement in Topolbampo in Mexico and Robert Owens's, "Icaria" community. In late 1894 Lane led a band of 220 settlers to Paraguay to form the New Australia colony. His belief in teetotalism did not sit well with men used to drinking alcohol. In July 1894 the community split, with a new site at nearby Cosme. The State Library holds a substantial collection of their publication, the *Cosme Monthly*.

Lane wrote another dystopian serialised novel, which appeared in the radical *Boomerang* newspaper, entitled *White or yellow? A story of the race-war of A.D. 1908* (1888). This was a cultural precursor to the fantasy of Australia in 2050 which appears in the more recent publication *Pauline Hanson: The truth: on Asian immigration, the Aboriginal question, the gun debate and the future of Australia* (1997).

Other dreamers imagined utopian futures. Francis Adams corrected the proofs of his socialist dream, *Songs of the army of the night* in his house called "Paradise" in Red Hill. Unlike his contemporaries, Adams was an admirer of Chinese civilisation. The utopian writer, "Austin South", also inspired by Henry George, presented a different future vision of Queensland with electrified cities free from class warfare and poverty in the year 2095 with "electric flying machines" as a form of transport. The two volume fantasy novel, *The curse and its cure* (1894) by the eccentric physician, entomologist and manufacturer of paw-paw ointment Dr Thomas Lucas, envisaged a ruined Brisbane in 2000 that was rebuilt in 2200 on the basis of Christian love, peace and prosperity. His fervent teetotalism and belief in natural medicines would have struck a chord in William Lane.

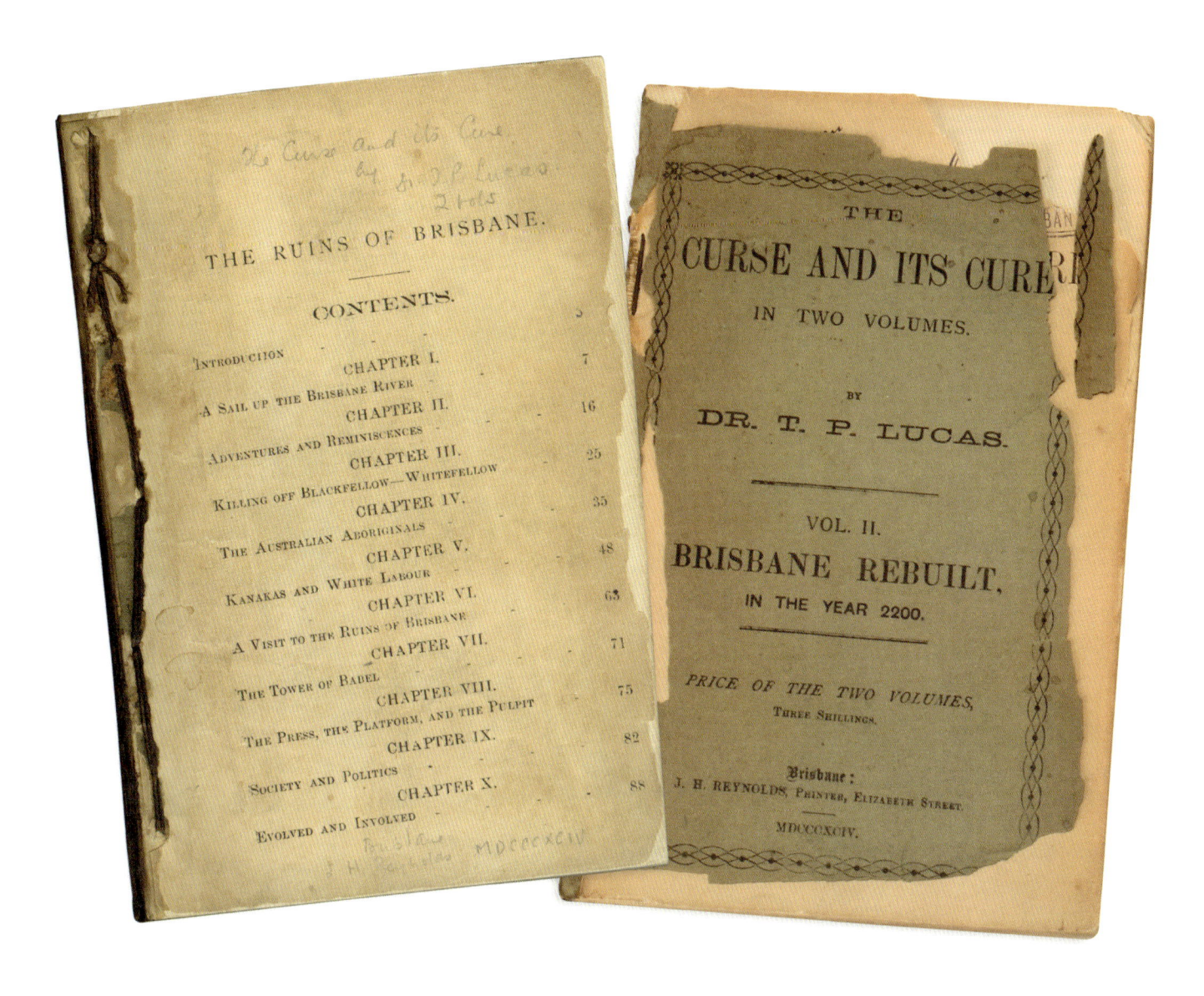

Writers like Steele Rudd (Arthur Hoey Davis) addressed current problems of rural poverty in his *On our selection* stories and through his *Steele Rudd's Magazine* begun in Brisbane in 1904. It championed authors like Barbara Baynton, Henry Lawson, Queenslander Vance Palmer and cartoonist Phil May. With his advocacy of Australian uniqueness, his stationery contained a kookaburra logo. By 1924, the Queensland Authors and Artists Association recognised Rudd's pre-eminence. His self-published book *The miserable clerk* (1926), with its cover by Percy Lindsay, recounted his own miserable days in the Brisbane Sheriff's Office. The book was a notable failure and was not even catalogued as part of his estate in 1935.

Queensland was a society that witnessed global landmarks. Lane would have been surprised to learn that the world's first labor government was sworn-in in Queensland in December 1899. Lasting only four days, it was a harbinger for a number of notable milestones, such as the election of Fred Paterson as the only Communist Party member of parliament in the British Commonwealth and the election of Liberal Neville Bonner as the first Indigenous Senator. In February 1912, the world's first general strike broke out in Brisbane over the issue of whether tram workers could wear

Above Science fiction novel, *The curse and its cure*, by Thomas Pennington Lucas, 1894. This strange work was published in two parts, the first a "dystopian" novel entitled *The ruins of Brisbane in the year 2000* and its utopian sequel *Brisbane rebuilt in the year 2200*. [RBJ A823.2 luc]

154 | Between the covers

Right Illuminated Address tendered to Arthur Morgan, Premier of Queensland, conveying the gratitude of the women of Queensland in relation to the granting of women's suffrage, July 1905. [ACC 6223]

Below Photograph of Arthur Hoey Davis and fellow members of the Committee of the Queensland Authors and Artists Association, together with a letter by Davis, relating to the magazine *Lone Hand*. [ACC 6411; OM 82-59]

> "In February 1912, the world's first general strike broke out in Brisbane over the issue of whether tram workers could wear their union badges on their uniforms."

their union badges on their uniforms. The issue of workers rights was taken up by seamstress Emma Miller, who helped form the first Brisbane Women's Union in 1890 as well as organise for the Australian Workers Union.

A strong supporter of the 1891 striking shearers, Miller also championed electoral reform. With existing plural voting on the basis of property ownership, she campaigned for universal suffrage from 1894 when she was appointed chair of the Women's Equal Franchise Association. The suffrage movement, supported by progressive men and women, was split between those like Elizabeth Brentnall and Women's Christian Temperance Union leader Margaret Ogg, who wished to maintain property qualifications as a condition of voting, and those like Liberal parliamentarian Charles Power (later a high court judge) and Sarah Bailey who wanted adult white franchise. With adult suffrage for European voters federally in 1902, Queensland waited until 1905 when the Morgan-Kidston Government amended the Electoral Act. The State Library holds an illuminated address presented to Premier Arthur Morgan by the Women of Queensland in acknowledgment of his role in securing women's suffrage.

This harmony between Labor and Liberals joined in coalition in 1905 was long since over when the 1912 General Strike erupted. Hard-line Premier Digby Denham, believing that Queensland was in a "state of siege and ... a state of war", wanted to deploy armed sailors from a British warship and a German vessel as well as Federal troops. As tensions mounted, Denham enrolled thousands of special constables including artist Lloyd Rees, University of Queensland Registrar

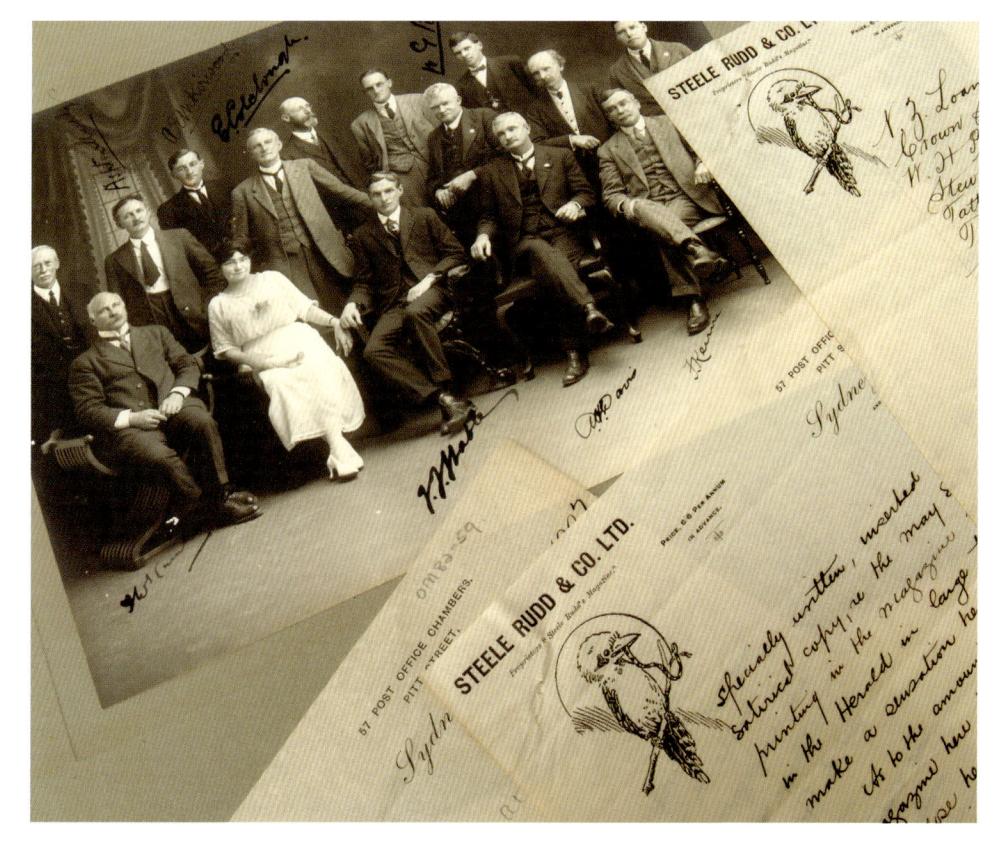

Dreamers and yarners | 155

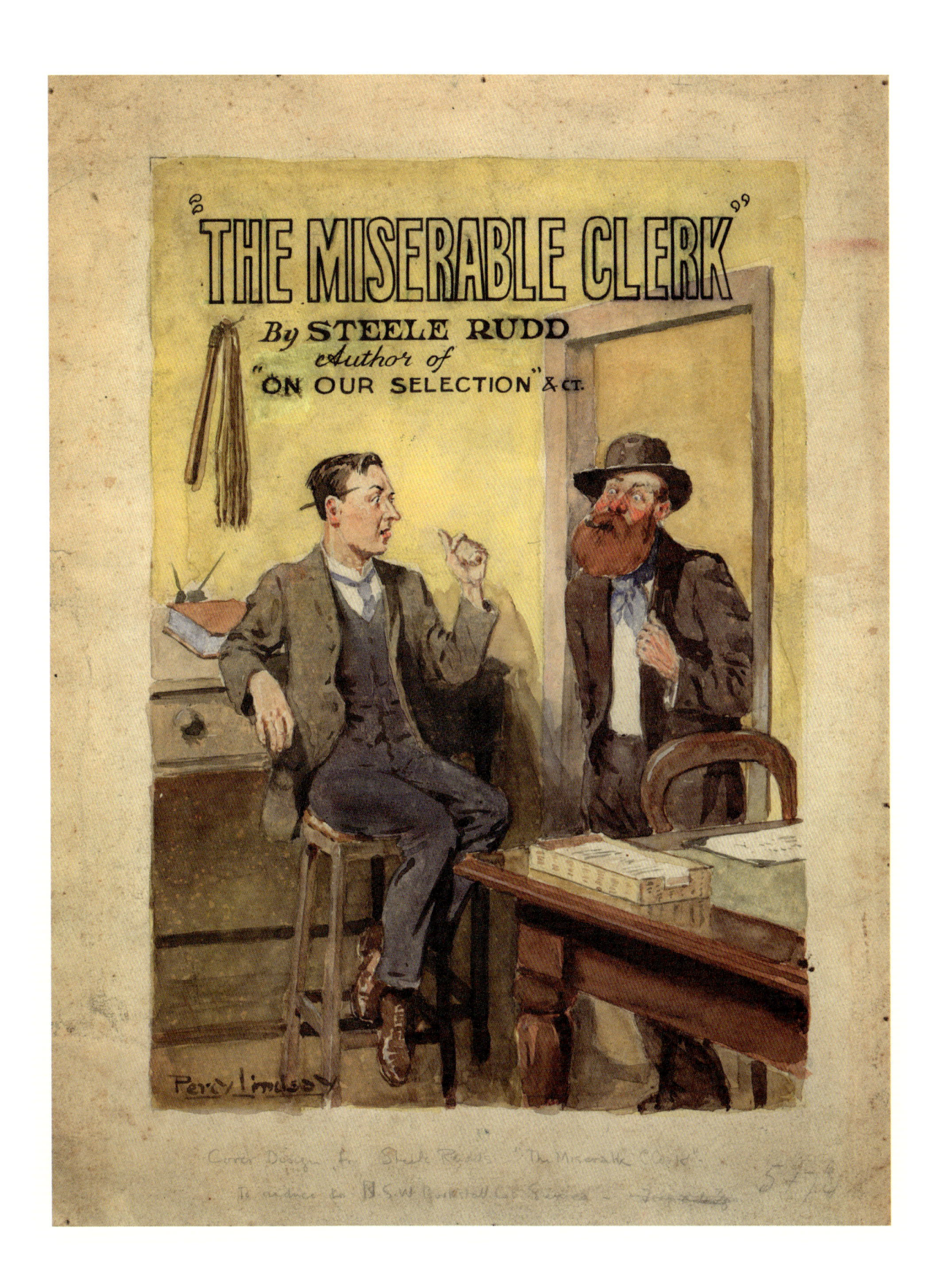

This page Original cover illustration by Percy Lindsay for Steele Rudd's book *The miserable clerk*, an account of the author's early career working in the Brisbane Sheriff's Office. It is the only book that the author had to publish himself and it lay forgotten for almost 40 years until reprinted in the 1970s. [ACC 6175]

> *Kate Dickson's book, Emma's umbrella, commissioned for the centenary of women's suffrage in 2005, shows Miller's trademark accessory floating across contemporary Brisbane, surveying the vast changes.*

Above *Emma's umbrella*, by Kate Dickson, a unique movable book commissioned by the State Library of Queensland for an exhibition to celebrate the centenary of women's suffrage, Brisbane 2005. [RBH MON DIC]

Francis Cumbrae-Stewart and the Brisbane Valley vigilante Boer War veterans, the Legion of Frontiersmen, the so-called "Prickly Pear Specials". Mounted police armed with fixed bayonets, rifles and swords faced demonstrators through the streets of Brisbane. Union leader Emma Miller's actions on the Black Friday march of 2 February 1912, when several workers were reportedly killed, showed quick thinking when she stuck her hat pin in Police Commissioner Cahill's posterior. Her statue with raised umbrella now stands in King George Square. Kate Dickson's book, *Emma's umbrella*, commissioned for the centenary of women's suffrage in 2005, shows Miller's trademark accessory floating across contemporary Brisbane, surveying the vast changes.

The election of the Ryan Labor Government in 1915 witnessed profound structural changes in Queensland. The introduction of state enterprises such as publicly-owned canneries, butcher shops, fisheries, hotels, sugar mills, pastoral properties and mines, was part of a dream to improve the living standard of all Queenslanders. The proposal by his successor EG Theodore to build a state smelter at Bowen witnessed the curtailment of the socialist experiment, as entrepreneurs like Sir Robert Philp feared the emergence of a militant industrial class. Only the State Government Insurance Office (now Suncorp) has survived.

Labor Premier Theodore's presence at a radical meeting displaying the slogan 'Workers of the World Unite' sat uneasily with his more pragmatic political philosophy. Although he was an advocate of workers' rights, he also was an entrepreneur. He would not have endorsed the views of radical critics like the future archaeologist Vere Gordon Childe, whose polemical denunciation of the conservatism of Theodore's government in *How Labour governs* (1923) did not really consider how power requires skilful compromise.

As Federal Treasurer in the Scullin Government, Theodore's talents as an innovative economic manager were destroyed by the 1930 Queensland Royal Commission to investigate his holding in the Mungana and Chillagoe state-owned mines. Nationalist parliamentarian and journalist Hubert Sizer, his old

Dreamers and yarners   157

Left EG Theodore had an imposing presence and was an impressive figure. As deputy to Labor Premier TJ Ryan and as Premier from 1919 to 1925, he sought to open up Queensland's resources and to challenge existing monopolies through the establishment of state enterprises, including timber and sugar mills, cattle stations and butcher shops. [Image No. 13619]

Above EG Theodore (1884–1950) at a workers rally, c. 1920. [Image No. 160265]

Below Original label for the "State" Cannery, one of a number of enterprises which were established by the Queensland Government in the years after the First World War to "provide a fair deal" for Queensland producers and consumers. [Ephemera Collection]

"Ideas given serious consideration were to divert the waters of the Tully, Burdekin and Clarke rivers inland, along with creating a series of dams on the Cooper River."

Above Albums owned by Dr John JC Bradfield documenting every facet of the construction of Brisbane's great project of the Depression years, the Story Bridge, 1935–40. [Albums APU 26-29]

opponent from the conscription fights of the First World War and the abolition of the Legislative Council in 1922, used his skills to discredit Theodore. Ideological fights over conscription were strong in Queensland where the Ryan Government was anti-conscription. On 9 July 1917 there had been a serious fight over conscription between loyalist women and members of the Women's Peace Army at the Brisbane School of Arts, (the site of the Servants Home, originally designed in 1865) and the outcome still resounded a dozen years later. Jack Lindsay's novel *The blood vote* (1937) attempted to capture the atmosphere of these struggles.

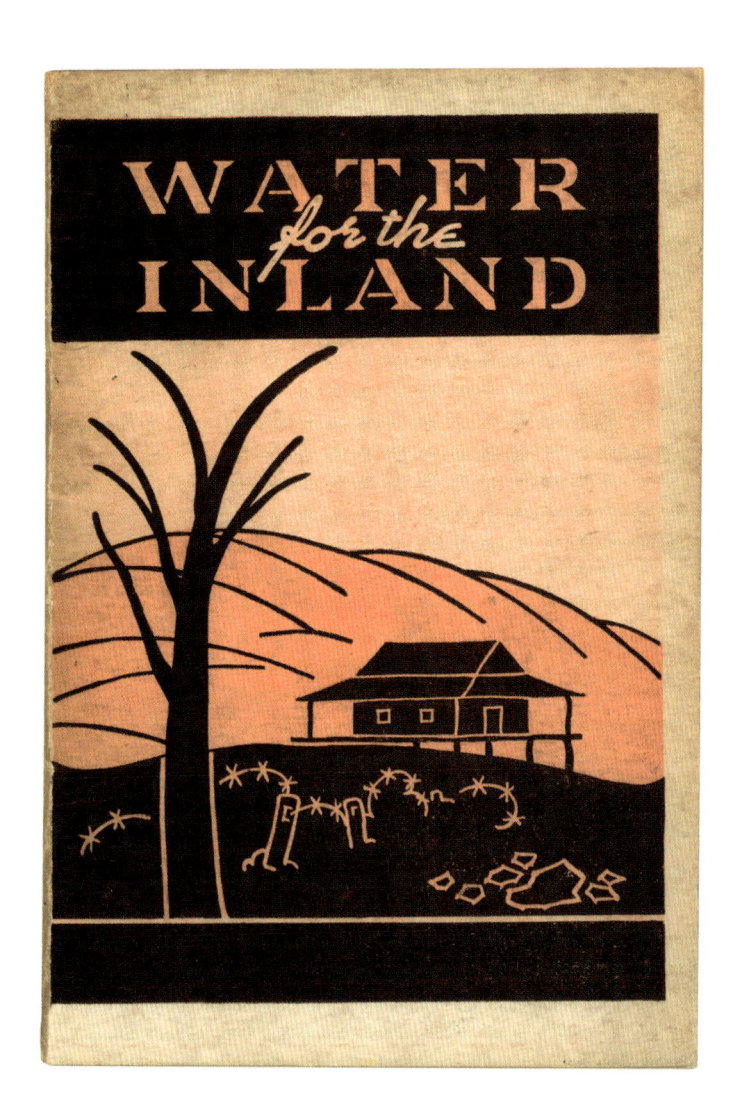

Leaving parliament, Theodore went into partnership with Frank Packer to found the *Australian Women's Weekly*. Novelist Vance Palmer's trilogy, commencing with *Golconda* (1948), captured the worth of a visionary like Theodore.

Other visionaries dreamed fantastical, grandiose schemes to improve the lives of Queenslanders. Dr John Job Crew Bradfield, the engineer who designed the Sydney Harbour Bridge, was appointed engineer in charge of constructing the Story Bridge from Kangaroo Point to Bowen Terrace in Brisbane in 1934. The State Library holds a series of presentation albums documenting the construction of his achievement. From his days as a young engineer in Sydney working on sewerage and storm water drains in the mid-1890s, Bradfield had been fascinated by the deployment of water resources. His most ambitious plan was to divert the waters of the Tully, Burdekin and Clarke rivers inland, as well as creating a series of dams on the Cooper River. His ideas were given serious consideration. The State Library holds a number of these assessments including FRV Timbury's *The battle for the inland* (1944) and Albert William Noakes's *Water for the inland* (1947). Other writers, without the technical reputation of Bradfield, came up with equally grandiose schemes. Ion Idriess, the author of

Above left *Water for the inland* by AW Noakes, outlining conditions in the Queensland outback and the principles of the ambitious Bradfield Water Scheme, 1947. [P 333.913]

Above right Entrepreneur Christopher Skase, became an adopted Queenslander in 1985 when he moved the headquarters of his Qintex Group to Brisbane. His flamboyant business career floundered in the early 1990s, when *Courier-Mail* artist, Tony Champ produced this cartoon. [Image No. 59937]

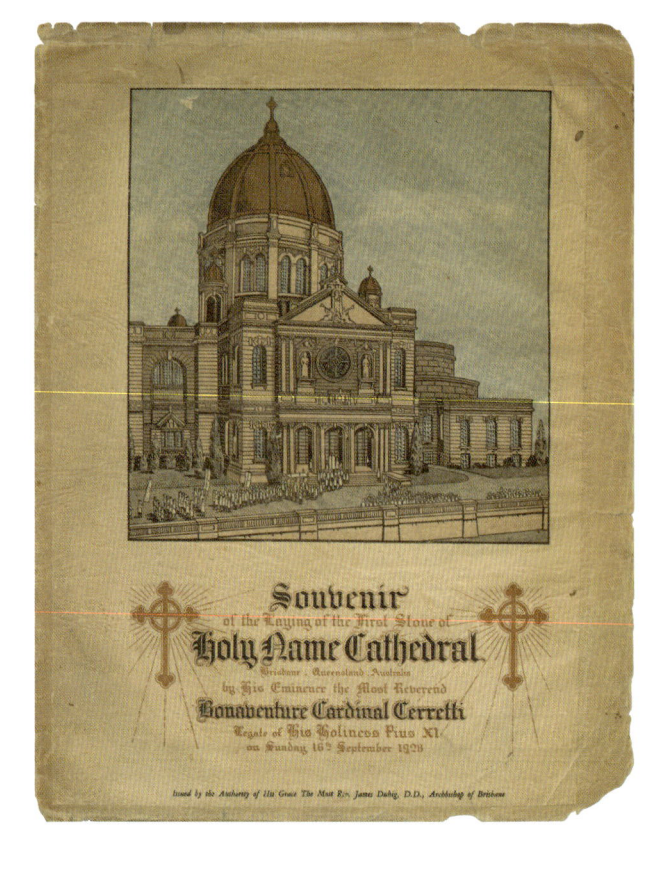

Above left Archbishop James Duhig, whose dream was to build a grand Catholic cathedral in the southern hemisphere. [Image No. 195199]

Above right Artist's conception of the proposed Holy Name Cathedral, which was never constructed. [Q 282.9431 SOU]

Inset Commemorative medal issued to celebrate the laying of the foundation stone for Brisbane's Holy Name Cathedral on Sunday 16 September 1928. [ACC 6570]

Lassiter's last ride (1931) and *Flynn of the inland* (1932), promoted his ideas about water for central Australia in *The great boomerang* (1941). Like Sir Thomas Mitchell's dream of a great port city at Normanton and Sir Thomas McIlwraith's determination to construct a railway to the Gulf of Carpentaria, these ambitious schemes were costly and impractical.

Other dreams, some in service to the glory of God, failed to eventuate. Archbishop James Duhig, renowned for his construction of Catholic schools and churches from 1917, conceived the plan for a magnificent cathedral in Brisbane. The State Library holds the commemorative medal to celebrate the laying of the foundation stone for the Holy Name Cathedral in September 1928, along with the souvenir program. A drawing of the proposed structure, which was never realised, shows a grand edifice modelled in part on Saint Peter's Basilica in Rome.

Other entrepreneurs with big dreams were more concerned about material advancement. Sir Bruce Small's development of the Gold Coast on American models, alongside Alfred Grant's developments, coincided with Brisbane Lord Mayor Clem Jones's vision of modern town planning. Christopher Skase, in the 1980s, took ideas of development to unimagined heights of folly.

Skases's Quintex consortium, with the Mirage developments on the Gold Coast and Port Douglas and ownership of Channel 7, faltered as he tried to purchase MGM Studios in Hollywood. His ostentatious lifestyle and his abandonment of creditors when he fled to Majorca saw his reputation destroyed.

The State Library's collections contain rich and diverse holdings documenting the causes of those who dreamed of better futures, whether material, creative or spiritual. The aspirations and battles in everyday life of ordinary people are captured in the many yarns held in the collections.

Chapter ten
The art of the book

By Erin Evans and Dianne Byrne

Between the covers

> "The history of the book is a story of both artistic and technical innovations, driven by the desire to document the world and to create a lasting record."

Opening image *The grub in the wood of time* with text by Mark O'Connor, made in Canberra and Paris, 1989. Four copies of this book were created, each handwritten by the author. The whole was a cooperative effort involving many talents. French-based bookbinder Sun Evrard conceived the idea, Australian artist John Tonkin designed the construction and Master of Woodcraft Frank Wiesner supplied the wooden pages. [RBHMON EVR]

Below Fragment of bandage from an Egyptian mummy with four lines of hieratic writing (a cursive rendering of hieroglyphs), c. 300–330 BC [RB 411.7 2nd cent. BC].

In one of his essays *Detached thoughts on books and reading* (1823) Charles Lamb confessed that there were certain types of books that for him were "false saints", mere bibliographic pretenders. His list included court calendars, directories, pocket books, almanacs and scientific treatises. With these exceptions, he could take up any volume: "I love to lose myself in other men's minds. When I am not walking, I am reading".

If Lamb were to wander today through the shelves of the State Library of Queensland, he would see not only the great iconic works that have shaped our view of the world and expanded our thinking, he would be astonished to see works that redefine and stretch the idea of what constitutes a book.

The history of the book is a story of both artistic and technical innovations, driven by the desire to document the world and to create a lasting record. Over the centuries, momentous changes have been made in pursuit of excellence and personal satisfaction, as well as portability, access to information and the lowering of production costs. The development of the book reflects the sociocultural, political and economic changes that have been part of society.

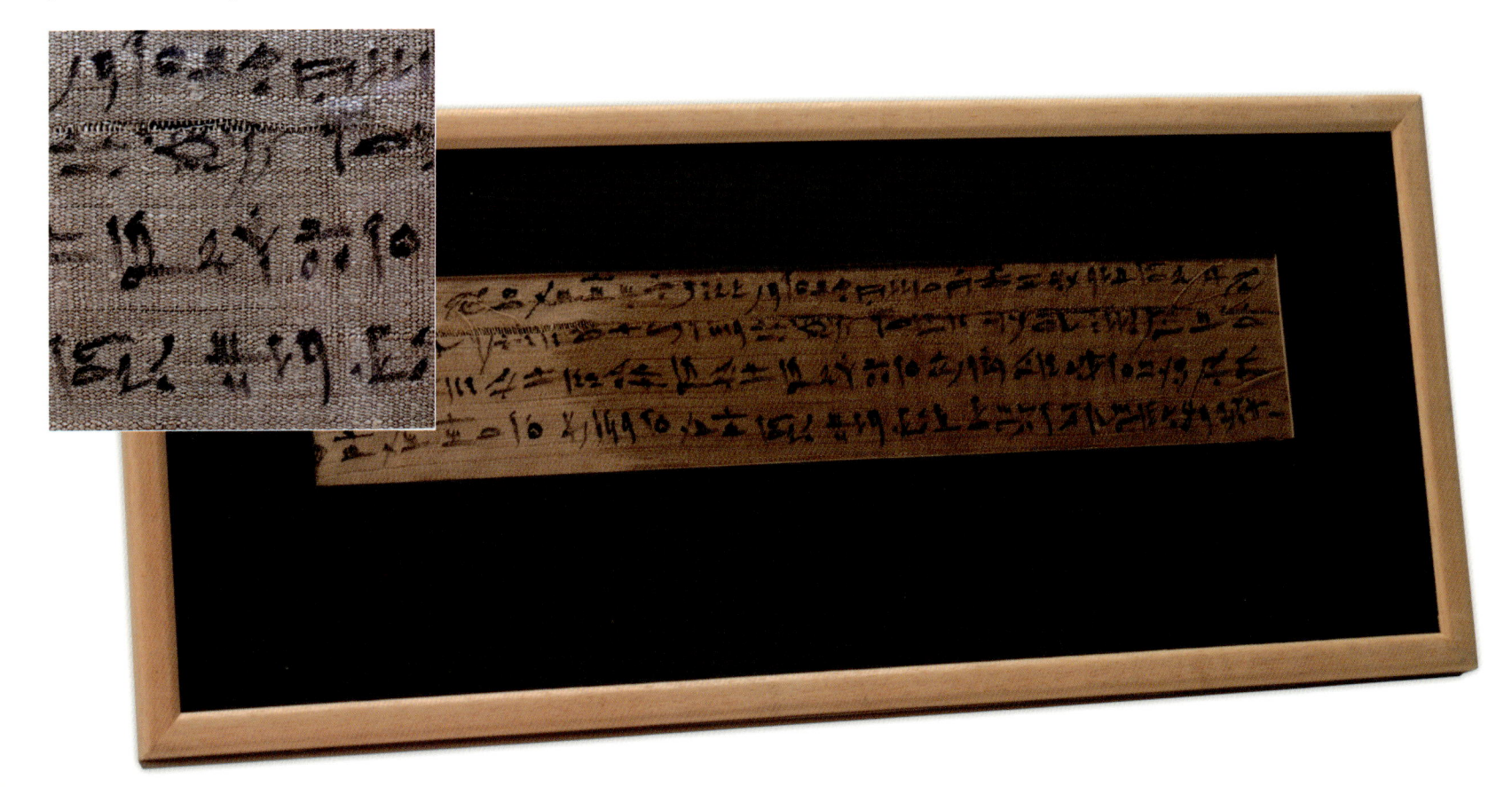

Writing appeared in the Middle East around 4,000 BC with the Sumerians who first utilised a series of pictograms, which laid the foundation for ideograms and symbols representing specific sounds. By 3,000 BC they had developed a form of writing known as cuneiform, characterised by wedged shaped linear markings. Around the same time, the Egyptians adopted the idea of pictorial writing and this developed into phonetic hieroglyphs, like the letters of the alphabet. The oldest materials in the State Library's collection are examples of Sumerian cuneiform clay tablets and Egyptian scripts carved into stone and inscribed on linen mummy wrappings and a fragment of papyrus.

Small rolls of papyrus or parchment, and longer book rolls or *volumen* were the principal means for recording and storing literary works until around the second century AD when the introduction of the codex (sheets folded and stitched together), brought written works closer to the form that we know today as the book. The codex changed the way individuals related to the written word. For the first time it was possible to locate a precise point in a text, leading directly to the advent of the table of contents. It further allowed the reader to place the text on a table and make notes while reading the text.

After the fall of the Roman Empire in the fifth century AD, monasteries stored books and preserved them from destruction. The copying and production of books was an intensive activity done as an act of worship and intellectual relationship with God. The monks produced exquisite illuminated texts that, while beautiful, did not engage the outside world or advance the education of the common man. The revival of cities in Europe from the twelfth century changed the conditions of book production and also extended the influence of books. The establishment of the first European universities, beginning with Bologna in 1119 AD, created a spirit of interest and inquisitiveness about the world and increased literacy. Universities facilitated an intellectual renaissance that brought about major advances in music, art and architecture. Book production was centred on these institutions, marking a change from the monastical period.

The introduction of papermaking and the invention of the printing press using movable type by Johannes Gutenberg

Above Among the oldest items in the State Library's collection are a Sumerian tablet with cuneiform text pressed into clay, **(right)** [RB 411.7 1850 BC] and a Roman marble block **(left)** [RB 411.7 2nd century AD]

Between the covers

> The State Library's collections are rich in publications capturing the increasing curiosity and exploration of the natural world from the 1600s onwards.

Left Sixteenth century woodblock depicting the Cornflower (*Cyanus maior*), one of a set designed for Pietro Andrea Mattioli's herbal *Commentarii in libros sex Pedacii Dioscoridis de medica materia*. Mattioli was personal physician to Ferdinand I, Archduke of Austria. His great work was first published in Italian in 1544, but the woodblock pictured here was used for the Czech translation of 1562, the German translation of 1563 and the Latin edition of 1565. It was acquired by the State Library in 1989. [RB 581.945 15—]

Below *Laertii Diogenis vitae et sententiae eorum qui in philosophia probati fuerunt* or *Lives of the philosophers*, by Diogenes Laetius printed in Venice in 1475. This is the oldest printed book in the State Library of Queensland's collection and the oldest printed book known to be held in Queensland. [RB 180 1475]

(c. 1455) heralded the entry of books into an industrial age and created a paradigm shift in the way information was transferred. The labour, time and costs involved in book production were dramatically reduced, resulting in increased availability and distribution. The oldest printed book in the State Library's collections is *Laertii Diogenis vitae et sententiae eorum qui in philosophia probati fuerunt (Diogenes Laertius' lives of the philosophers)*, published in 1475 in Venice by French engraver and typographer Nicholas Jenson. It is one of the first books to use the Roman typeface that Jenson perfected. The capital letters of the text are hand-drawn in the decorative manner formerly used on manuscripts.

The woodblock, *Cornflower*, held in the State Library, is one of the set designed for the Czech edition of Pietro Mattioli's herbal, *Commentarii in libros sex Pedacii Dioscoridis de medica materia* (1562) re-used in 1563 and 1565. The technique of woodblock printing, where the original image is hand carved into wooden blocks, had been employed in Europe since medieval times but reached a pinnacle with botanical illustrations as exemplified in the Mattioli blocks. Although the blocks could be reused many times, they were labour-intensive to produce and were prone to breakage.

The State Library's collections are rich in publications capturing the increasing curiosity and exploration of the natural world from the 1600s onwards. Among the most notable are early atlases and cosmologies of Gerhard Mercator (1612) and Peter Heylyn (1665). Heylyn was a believer in the counterpoise theory that a great southern continent must exist to balance the weight of the continents in the Northern Hemisphere. He also had a keen interest in utopian literature and in imaginary journeys, which were a favourite form of writing in the seventeenth and eighteenth centuries. The State Library has a number of examples of these in various European languages, including works by Captain Siden (1677–79) and Gabriel de Foigny (1693) in French, and Zaccaria Seriman (1764) in Italian.

The many works on explorations in the southern seas convey daring travels and unparalleled discoveries. The State Library holds the accounts drawn from the journals of Commodore Byron, Captains Carteret, Wallis and Cook, as well as the papers of Joseph Banks published in 1773. There also is an exceptionally fine copy of *The Journal of a voyage to New South Wales with sixty-five plates of nondescript animals, birds, lizards, serpents, curious cones*

Above Theologian and historian Peter Heylyn originally published his *Cosmographie, in four books containing the chronographie and historie of the whole world etc.* in 1652. This is the third edition, produced in London in 1665. It contains descriptions of Europe, Africa, Asia and America and is illustrated with large engraved folding maps. [RBQ 909.6 hey]

166 Between the covers

Cassowary of New South Wales.
London, Published Dec. 29, 1789 by J. Debrett.

A Kangaroo.
London, Published as the Act directs Dec. 29, 1789 by J. Debrett.

This page *The Journal of a voyage to New South Wales with sixty-five plates of nondescript animals, birds, lizards, serpents, curious cones of trees and other natural products* by John White, published in 1790. White arrived with the First Fleet in 1788. The flora and fauna which he collected around Sydney were used as the basis for the engravings in this work. [RBHMON WHI]

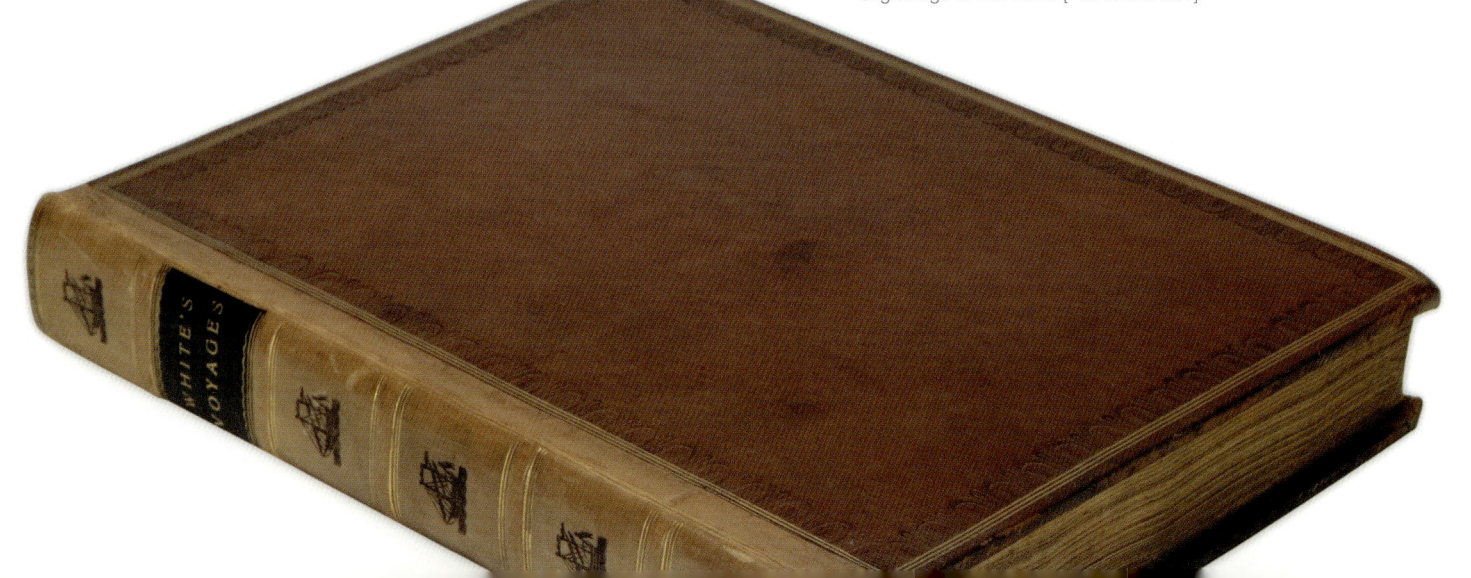

of trees and other natural products by John White (1790). This book is the first major work on Australia's natural history and is illustrated with some of the earliest recorded images by Europeans of the dingo, kangaroo, possum, emu and sulphur-crested cockatoo. Interestingly, many of the images were created from preserved skins, rather than from observation of the live animals.

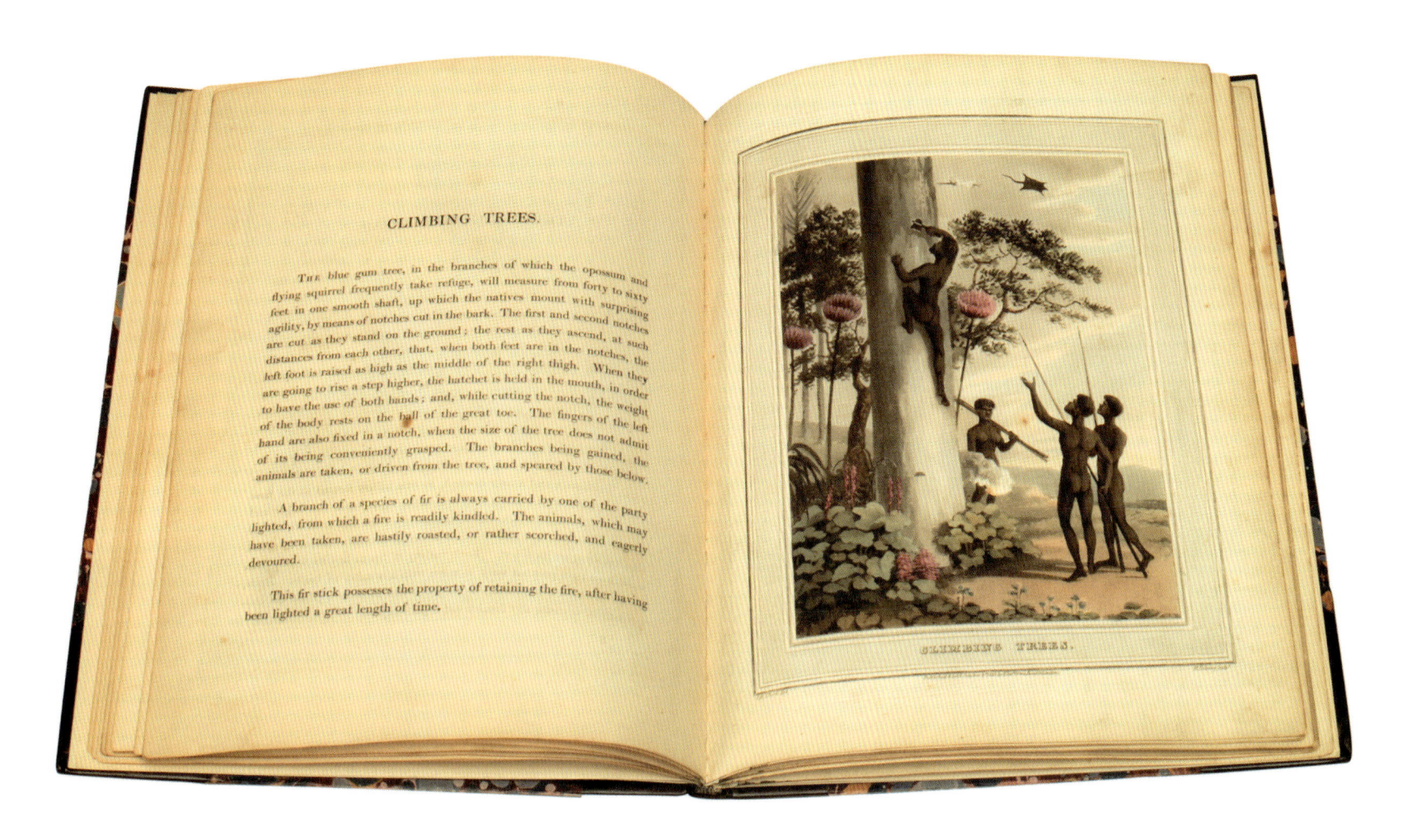

Another rarity is the first known work on the Aboriginal peoples of Australia. *Field sports, &c., &c., of the native inhabitants of New South Wales* (1813), by John Heaviside Clark, contains a series of beautiful hand-coloured aquatints depicting the life of the Indigenous inhabitants, especially showing them on hunting and fishing expeditions. The original sketches for the work have been attributed to John Lewin, who was probably Australia's first professional artist.

The unique flora of Australia was also a source of much wonder in the eighteenth and early nineteenth centuries, when many landmark works were produced, which today are among the State Library's treasures. The pinnacle is Joseph Banks' *Florilegium* consisting of over 700 large colour engravings of specimens collected during Cook's first voyage around the world in HMS *Endeavour*, 1768–71. Banks was an entrepreneur who sought medical applications for new plant species and personally financed the exploration's botanical research. At least 743 engraved copperplates of the specimens were made between 1771 and 1784; however, due to escalating costs and Banks' waning interest, the printing part of the project met with delays. Most of the exquisite engravings were not published until 1980.

Above *Field sports, &c., &c., of the native inhabitants of New South Wales* by John Heaviside Clark, London, Edward Orme, 1813. This book has been described as "the first known work solely devoted to the Aboriginal people of Australia" and contains 10 coloured plates depicting Indigenous people hunting, fishing and taking part in a corroboree. [RBHMON CLA]

Above Joseph Banks' *Florilegium* consists of over 700 large colour plates of botanical specimens collected during Captain Cook's first voyage around the world in HMS *Endeavour*, 1768–71. Watercolours from the original specimens were executed by Sydney Parkinson and engraved between 1772 and 1784. In 1980, the original copper plates were used to produce a new and complete edition. Plates 244, 254 and 285; [RB 581.99 1980-1990]

> *The unique flora of Australia was also a source of much wonder in the eighteenth and nineteenth centuries.*

The State Library also is fortunate to possess James Edward Smith's *A specimen of the botany of New Holland* (1793) and the wonderful hand-coloured floras of Robert Sweet (1827–28) and Ferdinand Bauer (1760–1826).

There are as well, beautiful works which illustrate the European world, both natural and urban from the 1700s. *Curtis's Botanical Magazine*, first published in 1787, is the oldest continuously published journal with coloured illustrations in the world. One of the great colour plate books of the nineteenth century, *Microcosm of London* (1808–10) by Rudolf Ackermann is also held in the State Library's collection. The 104 hand-coloured aquatint plates (from drawings by Augustus Pugin and Thomas Rowlandson) depict the life and architecture of London at the time.

The nineteenth century was a great age for book production, following the technical advances of the Industrial Revolution. By the 1850s, books which previously had been purchased in paper covers and custom-bound by craftsmen in small workshops, could be mass produced and offered in standardised bindings. Yet, just as access to cheap popular printed works was growing, a new generation of artists were emerging who were eager to bring back old crafts and to preserve and advance existing arts. One of these was illustrator and naturalist Henry Noel Humphreys (1810–79) who studied medieval manuscripts during his youth in Italy, and subsequently brought his passion for early illuminations to books which he produced using the printing technique of chromolithography. The State Library holds a copy of Humphreys' work *The origin and progress of the art of writing* (1853) which features an elaborate binding of papier-mâché and plaster of Paris. Also in the collection is an 1870 edition of Henry Kendall's

The art of the book | 169

Above *The Microcosm of London* by Rudolph Ackermann, was published in 26 parts from 1808 to 1810, and contains hand-coloured aquatint plates depicting the life and architecture of London. Much of the work on the *Microcosm* was reputedly carried out by French émigré women and children. [RB 914.211808]

Left *The Botanical Magazine or the flower garden displayed in which the most ornamental foreign plants, cultivated in the open ground, the greenhouse, and the stove, will be accurately represented in their natural colours* by William Curtis. This is the first of the popular gardening magazines which began to appear in the late eighteenth century. The State Library holds 12 volumes, printed in London and published between 1787 and 1798. [RB 580.5]

Above Details of two plates from *The Botanical Magazine*.

> *The modern private press movement maintains the tradition of producing bold creative works. The State Library is active in pursuing new examples both from Australia and overseas ...*

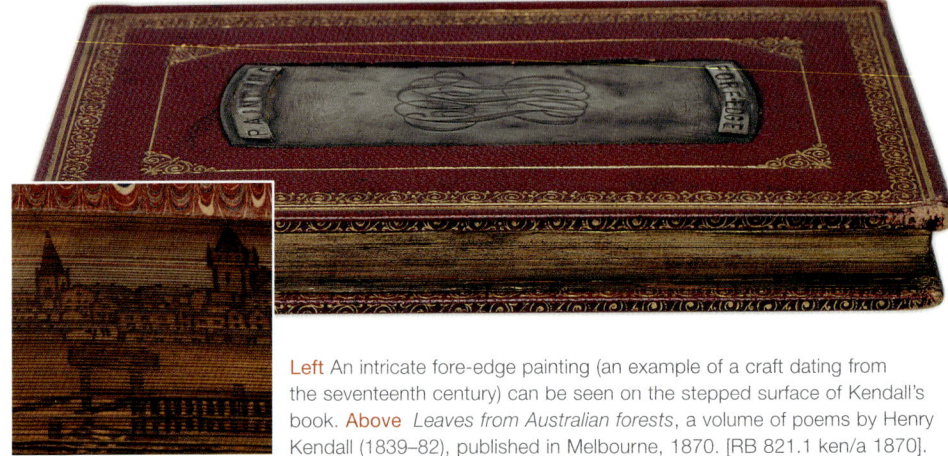

Left An intricate fore-edge painting (an example of a craft dating from the seventeenth century) can be seen on the stepped surface of Kendall's book. **Above** *Leaves from Australian forests*, a volume of poems by Henry Kendall (1839–82), published in Melbourne, 1870. [RB 821.1 ken/a 1870].

Above *The origin and progress of the art of writing* by Henry Noel Humphreys, published in London in 1853. The black papier-mâché covers are laid over a red parchment ground. [RB 411.09 1853]

Leaves from Australian forests with hand-marbled endpapers and a superb example of fore-edge painting, originally a seventeenth century art.

The ultimate exemplar of the movement to preserve ancient design and printing traditions and to bring these to a new audience as part of daily life was William Morris, who established the Kelmscott Press in 1891. Using his own typefaces and watermarks, and paper and inks made to his specifications, Morris published classics such as Chaucer's *Canterbury tales* as well as new works, including his own socialist treatise *News from nowhere*. His ideals of the appreciation of beauty continued to be endorsed by later generations. During the 1930s Depression, Northumberland miners treasured a copy of his *News from nowhere* even when they were forced to sell most of their other belongings.

Morris's example was followed by Jack Lindsay, PR Stephensen and John Kirtley who established the Fanfrolico Press, first in Sydney and then in London, in 1926. One of the valuable works held by the State Library is the 1926 edition of the anti-war comedy *Lysistrata*, by Aristophanes (411 BC), handsomely illustrated by Jack's father, Norman. In the space of six years, the press published 40 books, including editions of Kenneth Slessor's *Earth visitors* (1927), Nietzsche's *The anti-Christ* (1928) and the *Complete works of Petronius* (1927).

John Kirtley went on to establish his own Mountainside Press in Ferntree Gully in Victoria, where he produced an edition of RD Fitzgerald's *Heemskerck Shoals* (1949), recognised as one of finest pieces of hand printing done in Australia, although at the time it was not a commercial success. Eighty-five copies were produced on two types of paper with a two-page hand coloured map. The State Library is fortunate to hold a copy on each type of paper, as many unbound copies were used as underlay on the printer's floor, and others were employed to light the morning fires in the printing workshop.

The modern private press movement maintains the

Above left and top right *Lysistrata* by Aristophanes (411 BC) an anti-war comedy, translated by Jack Lindsay and illustrated by Norman Lindsay. This copy was published by the Fanfrolico Press in London in 1926. [RBHLIN FAN] **Above right** Norman Lindsay (at left), with brother Lionel, c.1903. [Image No. BC 988]

Above *Sangkuriang: (a legend from West Java)*, with collographs by Arthur Boyd and woodcuts by Indra Deigan, 1993. The epic oedipal story of a young man who kills his father and unknowingly falls in love with his mother, served as the inspiration for a dramatic series of illustrations depicting the beauty and awesome force of nature. [RBHMON DEI]

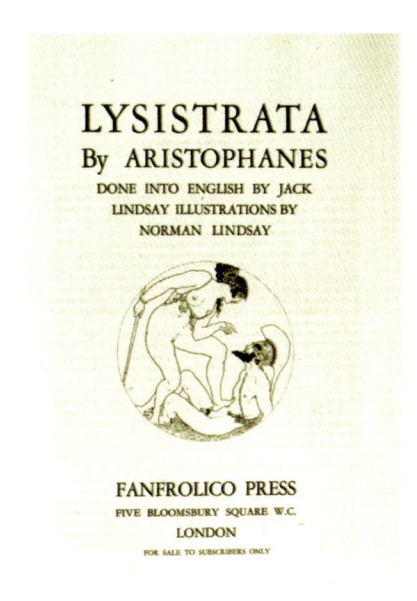

tradition of producing bold creative works. The State Library is active in pursuing new examples both from Australia and overseas, currently holding over 1,300 Australian privately printed titles. Recent acquisitions include works from Electio Editions in Melbourne and Locks' Press, which began in Brisbane but now publishes in Ontario in Canada. Wayzgoose Press is another contemporary Australian private press known for employing inventive typography to interpret and present texts by Australian poets. The State Library holds all of the Wayzgoose titles including *Dada: kampfen um leben und tod: a prose poem* (1996) by James H Duke, "Australia's first Dadaist".

Related to the private press movement are artists' books that could best be described as artworks in book format, or artworks which have their origin in the form or concept of the book. The term was coined in the 1950s to describe works which were produced by conceptual artists, for whom the book form provided a readily reproducible, cheap and identifiable vehicle for their ideas. Artists choose to make artists' books for many reasons, among them the intimacy of the relationship of the book with its reader and the sequential nature of reading. The most common Australian artists' book today is a limited edition handmade book. It may have images without words or words without images. It may assume a sculptural form or have a lyrical or poetical intent. Artists' books come in all forms, shapes and sizes and are made out of a variety of materials, including wood, handmade paper and stone. They interpret the concept of the book in some way, or use the format of the book to explore their chosen subject. These "books as art" aim to engage and challenge the beholder. The State Library owns around 900 of these unique, surprising, and often provocative items, of which the following are a sample.

Sangkuriang: (a legend from West Java) (1993) is an example of a collaborative artists' book which takes as its starting point the traditional Indonesian story of the creation of the Tangkuban Parahu volcano. To illustrate the episodes leading to the spectacular event, Arthur Boyd created ten

172 Between the covers

The art of the book | 173

Opposite (background) *The garden* by Katharine Nix, including the story *Three roses* by Garth Nix, published in a limited edition of 20 copies, Canberra, 2003.

Opposite (inset) The book has a rich, hand-sewn binding and a page marker woven of metallic and cotton thread with glass beads. **(left and centre)** One of the striking watermarked images impressed into rag paper. **(right)** [RBHMON NIX]

Above *Concrete poetry* by Bernadette Crockford, 1996. This book, which takes a concrete poem and uses it to create a concrete form, was designed, handset, printed and bound by Bernadette Crockford in 1996. The triangle opens out to square pages and further transforms into two different sculptural shapes. [RBHMON CRO]

collograph plates, painting thick-setting glue onto thin aluminium sheets. Indra Deigan then designed woodcuts printed from plywood blocks in response to his images. Indra Deigan donated her woodblocks, text blocks, preliminary drawings and proof prints to the library, and the Queensland Library Foundation purchased Boyd's collograph plates, drawings, and proof prints, so that the entire creative process for *Sangkuriang* is documented in the Australian Library of Art.

Katharine Nix's *The garden* (2003) is one of the State Library's most admired artists' books. It was made in collaboration with her writer son, Garth Nix, and the staff of the Edition + Artist Book Studio at the Canberra School of Art, where Nix was artist in residence. The inspiration was Garth Nix's story, *Three roses*, a fable about a medieval garden with magical coloured roses. Linking these images to her own love of Australian native plants, she created a series of large-scale images of flora in the form of watermarks impressed into handmade rag paper.

The medium of metal is the starting point for Paris-born jeweller Pierre Cavalan's untitled artists' book (1988). Enclosed within mahogany covers are pages cut from biscuit tins and oil and tea containers. The images on the tins become the book's content and illustrations.

Bernadette Crockford's *Concrete poetry* (1996) is very different in spirit and structure from the preceding works. A fold-out book in the shape of a triangle which can open out in a variety of ways and changes its structure to resemble different shapes, it represents the culmination of the artist's long search for a form in which to present her poetry.

Judy Watson's *a preponderance of Aboriginal blood* (2005) communicates a confronting message about Australia's Indigenous history. A direct descendant of the Waanyi clan from north-west Queensland, Watson was inspired to make the work after listening to a lecture on the state's disenfranchisement of Aboriginal people. The work consists of an installation of seven copper plates and 16 etchings which reproduce 1940s government documents overlaid with prints of vivid red ink. The artist uses the official records of the era when, under the State Electoral Act people with "a preponderance of aboriginal blood" were not eligible to vote, to graphically demonstrate the effect of the policy of isolation and containment.

174　Between the covers

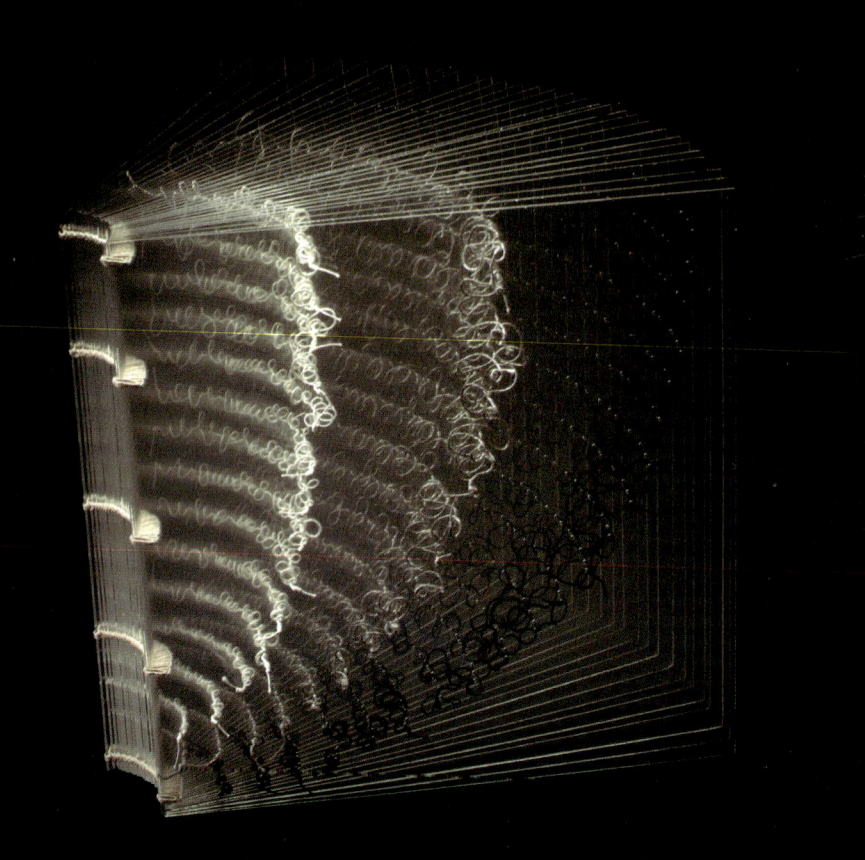

Above Two views of *Vessels*, produced in 2004 by book artist, printmaker and sculptor Adele Outteridge. [RBHMON OUT]

Below The dusky robin, a small bird native to Tasmania, was the inspiration for this altered book by Kylie Stillman, 2004. It is one of a series of open books, all bearing the carved impressions of bird species. [RBHMON STI]

Contemporary Brisbane artist Adele Outteridge's artists' book *Vessels* (2004) uses traditional binding methods to produce an exquisite sculptural piece created by linking individual sheets of perspex. When the book is closed, the threads which bind it come together to form what appears to be text. When the book is opened, the threads stretch out to create three ghostly vessels nestled within each other.

The State Library's collections also contain a number of "altered books", works which have been manipulated to create an object with a completely new aesthetic. For *Bruegel* (1990), Luke Roberts over-painted the words and illustrations in an art book to comment on the way that our knowledge of European art has been informed by reproductions. For *Dusky robin* (2004), Kylie Stillman took a scalpel to an existing book and carved through the pages of the volume an image of a small bird identifiable only by its size and shape. With the text no longer readable, the viewer "sees" the words as the textures and patterns of plumage.

As the element which immediately captures the attention of the book lover, bookbinding is an area where modern craftsmen and artists are venturing far beyond traditional practices and technical skill. Although the craft suffered a great decline after World War II, a group of devotees in Europe brought it back from the brink. The distinguished examples in the State Library attest to the vitality of today's practitioners and serve to refute Charles Lamb's statement that "the better a book is, the less it demands from binding".

Internationally acclaimed Swiss master binder Hugo Peller was one of the leaders of the revival in modern binding, which took place in the 1950s, and built his career on producing works of ravishing beauty and consummate craftsmanship. His binding for *Nahen* (1982) by Hans Erni, includes two sets of colourful morocco slip-cases which are designed to protect the book, but also serve to create a sense of mystery and expectation. German trained Friedhelm Pohlmann studied with Hugo Peller and like him

The art of the book   175

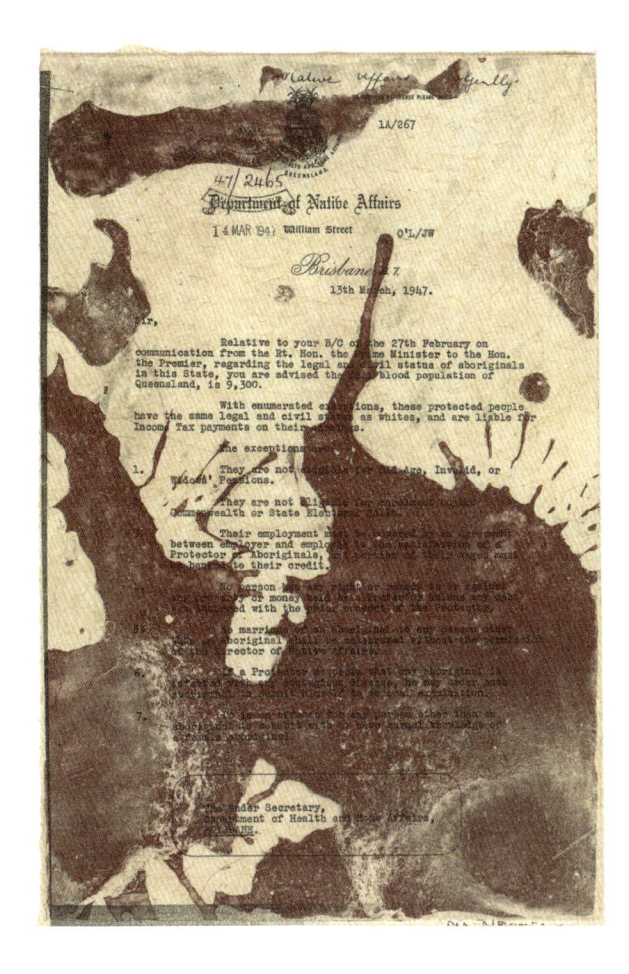

Above *a preponderance of Aboriginal blood* by Judy Watson, Brisbane 2005. This work is one of a unique limited edition of five numbered copies. The State Library's copy contains five artist's proofs, together with an "installation" of seven copper plates and 16 etchings. [RBHMON WAT]

Below An untitled artists' book by jeweller Pierre Cavalan, created in 1998. The metal pages are cut from metal olive oil containers and biscuit and tea tins. The pictures on the tins become the images in the book. [RBHMON CAV]

Left The mahogany covers of Cavalan's book have an attached metal plaque with a still life in relief.

Above *The little hole* by Ron McBurnie and Fred Pohlmann, produced in Queensland in 1996. The book consists of five etchings made by Ron McBurnie and printed by Rochelle Knarston on Arches paper. The book is designed and bound in full emu leather by Friedhelm Pohlmann. The State Library holds copy number one of an edition of 20. [RBHMON MACB]

Above left *How much land does a man need?* A short story by Leo Tolstoy, reprinted in a limited edition by Locks' Press, Brisbane, 1986. This copy was one of ten originally sold in sheets to individual bookbinders. The custom binding by Robin Tait incorporates cane toad skin. [RBHPP LOC]

Above centre *Nahen* by Hans Erni (1909–), published in Solothurn, Switzerland, 1982. This copy is part of a limited edition of 35 and consists of 12 engravings and two original signed drawings in red pen by Erni. It was bound by Hugo Peller. [RB 831.914 ERN/A 1982]

has brought a strong respect for traditional methods and bindings to the works which he now produces in Queensland. *The little hole* (1996), a collaborative work undertaken with printmaker Ron McBurnie, features a binding of emu skin which opens outwards to reveal a series of etchings that expand as the page is unfolded. The inventive binding style echoes the artistry of the book and is in harmony with its purpose, to lead the viewer into the structure and heart of the work.

Another work in which the binding has an integral part to play in the viewing and reading experience, is *The grub in the wood of time* (1989) the product of a collaboration between bookbinder Sun Evrard, Australian artist John Tonkin and woodworkers Frank Wiesner and Serge Amburger. Using timber from a fallen Queensland hoop pine found in a rainforest at Tamborine Mountain, the partners worked together to produce a wooden book consisting of five sawn pine pages and six pages of text. A handwritten poem by Mark O'Connor tells the tale of the tree and the wood that has been used to produce the book, while a parallel story is provided by the wood itself, chewed by generations of larvae of the Giant Hoop Pine Weevil.

The nineteenth century writer Amos Bronson Alcott noted that a good book "is opened with expectation, and closed with delight and profit". This expectation is more than satisfied by those parts of the State Library's collection that reflect the art, craft, history and impact of the printed book in all its guises.

Sponsors' Gallery of Excellence

Knight Frank

a: Level 11, AMP Place, 10 Eagle Street, Brisbane Qld 4000
p: (07) 3246 8888 f: (07) 3229 5436
w: www.knightfrank.com.au

KNIGHT FRANK

As part of the Millennium Arts Project, the redevelopment of the State Library of Queensland at South Bank on the Brisbane River will make it a world-class cultural destination.

This landmark building sets a new architectural benchmark in Queensland. It is the first major addition to Brisbane's arts precinct since the late 1980s and offers a more responsive State Library for all Queenslanders, with improved free access to state reference resources, larger display areas for the library's renowned heritage collections and an Indigenous Knowledge Centre.

The Brisbane property market is in the middle of its most dramatic transformation in recent history. Driven by the strength of the booming commodities market, the demand for suitable commercial, retail and residential space is fostering the growth and development of cutting-edge architecture in Brisbane.

Knight Frank, a leading force in the Australian property market, is also passionate about quality architecture. Knight Frank has been associated with some of the finest buildings in Australia, including the planning, leasing, sales and management of many major high-rises in Brisbane.

With this experience, Knight Frank understands how important the new State Library is as a showcase of contemporary and relevant architecture in the 'River City'.

Knight Frank is proud to be associated with the State Library of Queensland's new facility and *Between the covers: revealing the State Library of Queensland's collections*.

st.george
Good with people. Good with money.

a: Levels 1–5, 345 Queen Street, Central Plaza 1, St.George Annexe, Brisbane Qld 4000
p: (07) 3232 8888 f: (07) 3235 6770
w: www.stgeorge.com.au

ST. GEORGE BANK

St.George is Australia's fifth largest bank and one of the top 15 publicly listed companies in Australia, employing over 8,500 people.

Its national operations span all aspects of the financial industry including retail banking, institutional and business banking, and wealth management. At the bank's core is a close relationship with its customers—an important differential that distinguishes St.George from other Australian banks.

In Queensland, St.George is committed to expanding its operations to support the growing state economy. In the coming years we will be expanding our branch and ATM network in Queensland.

At St.George, we believe that everyone should have a chance to grow and reach their potential. That's why we strive to play a positive role in the community by supporting charities, the arts, sporting clubs, business programs and disaster relief initiatives.

St.George has a long tradition of supporting key initiatives in the community and, as such, we are proud to have embarked on this new partnership with the State Library of Queensland. The opportunity to be involved in such a progressive project is extremely exciting and it is very rewarding indeed to contribute towards preserving and sharing Queensland's unique culture and heritage.

Sponsors' gallery of excellence | 179

ALCAN

Alcan is proud to be part of *Between the covers: revealing the State Library of Queensland's collections*.

As part of doing things the right way, we partner with organisations and projects, like the State Library, which contribute to Queensland's social and educational environment.

Alcan is one of the world's leading bauxite and alumina producers. Australia is our major capital base outside of Canada, employing more than 3,500 people.

Brisbane is home to our Australian headquarters, as well as our Queensland Research and Development Centre and Alcan Engineering.

Our other interests include the Gove alumina refinery in the Northern Territory, bauxite reserves in the Northern Territory and Queensland, a production facility in Adelaide for Stelvin® wine screw caps and major shareholdings in Queensland Alumina Limited and the Tomago aluminium smelter in New South Wales.

a: Level 2, 443 Queen Street, GPO Box 1016, Brisbane Qld 4001
p: (07) 3218 3555 f: (07) 3221 7977
w: www.alcan.com.au

CHANNEL SEVEN BRISBANE

Channel Seven Brisbane commenced transmission in November 1959 and has since become an iconic free-to-air television broadcaster. Seven Brisbane's signal extends from Maroochydore in the north, to Coolangatta in the south and Ipswich in the west.

Seven has a proud history in News and Public Affairs, Sport and Entertainment programming of all genres, including its highly successful local lifestyle programmes, Creek to Coast, Queensland Weekender, and The Great South East.

Seven has always taken a vital interest in the South-East Queensland community and is very proud to be involved with such a magnificent project as the new State Library at Southbank and the publication of *Between the covers: revealing the State Library of Queensland's collections*.

a: Sir Samuel Griffith Drive, Mount Coot-tha Qld 4066
p: (07) 3368 7777 f: (07) 3368 7410
w: www.yahoo7.com.au

WILSON HTM INVESTMENT GROUP

Just like the Queensland State Library, Wilson HTM Investment Group has a long-standing history of helping Queenslanders. In existence since 1895, Wilson HTM has grown to be one of Australia's leading providers of private wealth management, investment banking and investment management services.

We have a long-standing commitment to supporting the communities in which we work primarily through the Wilson HTM Foundation. The foundation makes a number of significant annual donations substantially contributing to the mission and values of selected community organisations.

We are proud to support the Queensland State Library in providing learning opportunities and a knowledge base of Queensland history and culture for all Australians for the future.

a: Level 38, Riparian Plaza, 71 Eagle Street, Brisbane Qld 4000
p: (07) 3212 1333 or 1300 133 230 f: (07) 3212 1399
w: www.wilsonhtm.com.au

CLAYTON UTZ

Clayton Utz is delighted to support the State Library of Queensland.

At Clayton Utz our key goal is to provide commercially viable and innovative legal solutions for our clients. Our lawyers are results-driven, commercially savvy and recognised as bona fide leaders in their respective practice areas.

Our guiding philosophy is a practical approach and a thorough understanding of our clients and their business.

We are a national, full-service firm with a 170-year history of client service behind us.

Our strong sense of corporate responsibility is reflected in our involvement with a broad segment of the Australian community, including the State Library of Queensland.

a: Level 28, Riparian Plaza, 71 Eagle Street, Brisbane Qld 4000
p: (07) 3292 7000 f: (07) 3221 9669
w: www.claytonutz.com

Sponsors' gallery of excellence

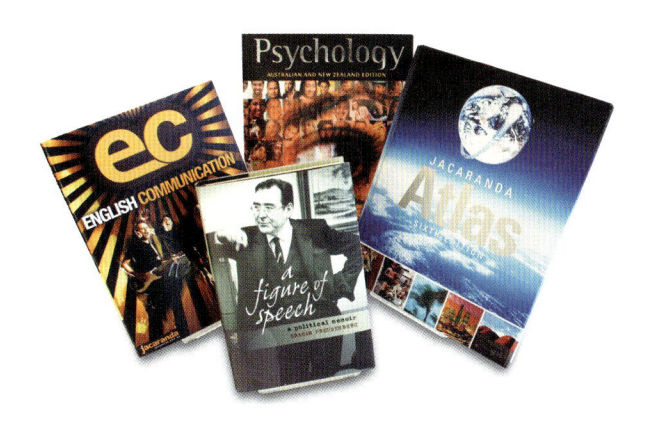

JOHN WILEY & SONS AUSTRALIA, LTD

As a large book publisher headquartered in Brisbane, Wiley Australia has contributed to the collection development of the State Library of Queensland over many decades. We are particularly proud of our innovative Queensland-focused publishing during the 1960s and 1970s under the Jacaranda imprint, some of which is highlighted in this book and showcased in the library.

We are the Australian subsidiary of the United States book and journals publisher John Wiley & Sons, Inc, a highly respected global publisher serving the vital information needs of researchers, professionals, teachers, students and consumers. Founded in 1807, the company celebrates its 200th anniversary in 2007.

We are proud of our enduring partnerships with prestigious libraries around the world, as we share with them a long tradition of commitment to literacy, culture and learning. In this context we are particularly proud of our long association with the State Library of Queensland.

John Wiley & Sons Australia, Ltd
Publishers Since 1807

a: 42 McDougall Street, Milton Qld 4064
p: (07) 3859 9755 f: (07) 3859 9715
w: www.johnwiley.com.au

XSTRATA QUEENSLAND LIMITED

Xstrata's operations in Queensland have made a significant contribution to the economic and social health and wellbeing of Queensland for many years—over 80 years in the case of Mount Isa.

In a similar way, the State Library of Queensland has made a significant contribution to the state, and Xstrata congratulates the library on its new building, which will help position it as a world-class contemporary cultural, educational and knowledge destination.

Xstrata's operations provide major benefits to Queensland. Its three commodity businesses in the state—copper, zinc and coal—run 10 major operations and employ more than 6,000 people. Since 2002, Xstrata has invested more than $8.5 billion in Queensland infrastructure and local operations and, since 2003, Xstrata has committed almost $7 million to community partnership initiatives in Queensland.

Xstrata Queensland Limited is part of Xstrata plc, which acquired MIM Holdings Limited in June 2003. It is a global mining company with operations and projects that span five continents and nine countries.

xstrata

a: GPO Box 1433, Brisbane Qld 4001
p: (07) 3295 7500 f: (07) 3295 7640
w: www.xstrata.com

Further reading

Adams, Francis William Lauderdale 1893, *The Australians: a social sketch*, T Fisher Unwin, London.

Archer, Thomas 1897, *Recollections of a rambling life*, Japan Gazette, Yokohama.

Astley, Thea 1979, *Hunting the wild pineapple, and other related stories*, Thomas Nelson, West Melbourne.

Banfield, Edmund James 1908, *The confessions of a beachcomber: scenes and incidents in the career of a professional beachcomber in tropical Queensland*, T Fisher Unwin, London.

Barton, Charles H 1885, *The Queensland timber industry and its prospects: a paper, read by request, before the Maryborough Chamber of Commerce*, Robinson & Company, Maryborough.

Bennett, Mary Montgomerie 1927, *Christison of Lammermoor*, Alston Rivers Ltd, London.

Carmichael, WB 1900, *Athletic Queensland: a history of amateur rowing, boxing and physical development, pedestrianism and cycling in Queensland …*, HJ Diddam & Co, Brisbane.

Childe, Vere Gordon 1923, *How Labour governs: a study of workers' representation in Australia*, Labour Publishing Company, London.

Colebrook, Joan 1950, *The northerner: a novel*, Invincible Press, Sydney.

Cornish, Hugh 1996, *Funny you should ask*, Queensland Arts Council Press, Brisbane.

Crooke, Ray 2000, *Island journal*, Bede Publishing, West End.

Davis, Arthur Hoey (Steele Rudd) 1899, *On our selection*, The Bulletin Newspaper Company, Sydney.

Eden, Charles Henry 1872, *My wife and I in Queensland: an eight years' experience in the above colony, with some account of Polynesian labour*, Longmans, Green, London.

Favenc, Ernest 1893, *The last of six: tales of the Austral tropics*, The Bulletin Newspaper Company, Sydney.

Favenc, Ernest c. 1900, *Tales for young Australia*, Empson & Son, Sydney.

Finch-Hatton, Harold 1885, *Advance Australia!: an account of eight years' work, wandering and amusement in Queensland, New South Wales, and Victoria*, Allen, London.

Harris, William Julius Henry 1970, *The bitter fight: a pictorial history of the Australian labor movement*, University of Queensland Press, St Lucia.

Haverfield, Eleanor Luisa c. 1908, *Queensland cousins*, Thomas Nelson & Sons, London.

Inglis, Gordon 1912, *Sport and pastime in Australia*, Methuen, London.

Lane, William (John Miller) 1892, *The working man's paradise: an Australian labour novel*, Edwards, Dunlop, Sydney.

Lang, John Dunmore 1847, *Cooksland in north-eastern Australia, the future cotton field of Great Britain: its characteristics and capabilities for European colonization: with a disquisition on the origin, manners, and customs of the Aborigines*, Longman, Brown, Green, and Longmans, London.

Lang, John Dunmore 1852, *Freedom and independence for the golden lands of Australia: the rights of the colonies and the interests of Britain and of the world*. Longman, Brown, Green, and Longmans, London.

Lea, Tom 1974, *In the crucible of the sun*, King Ranch, Kingsville, Texas.

Leichhardt, Ludwig 1847, *Journal of an overland expedition in Australia, from Moreton Bay to Port Essington, a distance of upwards of 3000 miles, during the years 1844–1845*, T&W Boone, London.

Lucas, Thomas Pennington 1894, *The curse and its cure in two volumes*, JH Reynolds, Brisbane.

McConnel, Mary 1905, *Memories of days long gone by, by the wife of an Australian pioneer*, M McConnel, Brisbane (privately printed).

Malouf, David 1975, *Johnno: a novel*, University of Queensland Press, St Lucia.

Mitchell, Thomas 1848, *Journal of an expedition into the interior of tropical Australia: in search of a route from Sydney to the Gulf of Carpentaria*, Longman, Brown, Green, and Longmans, London.

Noakes, Albert William 1947, *Water for the inland: a brief and vivid outline of conditions in the outback of Queensland in which is embodied the Reid and Dr Bradfield water schemes*, Rallings & Rallings, South Brisbane.

Petrie, Thomas 1904, *Tom Petrie's reminiscences of early Queensland (dating from 1837), recorded by his daughter*, Watson, Ferguson, Brisbane.

Praed, Rosa Caroline 1902, *My Australian girlhood: sketches and impressions of bush life*, T Fisher Unwin, London.

Rawson, Wilhelmina Frances (Mrs Lance) 1894, *Refer to me for everything: The Australian enquiry book of household and general information: a practical guide for the cottage, villa and bush home*, Pater & Knapton, Melbourne.

Russell, Henry Stuart 1888, *The genesis of Queensland: an account of the first exploring journeys to and over Darling Downs: the earliest days of their occupation; social life; station seeking; the course of discovery, northward and westward; and a resume of the causes which led to separation from New South Wales ...*, Turner & Henderson, Sydney.

Senior, William 1888, *Near and far: an angler's sketches of home, sport and colonial life*, Sampson Low, Marston, Searle, & Rivington, London.

Shaw, Flora Louise 1893, *Letters from Queensland, by The Times special correspondent*, Macmillan, London.

Tritton, Lydia Ellen c. 1920, *Poems*, RG Gillies & Co Ltd, Brisbane.

Weitemeyer, Thorvald Peter Ludwig 1892, *Missing friends: being the adventures of a Danish emigrant in Queensland (1871–1880)*, T Fisher Unwin, London.

Author Acknowledgements

A project of this complexity incurs many debts. First of all I'd like to thank Tess Livingstone who suggested me as a potential author of this book. Tess gave me a wonderful opportunity to explore a much beloved occupation, delving into Queensland's extraordinary history.

At Focus Publishing, I was given the opportunity to work with the publishing manager that all writers fantasise about—the one who listens carefully and offers constructive advice. Sandra Davies provided a collaborative partnership, with her intelligent, sympathetic and mindful support.

At the State Library of Queensland I should acknowledge the ongoing commitment of Vicki McDonald and Deb Stumm who steered this project to completion. Trudy Bennett, Simon Farley, Jorn Harbeck, Janie Meadows and Judith Murphy all brought interesting material to my attention.

At the State Library of Queensland my most enduring gratitude goes to Dianne Byrne. Our collaboration was filled with creative insights and bursts of joy as we hunted down historical and cultural connections to our collective past. Our brainstorming sessions where we talked through the contours of chapters was intellectually stimulating. Dianne's generosity with her time and knowledge alongside her commitment to excellence made our partnership singularly rewarding.

My former colleague from the University of Queensland, Dr Murray Johnson, continued that strong support and involvement that marked our days together on level three in the Gordon Greenwood Building. His expertise and advice is deeply appreciated.

My family has six generations connection with Queensland. In some respects, this book explores the diverse collective past that those of us produced by this contradictory culture share. Closer to home, my family were thrown into the project whether willingly or not.

My son-in-law, Jason Hilder, with his intimate knowledge of the outback as a lived reality, provided many suggestions and insights that were invaluable for ideas that informed my narrative. He could put many abstract ideas into tangible forms that will ring true for many Queenslanders. My little granddaughter, Gabriella Hilder took an active interest in the curious world of Queensland's past. She particularly enjoyed going through the beautiful illustrations of the flora and fauna. Most of all I owe an incalculable debt to my daughter, Dr Erin Evans, who took time off all her own projects to act as an editor, advisor and sympathetic ear as I endeavoured to complete a complex project in a short timeframe. We enjoyed many hours of discussions and debate that informed the finished product. Her generosity in devoting time and effort, her commitment to an area far from her own professional concerns and her good humour were invaluable.

Kay Saunders

Kay Saunders